Courtesy of the Government of Canada
Gracieuseté du gouvernement du Canada
publications.gc.ca

The Canadian Navy gratefully acknowledges the support of Raytheon Integrated Defence Systems in making this book possible.

CITIZEN SAILORS

CHRONICLES OF CANADA'S NAVAL RESERVE

Edited by

Richard H. Gimblett
and
Michael L. Hadley

DUNDURN PRESS

Toronto

Published by Dundurn Press Limited in co-operation with Department of National Defence and Government Services Canada.

All rights reserved. No part of this publication may be reproduced, stored in a retrieval system, or transmitted in any form or by any means, electronic, mechanical, photocopying, recording or otherwise without the prior written permission of the Minister of Public Works and Government Services Canada.

Copyright © Her Majesty the Queen in Right of Canada, 2010
Catalogue Number: D2-266/2010E

Project Editors: Michael Carroll and Jennifer McKnight
Copy Editor: Nigel Heseltine
Design: Kim Monteforte, WeMakeBooks.ca
Printer: Friesens

Library and Archives Canada Cataloguing in Publication

Citizen sailors: chronicles of Canada's naval reserve / edited by Richard H. Gimblett and Michael L. Hadley.

Issued also in French under title: Le Marin-Citoyen: Chroniques de la Réserve navale du Canada, 1910–2010.

Includes bibliographical references and index.

ISBN 978-1-55488-867-2

1. Canada — History, Naval. 2. Canada. Royal Canadian Navy — History. 3. Canada. Canadian Armed Forces. Maritime Command — History. I. Gimblett, Richard Howard, 1956–

VA400.N375 2009   359.00971   C2009-902462-4

1   2   3   4   5   14   13   12   11   10

We acknowledge the support of the **Canada Council for the Arts** and the **Ontario Arts Council** for our publishing program. We also acknowledge the financial support of the **Government of Canada** through the **Canada Book Fund** and **Livres Canada Books**, and the **Government of Ontario** through the **Ontario Book Publishers Tax Credit program**, and the **Ontario Media Development Corporation**.

Care has been taken to trace the ownership of copyright material used in this book. The author and the publisher welcome any information enabling them to rectify any references or credits in subsequent editions.

J. Kirk Howard, President

Printed and bound in Canada.
www.dundurn.com

Dundurn Press   Gazelle Book Services Limited   Dundurn Press
3 Church Street, Suite 500   White Cross Mills   2250 Military Road
Toronto, Ontario, Canada   High Town, Lancaster, England   Tonawanda, NY
M5E 1M2   LA1 4XS   U.S.A. 14150

Table of Contents

Foreword

Canada's Naval Reserve can proudly claim many significant achievements over the course of its history. One of them, and among the first, is the continued existence of the Canadian Navy.

From the outset, the Naval Reserve in Canada was founded with determination and a bit of bravado when Commander Walter Hose took Rear-Admiral Kingsmill, the director of the naval service, on a walk and planted an idea for an organization with a premise that still holds true almost 100 years later. During their conversation, Hose told the admiral that it would be difficult to get popular support for the navy across this vast country without direct contact with communities through a "citizen navy" — a naval volunteer reserve with units across the country. Despite the admiral's now famous response, "My dear Hose, you don't understand — it can't be done," a naval reserve was stood up in Victoria. Bringing the navy to Canadians across this nation is what this institution was founded upon and remains one of the most important roles of today's Naval Reserve.

This book chronicles the history of Canada's Naval Reserve and the vital role that naval reservists have played in the history of our navy and this nation. From the humble beginnings of "volunteer yachtsmen" to the integral formation of today, our "citizen sailors" have made an extraordinary commitment to Canada in choosing to serve their country while at the same time pursuing civilian careers or an education.

Canada's reserve sailors have made incredible sacrifices and continue to demonstrate the same determined attitude, persistence, and pride as their founder. Winston Churchill coined the term "twice the citizen" to describe reservists and that has certainly held true for ours, whether they served in the Royal Naval Canadian Volunteer Reserve (RNCVR), the Royal Canadian Naval Reserve (RCNR), the Royal Canadian Naval Volunteer Reserve (RCNVR) or the Naval Reserve (NAVRES) as it is known today.

This book and the history it chronicles are important to the navy and to Canadians. It is my privilege as commander of the navy to commend it to your reading and congratulate all who contributed to producing this fine historical reference.

P. Dean McFadden
Vice-Admiral
Chief of the Maritime Staff

Vice-Admiral Dean McFadden
(Chief of the Maritime Staff).

Department of National Defence.

Commodore Jennifer Bennett
(Commander Naval Reserve).

"Citizen sailors" have figured prominently in the first century of Canada's navy and today's Naval Reserve members carry the torch of our predecessors. While our missions, equipment, and alignment with the navy may have changed over the years, the spirit of reserve service has remained the same. We continue to serve with a "can do" attitude that exemplifies the motto of the Naval Reserve: "de l'audace, encore de l'audace, et toujours de l'audace."

You will discover as you read this book that we have become much more than the initial vision of the idealistic Commander Walter Hose, who believed that the navy should establish units in landlocked cities in an effort to promote the role of the navy. When the first half-companies were stood up, few would have conceived of the vital role that naval reservists would play in war and peacetime, and the impact we would have well beyond simply promoting the navy. The naval reserve of today is an integral part of the navy and we contribute to this partnership by providing unique and complementary skills at sea and ashore, at home and around the world.

Much like the Naval Reserve, this book project brought together a diverse team from across Canada, and they worked diligently to produce a wonderful tribute to and account of the history of Canada's citizen sailors. The fact that the contributing authors have all served in the reserve force is something that sets this book apart, and as you read their words you will sense the pride they hold in our history and the importance of commemorating our past, celebrating our successes, and understanding the foundation on which we will build our future.

I think that Admiral Hose would be very proud of what his Naval Reserve has become — a national institution of confident, professional Canadian officers and sailors, connecting with Canadians and continuing the tradition of outstanding service to our nation and our navy.

Thank you and "Bravo Zulu" ("well done") to the editors and the authors for such a wonderful tribute to the history of our organization and its members.

Jennifer Bennett
Commodore
Commander Naval Reserve

Acknowledgements

When approached to write a history of the Naval Reserve, my initial response — like that of so many others, it seems — was something along the lines of, "You don't understand, it simply can't be done." The appearance of this volume is proof yet again that, when it comes to Canada's naval reservists, things invariably do get done.

But I was not entirely wrong; the task could not have been achieved by myself alone, leaving me indebted to the many who helped make it happen. In the beginning, there were Captains Louis Christ and Anne Zuliani who made the approach on behalf of the Naval Reserve Formation Council — their collective confidence in me as de facto project manager, and consequent acceptance of my plan to get the volume done (including all the many changes to that plan along the way) was humbling. And in the end there was always the matter of the "bottom line," and I am grateful yet again to Captain John Pickford for the support of the Canadian Naval Centennial (CNC) project, and specifically the efforts of Commander Barry Houle and Major Francine Harding in managing the budget. We are grateful also for the generous financial assistance of Raytheon Integrated Defence Systems in making this book possible.

The most daunting aspect to preparing this history was that there was so little upon which to build in the way of existing publications or even accessible original records. The only book is Fraser McKee's *Volunteers for Sea Service*, published in 1972 as a thin volume, which he readily admits was only an introduction to the subject. A number of individual Naval Reserve divisions have produced their unit histories, but in objectively varied formats and content, and not enough of them from which to compile a complete picture. There remains much research to be done, and if this volume accomplishes nothing more than encourage budding historians as to the rich fields of research that exist in the operational, social, and civil-military relations aspects of our naval history, and leads to future endeavours to supplant this book, I shall be satisfied.

The confluence of a number of factors suggested a general line of approach. For one, I was already engaged in preparing a commemorative history of the navy for its centennial, since published as *The Naval Service of Canada, 1910–2010: The Centennial Story* (Dundurn, 2009). It is important for readers to appreciate how very different the history of the Canadian Navy is when viewed from the perspective of the citizen sailors of the Naval Reserve, which is the point of undertaking this separate volume as a companion to the previous. The approach used for the Navy's commemorative history — assembling different authors to write on their areas or periods of expertise — has been adopted here, but experts in areas of Naval Reserve history were not as easily found as they were for the navy as a whole, and many of the persons I identified were unknown to me as scholars.

Fortuitously, the Canadian Nautical Research Society (CNRS), was holding its 2008 conference in Quebec City in recognition of the 400th anniversary of the founding of that city. With Quebec also being the present home of Naval Reserve Headquarters, I am grateful to CNRS for recognizing the import of developing this area of Canadian maritime history by allowing the navy to partner with it for the 8th Maritime Command (MARCOM) Historical Conference. The opening of places in the conference program for a number of our authors provided a wonderful opportunity for us to gel intellectually and socially as a team.

The reader will come to know that team in going through the book and referring to the notes on contributors, but two persons deserve special recognition. Fraser McKee, author of the afore-mentioned *Volunteers for Sea Service*, is the acknowledged dean of our Naval Reserve history; without his early and enthusiastic support for the project, and access to his wealth of knowledge, rare archival records and photographs, this book could not have been accomplished, and we are honoured to have him pen as an epilogue what effectively is an "afterword" (as opposed to a "foreword") to this volume. Michael Hadley originally signed on as a "simple" chapter writer, but easily succumbed to my press ganging him as the "editor" (in the original "wordsmithing" sense of the word) of this volume; his skills and experience as a long-serving naval reservist and a distinguished naval historian were indispensable to his fashioning the individual author essays into an integral story, and I am honoured to have had him as a colleague on this project.

Leaving Michael to shape the chronicle of the Naval Reserve allowed me to direct my efforts to an aspect in which this volume departs from the *The Centennial Story*, that being where it acts as a reference work, filling gaps in technical and institutional matters where the Naval Reserve is overlooked in the standard histories. Those are addressed in part through a pair of appendices. Carl Gagnon, whose marvellous ship and aircraft side profile drawings once again grace our pages, searched through a wide range of archives and private histories to provide a graphic illustrated record of vessels of the Naval Reserve, a nautical dimension found nowhere else. Colin Stewart laboured with similarly fragmentary sources to establish a framework for brief histories of the Naval Reserve divisions that have been in existence over the past century. Jennifer Bennett, Louis Christ, Carl Gagnon, Richard Mayne, and Barbara Winters pitched in beyond their individual chapters to assist in this effort, as did many others in the various divisions.

Producing an illustrated history in two separate editions (one for each official language) proved much less challenging this time around, in that I was able to turn to many of the team who had been engaged in the *The Centennial Story*. Dean Boettger, Carl Gagnon and Kevin Sirko again did the initial compilation of images from the collections of the Library and Archives Canada (LAC), the Canadian War Museum (CWM), and the Canadian Forces Joint Imagery Centre (CFJIC). Additional assistance was provided by Andréa Belhumeur of the Naval Museum of Quebec, Valerie Casbourn of the Directorate of History and Heritage (DHH), Joseph Lenarcik of the Canadian Forces Base Esquimalt Naval and Military Museum, and Greg Looman of the DND Public Affairs production unit. Other images were obtained from the Imperial War Museum, as well as from private collections that are credited in the pertinent captions. Translation of the manuscript was coordinated by the Navy's Translation Bureau in Halifax, with the bulk of the superb French translation done again by Annie Williams. In the course of proofreading the translation, François Ferland and Hugues Létourneau made a significant number of observations on the English text, saving Michael and myself from untold embarrassment. To all these various persons and institutions, I extend our deep appreciation.

In the acknowledgements to the *The Centennial Story*, I noted what a pleasure it was to work with Kirk Howard's very professional team at Dundurn, and expressed my hope not to have to await another century for the next opportunity. Well, here it is less than a year later, a very fine sign for the future.

Richard H. Gimblett
Navy Command Historian
Ottawa, June 2010

Introduction

Michael L. Hadley

"There is nothing — absolutely nothing — half so much worth doing as simply messing about in boats." These memorable and oft-quoted lines from Kenneth Grahame's *Wind in the Willows* of 1908 may well strike an unusual note in a volume on the Naval Reserve. Yet they capture the playful seriousness with which generations of shore-bound Canadians have approached the lure of ships and the sea. Throughout its history, the Naval Reserve has played a number of vital roles, and in doing so has attracted many epithets. Whether earnest or jocular these have ranged from "a nursery of fighting seamen," to "Saturday night sailors," a "wavy navy," and even to "the shads" — the shadows of the regular force. But throughout that same history they have buoyed a remarkable channel through oft-uncharted shoal waters. For example, they once rescued the regular force from being stricken from the books altogether and being dismantled; they expanded the same regular force as much as 40-fold in times of crisis; they have augmented that force in times of need, while training and inspiring each succeeding generation. Ultimately, all of them have engaged in the earnest endeavour of national defence.

Citizen Sailors records the annals of a special kind of dual citizenship: Canadians working at sea in Canada's service, while at the same time meeting the demands of their civilian occupations in their communities at home. The tensions can be exquisite; the challenges sometimes daunting. But always this dual citizenship brings special personal rewards. It does so despite its dependence on the vagaries both of government policy and public recognition. Membership in the Nelsonian "band of brothers" — and sisters — has always been a transformative experience. This experience has been nourished by camaraderie, fellowship, and naval identity. For it has lifted individuals of differing cultural and linguistic backgrounds and aspirations out of their separateness in a vast land; and it has motivated them to form a community that spans this vastness from the Pacific to the Atlantic.

This volume both celebrates and critiques the experiences of well over 100 years of pursuing a wide range of personal and national ideals. These embrace seafaring, public service, national defence, adventure, and self-realization, and not the least of these, citizenship and nation-building. Those who have undertaken the journey as both citizen and sailor have not only gained in personal stature; they have contributed to the commonwealth of the nation.

This commemorative volume is the work of many: those who envisioned it, the serving members of the reserve and the permanent force who encouraged it, the thinkers in the

Canadian Forces and the Public Service of Canada who helped shape it, the members of the Naval Centennial Committee who funded it, and of course the writers who wrote it.

Most of the writers in this volume have served in Canada's Naval Reserve. Some of them have actually experienced the period of which they write. Only a couple of them, however, are professional naval historians. This feature underscores the notion of competent volunteerism so typical of being a naval reservist. Each writer has skillfully characterized a particular era of naval development. Although each of their contributions has been designed to stand alone, all are nonetheless linked by common threads and themes. These include nation-building, citizenship, duty, the integration of women and francophone Canadians, and of course the adventures and challenges of sea service.

Like the double-helix strands of DNA, the reserve and regular force have a close relationship. Indeed, as Louis Christ reminds us in our first chapter, "My dear Hose, it can't be done," their fates are intertwined. Thus his account of the earliest reserve experience reads like a primer on the roots of Canada's navy as a whole. And that's precisely as it should be. With deft brush strokes he paints a portrait of the reserve from its earliest origins in "marine reserves" of the 1760s, through the defence issues of 1812, the founding of the Royal Canadian Navy (RCN) in 1910, its struggle against enemy forces in home waters, and its temporary demise in 1922. In all this he highlights the tensions between national identity and colonial responsibilities. But at centre stage of politics, warfare, and naval prowess stands the commanding figure of Walter Hose who realized early on that indeed "it could be done." Long recognized as the "father of the Naval Reserve," he first elicited the concept of the citizen sailor that this volume celebrates.

The Naval Reserve badge.

Department of National Defence

In chapter 2, "Codfish, cruisers, and courage," David Parsons takes us back to 1900, a full decade before the actual founding of the Royal Canadian Navy. With poignant vignettes of the Newfoundland Division of the Royal Naval Reserve, he vividly describes the challenges of national and imperial defence in Newfoundland and overseas right up to 1922. He shows how fishermen became naval seamen, how they served not only coastal defence, but overseas with the Royal Navy (RN). He documents their heroism and sacrifice. Admittedly, Newfoundland did not join Confederation until 1949, and therefore what Parsons has written might be deemed a tribute to a hardy British colony in its defence

of British Imperial causes. Importantly, however, these great causes included Canada as we know it today. These early Newfoundland reservists are therefore a vital part of the Canadian story.

In drawing her portrait of the period of the Great Depression and the devastating effects of the First World War, Barbara Winters (chapter 3) has deftly blended a lively mix of politics, policy, and people. This is the period of the "Reserve Preserve" to which her title refers. It was a decisive time of financial deprivation, a time when population and politicians alike were recoiling from the horrors of war. To many it made no sense whatever to try to raise a navy to defend the country against non-existent bogeymen. Naval planners, by contrast, held radically different views. To their mind, this was precisely the time to develop a grand vision. In the event, the politicians won out; defence budgets were slashed to the bone, and even the regular navy tottered on the verge of extinction. Reservists "soldiered on" with resources so makeshift and scarce that their efforts strike the present-day observer as a comedy of errors. And yet, ironically, this ragged band of brothers held the naval idea together, and formed the basis for mobilization when the Second World War loomed on the horizon in 1938–39.

A naval reserve recruiting poster from the 1950s.

It is at this point that Richard Mayne (chapter 4) picks up the narrative of the war years 1939–45. This was the period in which, so the popular press would have it, the "People's Navy" emerged. Here Mayne explores the myth and the "facts." (Most of the sailors were "stubble-jumpers" from the prairies, said the myths; not so, say the "facts;" most really came from Ontario and British Columbia.) He recounts realities of naval life when "mere civilians" made up most of the navy. He picks up the old theme of a unilingual English-speaking force that offered little scope to francophone Quebec. In all this, deeds of derring-do and bravado ran counterpoint to bureaucratic intrigue, while well-educated but modestly trained reservists encountered their professionally-trained but less educated regular force mentors. In time, however, the harsh and demanding conditions of the war at sea melded the most disparate elements of personnel and technology into an efficient fighting force. But as Mayne observes, both the sea and the enemy inflicted some painful lessons. The story is replete with colourful characters and events.

Colour and character continue in the next phase (1945–68), as demobilization and the Cold War work their alchemy on the Naval Reserve. The phase is underscored by the long process of Canadianization

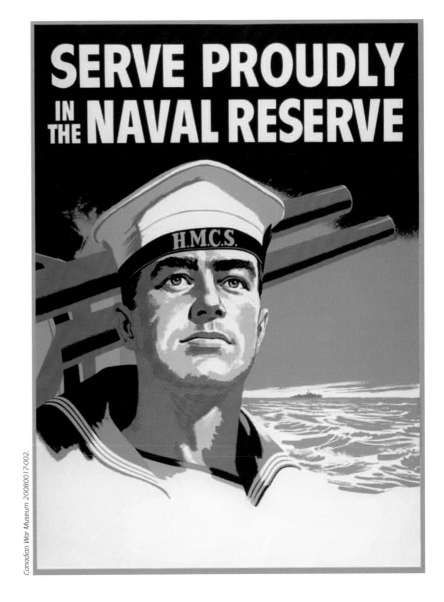

Canadian War Museum 20080017-002.

SERVE PROUDLY
IN THE NAVAL RESERVE

foreshadowed in earlier chapters. This meant unburdening the navy of the "Englishness" of inherited naval culture in the search for its own identity. Here Michael L. Hadley (chapter 5) explores the upbeat late 1940s and burgeoning 1950s. This was a time when reservists gained sea experience on a wide variety of operational warships, and trained with the air arm of the fleet. In the memories of many, these were the halcyon days when wartime lore and legend still felt vividly contemporary and relevant to current tasks. New recruits rallied to the flag. Among them came hundreds of "Untidies," university students who joined the UNTDs (University Naval Training Divisions). They were attracted by guaranteed summer employment, adventure, and both a university degree and a naval commission at the end of their studies. But as the threat of intercontinental ballistic missiles captured the media's imagination in the late 1950s, many Canadians — parliamentarians among them — soon concluded that no military force whatever would be able to defend the country. Hence none should be provided for, and the Naval Reserve should be dismantled. In the 1960s the politics of unification undercut all naval tradition by relegating distinctive uniforms and symbols to the dust heap. As Hadley's chapter title announces, the "Wavy Navy" in blue became officially the Sea Element (in green), and dubbed itself the "Jolly Green Giants."

But according to Ian Holloway's thesis in "The Quest for Relevance" (chapter 6), that metamorphosis left the Naval Reserve having to chart its own course. The reserve did so admirably in the years 1968 through 1990, despite the fact that most of what it did had

Canada Post Official 1998 First Day Cover commemorating the 75th anniversary of the establishment of the Naval Reserve. From left to right are stamps for HMC Ships *Sackville* and *Shawinigan*.

Copyright Canada Post 1998, reproduced with permission.

little real warfighting value. Of course, it continued with sea training aimed at supporting the regular force's fleet-in-being. The reserve's principal ships were the trawler-type gate vessels built in 1950–52 that evoked the unofficial sobriquet "pig boat navy." The gate vessel era ended with the arrival of the new Kingston-class maritime coastal defence vessels (MCDVs) in 1996. Yet throughout these difficult years it remained an upbeat organization, focusing not only on sea training, but on morale-building through adventure, bonspiels, regattas, and teams. In all this, the reserve saw itself as the custodian of naval tradition, while the regular force Sea Element bent to the style of unification. Some of this custodianship, like its occasional sidelong glances at Britain's White Ensign (which Canada's ships had worn until 1965), and the fading celebrations of Admiral Nelson's Battle of Trafalgar, were purely nostalgic and backward-looking. But hearkening back to these symbols did in some degree emphasize elements of the navy's distinctive character, which unification had attempted to wipe out. As it turned out, the reserve's virtual isolation as an institution from the regular force proved a boon, for it became expert in a trade rooted in the experience of the Battle of the Atlantic (1939–45). Surprisingly, that same trade was needed once again in North Atlantic Treaty Organization's (NATO's) Cold War strategy of resupplying Europe across the Atlantic in times of crisis. That trade, of course, was naval control of shipping (NCS).

Two key events influenced the policies and practices of subsequent years, and continue to do so: the end of the Cold War, and 9/11 — the devastating attack on the twin towers of the World Trade Center in New York in September 2001. In the long haul, as Bob Blakely argues in chapter 7, "This ain't your Dad's Naval Reserve anymore," the shift marked the emergence of an operational reserve. Between 1989 and 2010 it adapted to sharp-end missions and a Total Force concept that integrated permanent and reserve components of "One Navy." As we have seen, this type of renewal had been in process for some time. Now, however, international events accorded a sense of urgency. As Blakely explains, the Department of National Defence's (DNDs) White Paper 1987 had been, at best, out of joint with the times, for it addressed Cold War themes that would be irrelevant within two years of its publication. In 2005, however, the government issued a new white paper on international affairs and defence that signalled the government's intention of introducing significant change. The "new vision" that paper enunciated was to be "firmly grounded in the realities of the post–Cold War, post–September 11th world." This called for "the general and specialized operational competence of ... both Regular and Reserve" personnel. Central to this updating was the management concept of Transformation, a notion adopted not only by Canada, but by NATO.

"Transformation" is only the latest in a long list of concepts and terms that have emerged over the previous decades to describe radical change triggered by new security realities. They have evolved from MTR (Military Technical Revolution) of the 1980s and 1990s, to RMA (Revolution in Military Affairs) of the mid-90s, to "transforming transformation" of the current era. In Canada, the term refers to those initiatives underscored by the white paper of 2005 (Defence Policy Statement [2005]). Bob Blakely takes up the themes of transformation and professional competence to show how the Naval Reserve positioned itself to meet that new vision even before it was actually in place: new ships and professional specialties, "total force" integration of regular force and reserve, and realistic training for combat deployment. The Naval Reserve, he insists, is now a completely professional component of Canada's navy.

Casting his net wide, Hugues Létourneau (chapter 8) surveys what he calls "the naval presence" in Quebec. Arguing the case for Quebec as both a maritime province and a naval province, he outlines a seagoing culture beginning with New France and ending with the deep-sea ports of Montreal and Quebec City today. Central to his argument is the real and symbolic significance of the great St. Lawrence River: it has known the ships of New France in the 17th century, British and French ships in the 18th, transports in the 19th, enemy submarines and Allied naval forces in the 20th. Indeed, in the 20th century, Quebec was home to major Canadian naval establishments. But they were largely monolingual English. Given the broad historical dimensions of the naval presence in Quebec, he asks, what about the Quebec presence in the navy? His cultural and linguistic excursions are telling. The integration of francophones into the Canadian navy has been tentative and slow, sometimes grudging and ill-conceived. Against this broad cultural background he traces the work of isolated reserve divisions in their attempt to share a trans-Canadian responsibility for national defence, while advancing both the legitimacy and richness of Quebec culture. In the final analysis, while the Quebec presence has become more firmly rooted in the navy, the Quebec identity of the navy remains rooted in the naval reserve.

Woven throughout our narrative since 1942 is the role played by women volunteers. That year marked the founding of the Women's Royal Canadian Naval Service (WRCNS), or the "Wrens," as they were known. Strictly speaking, the organization was not part of the naval reserve, yet as a rich resource of "hostilities only" personnel their contribution to national defence was enormous. Though the WRCNS was disbanded in August 1946, many of its members responded to the navy's invitation in 1951 to join the naval reserve. The story of Wrens in the naval reserve is marked by the rise of women — in what had once been a male preserve — through all the naval trades, even to command of a warship and "flag rank" (commodore). Fraser McKee puts the final touch on this naval portrait by reflecting in his epilogue on what this account of service in the naval reserve ultimately means. He places the story of our citizen sailors in the context of a range of seafaring "fathers" from Champlain, d'Iberville, and Nelson, to Kingsmill and Hose. In doing so, McKee reminds us of the debt that Canada owes its volunteers for sea service. In evoking "the laws of the navy" he foresees a continuing tradition of innovation, flexibility, and commitment that will guide and develop Canada's naval reserve well into the future.

Each of the contributions in this volume is a snapshot of a crucial period, which, taken together, form a complete picture, a seamless narrative overview, of Naval Reserve history. Each writer has undertaken research in both primary and secondary sources, and has drawn upon personal experiences as well. For ease of reading we have limited the scholarly apparatus of endnotes to a bare minimum, and our bibliography to a convenient list of suggested readings. By subtitling the book "Chronicles of Canada's Naval Reserve" we are signalling that the definitive history is yet to come. It will appear when some enterprising historian takes all the threads in hand, and weaves the final pattern. The scope for further research and writing is great.

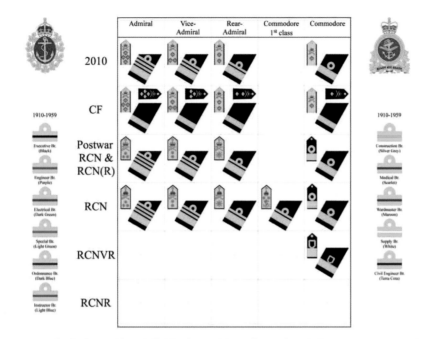

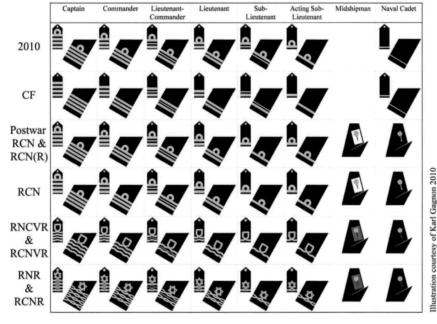

Illustration courtesy of Karl Gagnon 2010

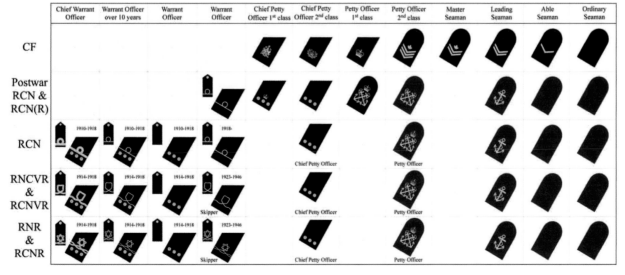

Rank insignia of the
Canadian Navy,
1910–2010.

Tradition and innovation define the reserves. For example, in a tradition reaching back at least to Britain's Admiral of the Fleet "Jackie" Fisher (1841–1920), the Bible served as a code-book for commenting on naval operations, squadron exercises, and daily affairs. Every yeoman of signals held a well-thumbed and personally annotated copy ready at hand on the bridge for immediate and highly inventive (if secular) use. A cryptic reference to an appropriate passage in one of the scriptural books set the recipient checking his own copy. Thus the story is told of Canadian reservists in the Second World War sighting an enemy submarine and then sending the terse signal "Rev13:1" (Book of Revelation: "And I saw a beast rising out of the sea having ten horns and seven heads"). The senior officer's ship responded with an equally brief signal to attack: "Ex 12:9" (Book of Exodus: "Do not eat any of it raw or boiled in water, but roasted over the fire, with its head, legs, and all the purtenances thereof"). According to naval lore, the Canadians did manage to "cook" their enemy submarine. Such accounts are doubtless apocryphal. But they underscore the playful earnestness of those who go "down to the sea in ships [and] do business in great waters" (Ps. 107:23–30). The stories lose nothing in retelling. As we launch the good ship *Citizen Sailors* and take it to sea we might imagine this old tradition coming alive once again in yet another unusual flag-hoist: "Pr. 25:11" (Book of Proverbs: "A word fitly spoken is like apples of gold in a setting of silver …"). These are precisely the words we have sought to speak about the naval reserve.

CHAPTER 1

"My Dear Hose ... It Can't Be Done": Splicing Traditions in the Early Years

Louis Christ

The day had gone well in Esquimalt aboard the cruiser HMCS *Rainbow*, but any visit by the director of the naval service was unnerving for a junior ship's captain. Still, it had gone well enough that Commander Hose decided to put his proposal to Admiral Kingsmill. It was spring 1912, and the navy was in desperate need of sailors as tensions were mounting in Europe.[1] "What about creating a citizen navy — a naval volunteer reserve with units across the country?" Kingsmill was not enthused. "My dear Hose, you don't understand — it can't be done."[2]

The idea of a naval reserve was not new to Canada, or to Hose. A few years earlier he had worked with the Royal Naval Reserve in Newfoundland, an organization whose sailors were seamen and fishermen trained to serve in warships in time of need. In Canada, "marine militias" and "marine reserves" had existed since shortly after the battle of the Plains of Abraham in 1759. Arising sporadically, they were established to counter specific threats, often from the United States, sometimes from an overseas enemy of the British Empire. All of them, even those with a true naval purpose, had been disbanded or atrophied once the threat was gone. Formed in January 1923, the Royal Canadian Naval Volunteer Reserve was different. It had a long-term, strategic purpose — to ensure the survival of the Royal Canadian Navy.

Department of National Defence, G-6573.

The ill-fated steam corvette, HMS *Charybdis*, came to symbolize the Dominion of Canada's first attempt at a naval reserve.

The marine reserve first appears in Canada in 1763 in the form of the Provincial Marine. It was formed to organize the ships and shore establishments of the Great Lakes, St. Lawrence, and Lake Champlain under the control of the governor of the Canadas. It could enrol local residents to man its vessels. By 1780 it consisted of 12 vessels of 10–16 guns with an additional two under construction. But early in the War of 1812 the Royal Navy assumed its station on the Great Lakes and the Provincial Marine was disbanded. Many of its members joined the Royal Navy to fill out its gunboat crews. Between 80 and 100 of the 970 British sailors engaged in the battle of Put-In Bay on 10 September 1813 were Canadians from the Provincial Marine.

The naval militia next appears in Canada in 1837 following the collapse of the Upper Canada Rebellion. Some of William Lyon Mackenzie's followers had seized Navy Island in the Niagara River. At the request of the governor of Upper Canada, a retired RN officer, Captain Andrew Drew, took charge of an ad hoc company of "naval militia" that included some experienced sailors. On the night of 19 December 1837 Drew's party set the American vessel *Caroline* ablaze and cut it loose to tumble over the falls in the early morning hours of 20 December. This amounted to an invasion of United States territory. Delicate and protracted negotiations averted a war.[3]

The *Militia Act* of 1846 marks the first official Canadian recognition of a corps of military volunteers. It was passed in response to the U.S. presidential cry of "Fifty-four Forty or Fight" that had rallied Americans to fight Great Britain if it did not cede to America all land west of the Rockies to 54° 40'N. This was the American policy of Manifest Destiny. The act was innovative in creating an official volunteer force — and the principle of citizen soldiers defending Canada. Typically, members received nothing but a weapon, and were responsible for the costs of their own uniforms, training, and horses. The act also authorized the first formal body of naval volunteers in Canada, a "Provincial Naval Corps" that was to operate on the Great Lakes. Nothing came of it. A subsequent *Militia Act* in 1855 authorized the formation of "Volunteer Marine Companies" consisting of a captain, a lieutenant and 50 men. For the first time it covered the costs of drills and uniform. Once again, nothing came of it. Twice the name changed, from "Marine and Naval Companies" (1862) to "Naval Companies" (1863). But still nothing much came of it. Not until the Fenian raids of 1866 did volunteer forces become active. Naval volunteer companies of 55 to 65 men came from Kingston, Cobourg, Toronto, Oakville, Hamilton, Dunnville, and Port Stanley. They armed and operated small vessels on the lakes and rivers of Upper Canada — but only until the Royal Navy brought up forces from the coast.

Library and Archives Canada, PA-123950.

The crew of CGS *Canada* in 1905 performing naval militia drills on their winter cruise to Bermuda.

The end of the Fenian threat saw the volunteer naval companies dropped from the Militia List. Yet the *Militia and Defence Act* (1868) of the newly formed Dominion of Canada did authorize marine militia units. These consisted of volunteers whose normal occupation was in ships plying Canadian waters, and a naval brigade of infantry that could be employed in ships. The 1st Division was formed in Halifax in 1868. A year later, marine companies were formed in Quebec at Bonaventure, New Carlisle, and Carleton. Having no apparent role in peacetime, they languished and were disbanded in 1874. Ultimately, the act of 1868 "resulted only in the building of a few gunboats and cutters to defend the Great Lakes and seacoasts and protect the fisheries."[4]

The Canadian militia tradition, including that of the naval militia, had developed out of a need to protect Canada from American invasion. The 1871 Treaty of Washington made future war with the Americans unlikely. But the Fenian raids of 1866 and the Northwest Rebellion of 1885 highlighted the important role that militia could play in a domestic emergency. On the Great Lakes a marine militia often provided a first response — but nothing more. For even here, naval security remained the responsibility of the Royal Navy and did not factor into Canadian plans in any significant way. Canada saw its unique maritime security responsibility as lying with the fisheries.

Rear-Admiral Charles Kingsmill sits for his official photograph soon after arriving in Canada to command the Marine Service, May 1908.

Library and Archives Canada, PA-108013.

At the time of Confederation (1867) the task of maintaining a Canadian maritime presence in coastal waters fell to the Department of Marine and Fisheries of the new dominion government. This was important to Canadian sovereignty, as Britain proved reluctant to enforce Canadian fishing agreements. Indeed, it came to resolve all disputes with the Americans by sacrificing Canadian interests. Six armed schooners of the "Dominion Cruiser Fleet" became the Marine Police, charged with fisheries protection and seizure of offending vessels. Commanded by former ship's captains of the Royal Navy, its sailors were hired on voluntarily and laid off each fall. International disputes and the American abrogation of the fisheries provisions of the Treaty of Washington in 1885 secured the future of the Fisheries Protection Service on the East Coast. A civilian agency, it formed the base from which Canada's navy would grow.

At the same time, a number of influences — technology, international crises, and internal politics — led Canada to acquire its first ship for naval purposes. The *Militia Act* (1868) and Britain's *Colonial Naval Defence Act* (1865) supported the proposition that Canada "would not be averse to instituting a ship for training purposes." In 1881, amid rising international tensions, the Admiralty sent HMS *Charybdis*, a steam-driven sailing ship "worn by years on the China station." Tensions eased and *Charybdis* rotted at its moorings. Referred to as "Canada's White Elephant" and a "rotten tub," it was returned to the British navy at Halifax in 1882 after causing the death of two civilians who fell through its rotting gangway and damaging other shipping in Saint John, New Brunswick, harbour after breaking loose in a gale. The *Charybdis* experience scuttled notions of a Canadian navy for a generation.

Concerns for a larger role for Canada in naval affairs returned to prominence at the end of the 19th century as international tensions and imperial rivalries rose once again in Europe. It was also a time in which the new nation was trying to define its own national identity. Talk of contributing funds directly to Britain rather than building ships at home seemed contrary to the national interest — apart from the fact that direct support to Britain inflamed the suspicions of isolationists and French Canadians.[5] Enter the Toronto branch of the Navy League, a pro-navy lobby group founded in 1895. Against the backdrop of Britain's growing naval arms race with Germany, its honorary secretary, H.J. Wickham, published a naval defence plan in th*e Globe*, a Toronto newspaper, on 20 June 1896. This was just three days before the federal election that would bring Wilfrid Laurier's Liberals to power. Wickham proposed a naval militia that would partner with the land militia, have both permanent and reserve forces, and training schools on both coasts. His plan proposed the conversion of the Fisheries Protection Service into a coastal defence force. Later that year Wickham proposed an additional program that would see Canadians made available to the Royal Naval Reserve to help arm merchant vessels in a crisis. Wickham's ideas failed to move the government. Yet he continued to press them until 1910.

Still, by the beginning of the 20th century it was clear that something had to be done to establish a Canadian naval presence along the East and West Coasts. The United States was on the verge of world power status and Britain was increasingly preoccupied with the threat posed by the growing German navy. Gradually, support grew among politicians and navalists for a distinct Canadian navy — and for the formation of a reserve along the lines proposed by the Navy League. On 24 November 1902 Frederick Borden, Laurier's minister of militia and defence, spoke publicly at least twice of the government standing ready "to form the nucleus of a navy" for Canada.[6] This "nucleus" was to be a naval militia that would augment the Royal Naval Reserve, but would have training vessels provided by the Canadian government. Recent activities of the Newfoundland reserve (see next chapter) had demonstrated the value of such training. They had been led by then-Lieutenant Walter Hose, who in 1923 would become director of the Naval Service of Canada.

Next, on 2 April 1903, the *Globe* reported on the development of "a scheme for establishing gun sheds on the sea coasts of Canada, where the fishermen may be trained in naval artillery." Based on the successful training of a few sailors in the Fisheries Protection Service with rapid-fire guns in 1901 and 1903, this was the brainchild of the new minister of marine and fisheries, Raymond Préfontaine. The report further suggested that the reservists would train in three vessels — one each at Esquimalt, Toronto, and Halifax — to be provided either by the British government or the dominion itself. In the House of Commons on 23 June 1903 Préfontaine was obliged to concede that the "matter of the naval reserve is under consideration." Haggling over jurisdictions followed, and funding emerged as a major issue. Ultimately, the matter was referred to the Colonial Defence Committee whose secretary wrote to the colonial secretary, Joseph Chamberlain, on 28 July 1903: "Canada should take the same precautions [as the naval militias of the American Great Lake states]

Library and Archives Canada, PA-020729.

With the white-hulled Canadian Government Ships *Canada* (right) and *La Canadienne* anchored in the background, *Canada*'s steam launch ferries guests ashore at the 1910 summer festival in Canso Harbour, Nova Scotia.

and should raise and train a naval force and organize it to man the vessels at her disposal at the outbreak of war."[7] As far as the Canadian government was concerned, America was no longer a threat, and if defence against American attack were the purpose of a naval reserve, then it had no value.

As early as 1902 Laurier had acknowledged that the defence of Canada lay in accepting the Monroe Doctrine and fostering good relations with the United States. Key players in London and the British Admiralty had also come to this view, realizing that Royal Navy resources were being spread too thinly. In the words of Admiral Walter Kerr, RN, it was impossible for the Royal Navy "to be a superior force everywhere."[8] Certainly, Britain owed its prosperity to its control of the seas. But by the end of the 19th century significant advancements in worldwide communications, facilitated by improvements in wireless telegraphy and submarine cables, made the deployment of ships in response to a crisis more efficient. This supported a strategy increasingly focused on home defence. Thus, when Admiral Sir John Fisher was appointed First Sea Lord in 1904 he initiated a plan to withdraw the main British force from North America and the West Indies, and to leave Canada to get along with the United States. In doing so, he relied on Britain's exceptional worldwide communications and supply network. Though reduction of forces caused some apprehension in Canada, it sharpened the Canadian focus on the need to look out for the nation's own interests.

By 1904 the Department of Marine and Fisheries was the largest government department. It had broad responsibilities including all things related to fisheries, navigation, harbours, shipwrecks, and the welfare of seamen. Later that year it came to embrace the St. Lawrence and the exercise of sovereignty in the Arctic. It had a fisheries protection fleet of eight armed cruisers and a marine fleet of six icebreakers, as well as 18 or so other vessels over 24.4 metres in length. In that year the department took delivery of its newest and largest vessel (61.0 metres and 526 tonnes) CGS *Canada* (the abbreviation stood for Canadian Government Ship). A second ship of similar displacement, the 53.4-metre CGS *Vigilant*, soon followed. Coincident with the acquisition of *Canada*, Minister Préfontaine drafted new legislation for a naval reserve that would train on the vessel. The bill failed for a number of reasons, not least of which was money. World events again intervened and the concept of a marine reserve idled.

Canada's pervasive maritime concern was how to deal with American poachers in its fisheries, so the Fisheries Protection Fleet remained, and it was the next best thing to a

Commander Walter Hose and HMCS *Rainbow*.

Library and Archives Canada, PA-141880.

navy. Its two newest vessels looked like small modern warships. Their crews dressed in uniforms much like those worn by British sailors; they flew the Blue Ensign with a Canadian coat of arms, were commanded by former officers of the Royal Navy, and were fitted with quick-firing guns. But grassroots support for a true Canadian navy had been growing, punctuated by a great deal of communication between the Navy League branches in Toronto and Victoria and successive ministers of marine and fisheries. Following up on Wickham's paper of 1896, the Toronto branch in 1898 proposed the formation of a naval reserve of 5,000 men to augment the Canadian militia. It would be subject to regulations "similar to those of the Admiralty as far as local conditions permit." The government, it argued, would obtain "suitable vessels for such crews and instructors as may be necessary, paying a reasonable sum for their use." It even suggested that "the fishermen of Canada might do their training in the winter months in a warmer latitude." The driving force behind the Toronto proposals was again H.J. Wickham and the position was unequivocal: "Canadian money should be spent in Canada, making naval preparation go hand-in-hand with the development of a truly Canadian Maritime policy, the encouragement of Canadian Shipbuilding, the proper equipment of Canadian national ports, and the employment of our maritime population, than whom no finer seamen exist." Early in 1908 the new minister of marine and fisheries, Louis-Philippe Brodeur (Préfontaine had died in December 1905), responded to Wickham and spoke of the government's plans for the fisheries fleet, which "would be governed by the rules of naval discipline." He also wrote of plans to "establish a Naval Reserve on a basis which would command the confidence and support of the Canadian people." Not every branch agreed. The Victoria-Esquimalt branch, for example, pressed instead for "a substantial contribution to the Imperial Navy, upon which the very existence of Canada as a portion of the empire depends."[9]

The first RNCVR volunteers gathered for inspection at Esquimalt, 29 April 1914.

Department of National Defence, E-15243.

In the light of Laurier's growing global context, a militarized Fisheries Protection Service came to seem woefully inadequate. The dreadnought scare of 1909, resulting from Britain's fear that it was falling behind Germany in the naval arms race, brought matters into focus. Still, making direct financial contributions to imperial defence was not palatable to key voters. A distinct Canadian navy emerged as the middle ground — though not on the basis of a sound policy debate, nor on any degree of national consensus. The likelihood of a positive outcome, however, had increased in 1908 with two key appointments: the distinguished, and recently retired, Rear-Admiral Charles

Kingsmill, RN, as director of marine services; and Georges Desbarats as deputy minister. These appointments proved inspired, for until that time the government had paid little money and less attention to its marine forces.

Ultimately, Canada's solution found expression in the *Naval Service Act* of 1910. The act provided for a naval reserve of qualified mariners, and a volunteer reserve of amateurs who, in case of emergency, could be placed on active service in Canada or at the disposal of the Royal Navy. It also provided for a naval college. Yet none of these provisions was implemented at the time. On 21 October 1910 the 9,980-tonne HMCS *Niobe*, the first of two cruisers bought from the Admiralty for the fledgling Canadian naval service, steamed into Halifax harbour. Imperialists and Quebec nationalists alike were critical. At a Montreal rally held the night before *Niobe* arrived in Halifax, Henri Bourassa and others railed against Laurier's policy. The Toronto Conservative press was "openly scornful," jeering that *Niobe* had been "on her way to the scrap heap" when Ottawa made the decision to create its navy.[10] Commanding officers for *Niobe* and *Rainbow* were loaned from the Royal Navy. Among them was Commander Walter Hose, who assumed command of *Rainbow* in 1911 and transferred to the RCN in 1912.

In 1911 Laurier's 15-year government went down to defeat at the hands of Robert Borden's Conservatives. As a result, the new naval service suffered collateral damage as Borden sought to make good on his election promise to repeal the *Naval Service Act* and return to an upscale, militarized version of the Fisheries Protection Service. He put his *Naval Aid Bill* before parliament on 5 December 1912. The key tenet of the bill was that militia forces, like a coastal force, were inherently defensive; navies, on the other hand, were potentially offensive as they travelled the globe and risked becoming embroiled in faraway intrigues. The *Naval Aid Bill* was rejected on 30 May 1913, leaving Canada's naval policy "in total disarray." In the interval, both *Niobe* and *Rainbow* had been laid up for want of funds and the RCN declined from its peak of about 800 officers and men in 1911 to about 350 by mid-1913.

The idea of a naval reserve had continued to percolate. Speaking with Admiral Kingsmill in the spring of 1912 Hose had proposed his concept of "a citizen navy, a naval volunteer reserve with units across the country." Kingsmill's charitable reply, as we saw in the opening scenario of this chapter, was sheer incredulity: it simply could not be done. But Hose had formed a strong opinion on the potential for such a force. His experience with the naval reserve in Newfoundland, and with the rising fortunes of the militia under Sam Hughes, had proved the point.

Early in 1913 some enthusiastic Victoria yachtsmen and businessmen came upon the idea of forming a volunteer naval company. Hose encouraged this group and some former members of the Royal Naval Volunteer Reserve to approach Douglas Hazen, minister of marine and fisheries, on a visit to Victoria. He approached Hazen himself. Hazen was outwardly sympathetic, encouraged the group, and allowed them to use the Esquimalt facilities. Ottawa did not initially support the idea, but in July 1913 granted permission for them to commence training. They did so with the encouragement and assistance of the crew of the *Rainbow* and its commanding officer. The group had no official status, nor did it have money for uniforms or pay. Their instructors came both from RCN and RN ships.

Now in proper attire, the Victoria RNCVR parade in front of the provincial legislature in Victoria, British Columbia, in 1914.

Library & Archives Canada, PA-115374.

Perhaps surprisingly, Kingsmill himself was unsympathetic, and reprimanded Hose for his actions. But Hose had already commenced training and turned a blind eye. Training continued and by July 1914 the Victoria volunteers numbered 140. "Both for this, and for his advocacy of reserves during the dismal wasteland years of the Great Depression, Hose has become known as 'Father of the Naval Reserve.'"[11]

Ottawa caught up with the volunteer movement as the threat of a major war in Europe loomed, and officially established the Royal Naval Canadian Volunteer Reserve in May 1914. Patterned after the Royal Naval Reserve, the new RNCVR was to be a volunteer reserve of "seafaring men and others who might be deemed suitable." With an establishment of 3,600 men it was to be "organized into three main regional divisions with companies of 100 men" at major centres in the regions. Nothing was done to recruit at the time, but the Victoria volunteers were called upon to fill out *Rainbow*'s crew shortly after Canada went to war in August 1914. *Niobe* on the East Coast required similar augmentation, largely from the Newfoundland reserve. With men and material scarce, and ships unavailable, the RCN established a St. Lawrence patrol with private yachts purchased in the United States and Canada, and with vessels borrowed from other departments. The force operated from Halifax during the winter and from an improvised base in Sydney for the rest of the year.

By February 1916 the number of volunteers for naval service had grown so large that the minister of the naval service created the Overseas Division of the RNCVR to recruit Canadians for service in the Royal Navy. Canadian ships simply could not accommodate all those volunteering. Up to 5,000 men were authorized. Some were commissioned in the

RNVR on arriving in England and were empowered to up-rate their sailors based on their experience. By the spring of 1917 nearly 1,200 recruits, most with seagoing experience, had been shipped to Britain.

The strategic picture changed suddenly and irrevocably for the RCN in 1916. German submarines demonstrated their ability to cross the Atlantic and return home without refuelling. The merchant submarine *Deutschland* undercut British patrols and delivered trade goods to the United States, while later in the year *U-53* sank five Allied merchant ships off Nantucket. For Canada this was but a prelude. In November the Admiralty advised the Canadian government that its 12-ship flotilla should be tripled in size, but could offer no assistance. "Hun Pirate Deviltry," as the *Halifax Herald* called it, began in the spring of 1918 when German U-cruisers with torpedoes and 6-inch guns attacked shipping close off Nova Scotia: they sank ships, captured the Canadian steam trawler *Triumph* (which the Germans fitted as a raider), destroyed a tanker off Halifax harbour, cut the transatlantic cable, terrorized the fishing fleet, and set the media agog.[12] U-boats underscored the perilous state not only of Canadian naval forces, but American as well. In the final analysis, the RCN did a credible job in exceptionally difficult circumstances, but its popular legacy was discouraging.[13] In the words of the *Halifax Herald:* "What is the good of a fleet of patrols that cannot catch submarines?" So ineffective seemed its defence against U-boats that these episodes were not included in the navy's official history. By contrast, the successes of the Canadian army on the Western Front were both brilliant and well-publicized. Postwar desire to reduce defence spending undercut the navy further, and the Canadian government quickly reduced the naval service to "a severely restricted reserve force with two destroyers, HMC Ships *Patrician* and *Patriot*, and a few trawlers."[14] As Hose himself lamented, "when demobilization came, Canada was left practically without a ship, without a gun and without a rating."[15]

Hose moved to Ottawa in December 1918 to demobilize the patrol service that he had commanded during the war, and became director of the naval service on 1 January 1921. Discussions on a permanent naval policy for Canada remained unsettled until December 1921 when Mackenzie King's new Liberal minority government abruptly altered course in the naval debate. No longer facing the prospect of war, and secure with "special relationships" with Britain and the United States, it was no longer necessary to think of a deep-sea naval fleet. Mackenzie King's approach marked a move toward the political isolationism and "near-neutralism which permeated Ottawa and Quebec in the 1920s and 1930s."[16] The Washington Conference on Naval Disarmament (November 1921–February 1922) encouraged the government's approach to reducing defence spending. Yet how best to do so while retaining an effective naval force proved a singular challenge.

"Effectiveness" became the conceptual foundation in subsequent debates and proposals. Writing on behalf of the Naval Committee in its proposal to the minister on 28 February

Library and Archives Canada, 1983-28-893.

With the outbreak of war, the RNCVR was authorized to undertake a major recruiting campaign.

TR 24, built in late 1917, was one of a class of sub-chasing trawlers for the Atlantic patrol.

Department of National Defence, CN-6464.

1922, Hose put it this way: "In speaking of an efficient Navy the Committee does not mean so much a numerically efficient Navy for war purposes, as an internally efficient Navy, that is to say one in which discipline, esprit de corps, training and morale generally are such as will permit the Service to function." Hose had proposed two "efficient" institutions. The first was a small fleet of five warships costing $2,275,000 annually. The second was a reserve navy supported by a permanent force training cadre at an annual cost of $1,500,000. His plan for a naval reserve sacrificed operational capability in favour of institutional viability. Hose pressed his point with Desbarats and the minister, and by the evening of 21 April, when Desbarats finalized his memorandum to the minister for presentation to the Privy Council, he had convinced the minister of its merits. The Privy Council accepted the plan on 24 April.[17] Subsequent debates in the House continued to wrestle with seemingly intractable difficulties associated with the proposal.

By May 1922 the debates coalesced and Hose's plan for a reserve navy had gained the upper hand. The new minister of militia and minister of the naval service, George Graham, defended the operational competence of a part-time service. In a memorandum drafted by Hose, he recognized that "amateur sailors" could effectively carry out the navy's essential missions. These included coastal defence, minesweeping, patrols, and examination services. These were precisely the roles that the government was prepared to support. Indeed, he observed when debating in the House of Commons on 12 May 1922, "the trend of public opinion" on naval disarmament outlined in the position of Canada's representative at the Washington Conference, was to reduce expenditures "within the limits of safety, and without any sacrifice of national dignity."

Hose's plan proposed a bare-bones regular navy on each coast in addition to a reserve force. The 1,500 members of the reserve force would be trained at different times of the year to keep the small permanent force busy throughout. As volunteers, the members of the

Esquimalt Naval Museum, VR999.684.1.

"Holds full of water — send help!" HMCS *Galiano* was the only RCN vessel lost in the Great War. She went down with all hands (an RNCVR crew) in a storm off Vancouver Island on 30 October 1918.

reserve force would remain in their civilian jobs. But following the militia model, they would engage in full-time training for periods of two to three weeks each year. To that end, they could use army training facilities across the country to avoid any expense for new construction. Perhaps most importantly, "the [reserve] force would consist of Canadians who would be on hand for any future expansion of the Canadian Navy." The prime minister himself defended Graham's views in the House on 12 May 1922: "That is a broad policy … for the years that lie ahead.… And that policy will be carried on in the light of our country's present financial condition and in the light of conditions generally throughout the world." He marked the end of days of waffling about in naval affairs when he declared four days later that "the present Government has a permanent naval policy." Mackenzie King's approach was consistent with the mood of the people. His decision to reduce the naval budget was widely accepted by the Canadian public.

Hose viewed the final plan not as a political expedient. He saw it instead as a means to establish nationwide awareness and support, as well as a foundation of trained sailors on which to build the future navy. His experience with the Newfoundland RNR and the Victoria volunteers convinced him of the plan's merits. Additionally, his crucial experience as captain of patrols, commanding up to 136 vessels operated by reservists during the war, confirmed this view. As he said, he knew professionally of "the practicability of a naval

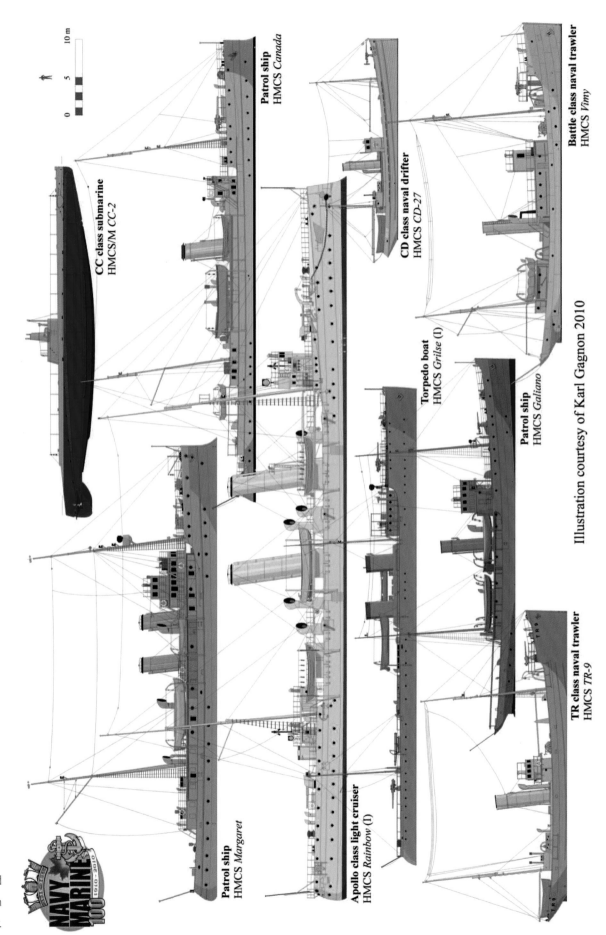

CC class submarine
HMCS/M *CC-2*

Patrol ship
HMCS *Canada*

CD class naval drifter
HMCS *CD-27*

Battle class naval trawler
HMCS *Vimy*

Torpedo boat
HMCS *Grilse* (I)

Patrol ship
HMCS *Galiano*

Patrol ship
HMCS *Margaret*

Apollo class light cruiser
HMCS *Rainbow* (I)

TR class naval trawler
HMCS *TR-9*

Illustration courtesy of Karl Gagnon 2010

0 5 10 m

Selected vessels manned
by the Naval Reserve in
the Great War.

14

volunteer force drawn from the length and breadth of the country, [which also] brought some knowledge of the navy to the prairies and the interior generally."[18]

By July 1922 the strength of the RCN had fallen to 402, and by end of 1928 the fleet consisted of only six ships: HMC Ships *Patriot, Ypres,* and *Festubert* at Halifax, and *Patrician, Armentières,* and *Thiepval* at Esquimalt. The naval secretary at the time, Paymaster Commander J.A.E. Woodhouse, left an account of the rationale by which the naval service arrived at the course it would steer between the wars. "If a Dominion is to spend money on the Navy," he wrote, "its people must be convinced a Navy is necessary."[19] This was a difficult challenge, for "in Canada a large majority of the people live far from the sea and do not visualize the necessity for safe sea communications." It was imperative, therefore, "to educate the people." And the "most effective method" to do so was "to bring the Navy to their doors, into the lives of families and friends." But given the fact that the personnel in Canada's small navy live on or near the naval bases at the coasts, "a reserve force distributed across Canada would bring the Navy home to a great number of inland people," and would do so within the navy's budget. Not only would it provide recruiting opportunities and access to the local press, but "give the Director of the Naval Service opportunity to visit the Reserve Centres throughout the country and address Chambers of Commerce, Rotarian Clubs, etc., on the elements of Naval Defence." Significantly, it "would be the first step in the conversion of Quebec."

The plan led to the creation of the first strategic Canadian naval reserve, consisting of two distinct components. First was the Royal Canadian Naval Reserve, authorized by Privy Council order (P.C. 80) of 15 January 1923. Originally organized in nine port divisions, it was reduced to five: Charlottetown, Halifax, Quebec, Montreal, and Vancouver. A registrar for each division would see to the welfare of its sailors and act as a link between the RCN and the RCNR. Besides being British citizens, physically fit, and of good character, candidates normally had to work on the sea in their civilian occupations. It had an authorized complement of 70 officers and 430 men. A second division was the Royal Canadian Naval Volunteer Reserve authorized by P.C. 139 of 31 January, 1923. The RCNVR was authorized 70 officers and 930 men in companies of 100, and half-companies of 50 in Calgary, Charlottetown, Edmonton, Halifax, Hamilton, Montreal, Ottawa, Quebec, Regina, Saint John, Saskatoon, Toronto, Vancouver, and Winnipeg. Applicants for the RCNVR had to be British citizens, aged 18–32 and physically fit. They enlisted for a three-year term and had to perform at least 30 drills annually at home and undertake two weeks of training each year at either Halifax or Esquimalt. Men were paid 25 cents per drill, officers nothing. While undergoing annual training both officers and men were paid according to the RCN scale for their rank and qualifications. The first commanding officer of the RCNVR was Lieutenant Frank Mead, for the English half-company in Montreal on 14 March 1923; he was followed the next day by Lieutenant Ralph Howard Yeates for the half-company in Hamilton.

The RCN had been formed during an unresolved debate about whether Canada needed a navy at all. The more accepted view at the time was that a militarized Fisheries Protection Service was adequate to meet Canada's needs. Canada would depend on its special relationship with the dominant naval power of the day — first Britain, later the United States —

to meet its broader maritime security needs. There had been no consensus among the Canadian people on the need for a unique Canadian navy; hence there could be none among politicians. Shortly after the formation of the RCN, politicians of all stripes came to realize that taking any stand on the navy would be hazardous in an election, and determined that it was safer to avoid formulating any naval policy at all. Interest waned, the world grew weary of war and defence spending, budgets were cut — and the RCNVR was born. It had been made possible by the traditions of previous marine militias and naval reserves in Canada. Yet it was unlike any of them. It had not been created to meet an immediate threat, but to assure the survival of Canada's navy in the long term. It was dispersed to population centres across the country where its sailors would spread the word to Canadians about the importance of the navy to Canada's maritime security and economic well being — and train for future conflict.

Notes

1. The standard secondary sources for the period are Gimblett ("Reassessing the Dreadnought Crisis of 1909"), Gough ("The End of Pax Britannica"), Hadley and Sarty (*Tin-Pots and Pirate Ships*), McKee (*Volunteers for Sea Service*), Milner (*Canada's Navy*), Sarty ("Hard Luck Flotilla"), Tucker (*Naval Service of Canada*). They are referenced explicitly in the notes and listed in the Suggested Readings at the end of this volume.

2. Directorate of History and Heritage (DHH), Hose Papers, Folder B, File 3, 3–4, Admiral Walter Hose, "The Early Years of the Royal Canadian Navy" (address to the Royal Canadian Navy Golden Jubilee Dinner, Hamilton, 19 February 1960).

3. L.N. Fuller, "The Burning of the Steamer Caroline," *Patriot War of 1837: The Canadian Rebellion*, NNY Genealogy/Stories in Stone — Genealogy Research for Northern New York. *www.nnygenealogy.com/pages/patriotwar/patriotwar-caroline.html* (accessed 18 June, 2010).

4. Canadian Military Heritage, "The Issues Crystallize," *The Naval Bill*, Volume 3 (1872–2000), Chapter 3. *www.cmhg.gc.ca/cmh/page-594-eng.asp?flash=1* (accessed 18 June, 2010).

5. Paul Kennedy, "Naval Mastery: The Canadian Context," in W.A.B. Douglas, ed., *The RCN in Transition* (Vancouver: UBC Press, 1988), 15–33.

6. *The Canadian Annual Review of Public Affairs* (Toronto: The Annual Review Publishing Company, 1902), 145.

7. U.K. National Archives, ADM 1/8904, Secretary Colonial Defence Committee to Chamberlain, 28 July 1903.

8. Barry Morton Gough, "The End of the Pax Britannica and the Origins of the Royal Canadian Navy: Shifting Strategic Demands of an Empire at Sea" (paper presented at the conference *The Navy in the Modern World*, Halifax, Nova Scotia, 16 October 1985), 2.

9. Nigel D.Brodeur, "L.P. Brodeur and the Origins of the Royal Canadian Navy," in James A. Boutilier, ed., *The RCN in Retrospect* (Vancouver: UBC Press, 1982), 13–32.

10. Marc Milner, *Canada's Navy: The First Century* (Toronto, Buffalo, London: University of Toronto Press, 1999), 19–20.

11. Michael L. Hadley and Roger Sarty, *Tin-Pots and Pirate Ships* (Montreal: McGill-Queen's University Press, 1991), 73.

12. *Ibid.*, 233–62.

13. *House of Commons Debates*, 26 July 1919, 2812–52; also Hadley and Sarty, *Tin-Pots*, 302.

14. Barry D. Hunt, "The Road to Washington: Canada and Empire Naval Defence, 1918–21," in Boutilier, ed., *The RCN in Retrospect*, 44–61. The cruiser *Aurora* and the destroyers *Patriot* and *Patrician* arrived in Halifax in December 1920.

15. Hose, Address, 5.

16. Paul Kennedy, "Naval Mastery," 15–33, 23.

17. Library and Archives Canada, MG 30 E89, vol. 6, Georges J. Desbarats Papers, diary entries for 21 and 24 April 1922.

18. Hose, Address, 5.

19. James George Eayrs, *In Defence of Canada: From the Great War to the Great Depression* (Toronto: University of Toronto Press, 1965), 171.

CHAPTER 2

Codfish, Cruisers, and Courage: The Newfoundland Division of the Royal Naval Reserve, 1900–22

W. David Parsons

Rich in maritime culture and lore, Newfoundland stands as a rocky and storm-beaten bastion against the surging Atlantic. To generations of deep-sea mariners it has offered safe haven. Its vivid place names bear witness to happy landfalls in centuries past: Harbour Grace (1583), Heart's Content (1612), and Come By Chance (1706). Indeed, the "Island" has been marked by over a thousand years of recorded seafaring history: Vikings at the end of the 10th century, the voyages of John Cabot (1497), Jacques Cartier (1535–36), and the coastal surveys of James Cook (1760s). Since the earliest days, rugged and enterprising seafarers have worked the Grand Banks in tall ships and open dories. In the Second World War St. John's served as naval base for the escorts of Atlantic convoys. Even though Newfoundland did not join Confederation until 1949, many would argue that the province spawned the first "Canadian" naval reserve. Unquestionably, the hardy British colony gained fame as a "nursery of fighting seamen" in defence of British imperial causes. And these causes included Canada as we know it today.

The Newfoundland Division of the Royal Naval Reserve was a component of Britain's Royal Naval Reserve that had been created in 1859. The Newfoundland Division enjoyed an active, though relatively brief, lifespan. Both shared a common concept: training for mobilization in emergency. Men were recruited from seamen in the merchant and fishing fleets, and would be trained by the Royal Navy for short periods both ashore and afloat. The Newfoundland Division was born in 1900 of the Admiralty's desire to support imperial defence as cheaply as possible. It was disbanded 22 years later for the same budgetary reasons. Its defining moment, of course, was the First World War, or what was known as "The Great War." In that conflict the reservists of the Newfoundland Royal Naval Reserve served with distinction all over the world with the Royal Navy and with a young Royal Canadian Navy, which was just four years old at the outbreak of war. Their memory lives on in the traditions of Canada's navy today.

The division had had cautious beginnings. When British forces withdrew their garrisons from the colonies in the 1870's, Britain urged the colonies to organize and finance their own defence as part of a unified imperial defence plan. The Newfoundland government rejected the notion, mainly for financial reasons.[1] By the early 1880s Lord Thomas Brassey, a civil lord of the Admiralty (1880–83), recommended during a visit to Newfoundland that an effort be made to enrol the fishermen in the Royal Naval Reserve. (He had visited Newfoundland earlier when circumnavigating the globe in his yacht *Sunbeam* in 1877–79.)

The North America and West Indies Squadron of the Royal Navy in St John's harbour, circa 1900.

Library and Archives Canada, C-023333.

Between 1898 and 1902 the Newfoundland government began evolving a policy to meet both local defence and the obligations to support British Admiralty policy and plans. In 1900 it committed itself to forming a local division of the Royal Naval Reserve.[2]

That year, during a tour of the northeast coast aboard HMS *Charybdis* (not the ill-fated earlier vessel, but a cruiser built in 1893), the governor of Newfoundland, Sir Henry MacCallum, undertook to engage 300 fishermen in the Royal Naval Reserve. Fifty of these fishermen were selected to take a six-month training cruise from November 1900 to May 1901. This proved so successful for both Britain's Royal Navy and the participants that arrangements were made to continue it the following year.[3] In fact, Newfoundland reservists formed part of the naval force aboard HMS *Charybdis* when it deployed to Venezuela in 1902 to protect British and foreign interests threatened by the Venezuelan dictator, President Cipriano Castro. It was here, in what was called at the time Newfoundland's "first naval incident," that the Newfoundlanders demonstrated their prowess as handlers of small boats. Whether landing marines or competing in fleet regattas, they were demonstrably without equal.[4]

At the Colonial Conference in London in June 1902, Sir Robert Bond, the prime minister of Newfoundland, offered a two-part proposal to meet Newfoundland's share in imperial defence: the Royal Navy should establish a cruiser base in St. John's harbour, and the Newfoundland Royal Naval Reserve contribute personnel.[5] To his mind, this solved the government's embarrassment over lack of preparation for the defence of the colony. Not only would this satisfy both the Admiralty and the British War Office, but it would cause a minimal drain on the Newfoundland exchequer. The actual training of reservists had begun.

The Admiralty agreed to send its 2,512-tonne, three-masted barque HMS *Calypso* as a drill ship for the Royal Naval Reserve, while remaining attached to the Bermuda Squadron in the Caribbean. Built in 1883 as the last British sailing corvette, it carried an armament of four 6-inch breech-loading guns, 15 5-inch guns, and 10 machine guns, as well as two torpedo tubes. It could reach 15 knots under steam, but projected a gallant image of old-world sea power with all canvas set. As the *Evening Telegram* reported on 15 October 1902, it sailed through the narrows of St. Johns harbour, skippered by Commander F.M. Walker, RN. Its permanent staff of Royal Navy personnel consisted of the commanding officer, a surgeon, and a paymaster, as well as instructors for drill and gunnery. Regular force ratings such as stokers, carpenters, and storesmen maintained the vessel. A schoolmaster offered lessons to those reservists who wished to advance their education.

Its arrival had not been without its critics. Some suggested the ship be anchored in a remote cove in Placentia Bay so that unruly seamen would not disturb the city. Others outside St. John's feared that the "big city" would tempt the fine fishermen away from the outports. For practical and probably commercial reasons, the decision was made to dock it in St. John's at the Reid Newfoundland wharf near the railway station. The masts and funnel were removed, and the decks covered in order to provide accommodation and a "drill hall" to train reserves. There it remained for the next 20 years, training over 1,400 seamen from 1900 to 1914.

Although many partook of only one year's training, others returned for five periods or more. Some of these made what was known as "the cruise down south," a voyage in a

HMS *Calypso* underway in full sailing splendour, circa 1890.

The Rooms Provincial Archives of Newfoundland, B-17-22.

deep-sea Royal Navy warship of the West Indies Squadron.[6] Training included drill, rifle practice, firing the ship's guns (which had been removed and placed near Fort Amherst at the entrance of St. John's harbour), and — deemed of special use when boarding enemy ships — handling a cutlass. This was precisely the type of training that any Royal Navy recruit would undergo. As in the Royal Navy, the seamen were paid one shilling three pence per day (about 33 cents) and one shilling six pence when promoted to qualified seaman. On completion of five years training, they would receive a bonus of five pounds. For many, this extra cash came at a time when it was unlikely they would have been profitably employed in the fishery. At the end of the "cruise down South," every effort was made to assure the seamen's return home in time for the season's fishery or seal hunt.[7]

In the spring of 1914, Commander Anthony MacDermott, RN, was appointed commanding officer of HMS *Calypso*. He guided the Newfoundland Division throughout the war years until 1919. MacDermott lived aboard ship with his wife and children, and their nanny, a Miss Kathleen Dyer, whom he signed on as crew in 1916 so she could officially live aboard ship.[8] That would seem to make her Newfoundland's first female reservist.

When the "guns of August" blazed forth in Europe to open the "war to end all wars," Newfoundland's active enrolment stood at nearly 500 men. On 3 August 1914 a royal proclamation had summoned all reservists to report aboard HMS *Calypso*. By the end of the month nearly 400 reservists had joined the ship.[9] Of those who did not report right away, some were finishing the season's fishery, while others had migrated to Canada. Yet others were counted among those who had lost their lives in the sealing disasters of the spring of 1914: SS *Southern Cross* had sunk in a storm with the loss of all 175 crew, and 75 sealers from SS *Newfoundland* had perished when caught on the ice in a blizzard.[10]

Hostilities thrust Newfoundland's reservists into a variety of tasks and theatres of war. They operated the wireless stations at Cape Race and Mount Pearl, and the cable stations at Heart's Content and Cape Ray. They served in home waters, in the North Sea and English Channel, from the Mediterranean to Archangel, as well as in the Gallipoli landings. They crewed various classes of vessel from battleships to cruisers, trawlers, and sailing cutters. Indeed, the first Newfoundlanders to go on active wartime service were the 106 seamen of the Newfoundland Division of the Royal Naval Reserve who brought the crew of HMCS *Niobe* to its wartime complement. When it arrived in St. John's harbour on 6 September 1914 with its 298 Royal Navy seamen and 333 Royal Canadian Navy seamen, the reservists went aboard, and steamed out on a war footing.

The unannounced swiftness of this arrival and departure caught Newfoundland's governor, Sir Walter Davidson, completely off guard. As chairman of the Patriotic Association, which had been formed to conduct the dominion's military affairs, he was upset that he had not been informed of *Niobe*'s arrival and been invited aboard. Commander Anthony MacDermott, the commanding officer of HMS *Calypso*, informed the governor that by order of the Royal Navy all ship movements were secret, and by keeping silent both he and *Niobe* had been obeying orders. The governor did not interfere with the Royal Naval Reserve again.[11] When HMCS *Niobe* was paid off in the summer of 1915, the Newfoundland reservists were given a short leave in Newfoundland before being deployed overseas to serve where they were most needed. They had proven in all respects equal to the Royal Navy's seamen. As will be elaborated below, many Newfoundlanders subsequently served with fleet units as diverse as ships of the auxiliary fleet, defensively armed merchant ships (DAMS), minesweeping trawlers, the 10th Cruiser Squadron, and the legendary "mystery ships."[12] There were Newfoundlanders on the battleships and cruisers of the Royal Navy.

David Parsons collection.

Commander Anthony MacDermott.

The Rooms Provincial Archives of Newfoundland, A-11-165.

Trainees get a tour around
St John's harbour.

One Newfoundland reservist was lost at the Battle of Jutland, the major big-ship, big-gun sea battle between the fleets of Britain and Germany. Each of these naval tasks had its dangers and challenges, and each remains an icon of meritorious sea service.

The 10th Cruiser Squadron consisted of merchant ships — designated as armed merchant cruisers, or AMCs — requisitioned and armed by the Admiralty, and crewed largely by reservists. Most of these vessels were merchant ships — a few of them passenger ships. Judging from mail written from them, there were no luxury liners. Newfoundlanders got their sea billets after shore training either at HM Ships *Vivid* (Plymouth), *Victory* (Portsmouth), or *Pembroke* (Chatham). Their task was to blockade the seas between the north of Scotland and Iceland to prevent neutral ships destined for Norway, Sweden, Denmark, and Holland from carrying contraband that could be transshipped to Germany for use in the war. Any suspicious ship would be stopped and searched. If suspected of carrying contraband, the ship would be sent to a port in Scotland under a prize crew for further examination. This whole operation of detain-and-search required crossing open waters with a boarding party in an open boat either under oars or sail — regardless of the weather or sea state. This is a hazardous task, for the region is notorious for foul weather — blizzards during the long winter months, fog, gales, and storms all year round. This is where Admiral of the Fleet Earl Beatty acclaimed the Newfoundland reservists. Their skill in handling the small boats across rough waters, a skill honed in the fishing grounds of the Newfoundland coast, made them in his eyes "the best small boat seamen in the Royal Navy."[13]

Service aboard armed merchant cruisers was dangerous. Fifty-eight Newfoundlanders died in the early spring of 1915 when HM Ships *Viknor* and *Bayano* were sunk by enemy action, and HMS *Clan MacNaughton* foundered in a storm. Eight Newfoundlanders received citations for bravery.[14] Pitched battle on the high seas was always a possibility that could quickly become reality. This is precisely what happened when, as *The New York Times* announced on 26 March 1916, "German Raider *Greif* and British Converted Cruiser *Alcantara* Battle to the Death." Disguised as a neutral Norwegian merchantman, the SMS *Greif* had been attempting to break through the blockade when accosted by the 10th Squadron's HMCS *Alcantara* on 29 February 1916. The encounter is unique in naval history: the only battle between two armed merchantmen. Both ships sank with heavy loss of life: *Greif* by gunfire, and the badly damaged *Alcantara* by a torpedo from a British destroyer. Among the many Newfoundlanders serving in *Alcantara* two died.[15] Nearly 300 Newfoundland reservists had served in the 10th Cruiser Squadron from 1914 until

Men of the Newfoundland Division RNR at field training near Halifax Dockyard, presumably 1902.

Department of National Defence, CN-5002.

7 December 1917, when the squadron was disbanded. With the United States now a combatant ally, the Americans would now control cargos from their North American source.

Mystery ships, or Q-ships, were Britain's response to the threat of German submarines. Newfoundlanders served in these as well. (Seaman John Joseph Power was killed aboard Q 20, HMS *Bayard*, when it was run down in a collision.) So "treacherous" were Q-ships, in fact, that the Germans regarded them as piratical craft. In those days, submarines were little more than submersible torpedo boats. They generally submerged to hide, and surfaced to attack. Disguised as unarmed vessels — tramp steamers, colliers, trawlers, or schooners — Q-ships were designed as bait to entice a submarine to surface and attack. Once the submarine was in range, the Q-ship would drop its disguise and open fire. Such ships sank 15 submarines. Yet their greater value lay in causing the submarine to avoid attacking seemingly defenceless small ships altogether. Thus the *ruse de guerre* saved many smaller vessels from the guns of the underwater craft.

Seamen of the Newfoundland Division of the Royal Naval Reserve served with distinction throughout the Gallipoli campaign. Some were aboard HMS *Cornwallis* when it fired the first shots at the Turkish forts. When the landings took place on 25 April 1915, Newfoundland reservists operated the boats to take the soldiers ashore; they ferried supplies and transported the wounded from the beaches to the hospital ships. They were there in January 1916 when the last soldier was evacuated from the beaches at Suvla Bay and Cape Helles. Others were part of the crew on the trawlers clearing the mines, and on the drifters laying anti-submarine nets to protect the battleships, which were lying at anchor bombarding the shore.[16]

Trainees aboard HMS *Calypso*, 1915.

The Rooms Provincial Archives of Newfoundland, B-51-85.

The largest number of Newfoundland reservists served in auxiliary ships. These were the trawlers, drifters, paddleboats, and yachts requisitioned by the Admiralty. In 1912 the Admiralty had investigated the use of trawlers to sweep for mines. Trawlers had evolved over the years for the fishery in the North Sea and off Iceland, resulting in a sturdy sea-worthy craft. The experiment was successful. The Admiralty consequently requisitioned a number of trawlers and later had them built specifically for the navy. These small ships were used for minesweeping, laying nets to protect harbours, and to prevent submarines using the Channel. They were used to spot submarines, and also in convoy duty. Although these trawlers were the fishing boats of the North Sea and quite different from the type of fishing craft to which a Newfoundlander was accustomed, these men adapted and served well on these ships. But there was a toll to be paid: more than 30 Newfoundlanders were lost in this arm of the navy.[17] Equally important to the war effort were the DAMS — defensively armed merchant ships — on which Newfoundlanders served as gunners and deckhands. More than 20 lost their lives. These vessels formed Britain's lifeline by carrying cargo from all parts of the world. Armed to repel submarines and enemy raiders, they supplied Allied fighting forces in France and Belgium, the Mediterranean to Salonika, Mesopotamia, as well as Africa and to India.

Most of the casualties of the Newfoundland Division of the Royal Naval Reserve occurred at sea when their ships sank. Of course, others died of illness or accident. But

Imperial War Museum, Q 13682.

Newfoundland seamen were embarked in HMS *Cornwallis* supporting their comrades ashore during the bombardment of Gallipoli.

Two Newfoundland seamen in HMS *Alcantara* were killed on 28 February 1916, in her sinking of SMS *Greif*, a converted merchantman serving the Germans as an armed raider.

David Parsons collection.

even ashore they were within enemy reach. Thus on 3 September 1917 four Newfoundland reservists were among the 135 seamen killed at the shore base HMS *Pembroke* (Chatham) when a German Gotha bomber dropped two primitive bombs on the drill hall. The glass and metal structure collapsed causing not only the deaths, but more than 40 wounded.

Meanwhile back home, in and around Newfoundland, national defence continued, though not without a tug-of-war between British Admiralty plans and Canadian aspirations. The Canadian government wanted the centre for North American intelligence-collecting to be in Halifax. The Admiralty, however, was reluctant to relinquish control of intelligence gathering to the Canadians, and built the wireless station outside of St. John's at Mount Pearl. It became operational in 1915. The operators were "Marconi" men seconded to the Royal Navy, while the Royal Naval Reserve supplied a company of reservists for guard duty. This wireless station was one of 19 built around the world to transmit information to the Admiralty in London. The station at Mount Pearl was responsible for transmitting the information and intelligence coming from the United States and Canada. In 1917, the intelligence centre was transferred to Halifax.

By 1917 German submarines had proven their ability to cross the Atlantic and return home without refuelling. The cargo-carrying *U-Deutschland* had made two commercial voyages to the United States in 1916, the year in which the combat submarine *U-53* wreaked havoc off New York, sinking ships while 20 neutral American destroyers looked on.[18] Ships of the Newfoundland Merchant Navy were attacked and sunk by German predators. On 8 August 1916, for example, SS *Stephano* was sunk according to "Prize Rules" (i.e., after allowing all passengers and crew to take to the lifeboats) by *U-53* off Nantucket Lightship, while an American destroyer stood by and observed the action. SS *Eric* was sunk by *U-156* on 26 August 1918. The schooner *Jean* was sunk in March 1917 and the schooner *Duchess of Cornwall* was sunk in December 1916, both by surface raiders. The schooner *Dictator* was sunk by *U-151* in June 1918. The war had come close to the shores of Newfoundland.

Rumours abounded about German submarines refuelling in isolated harbours in northern Newfoundland and Labrador, and prompted the formation of patrols to investigate these reports. Now in charge of home defence, Commander MacDermott organized what was locally known as the "Newfoundland Navy" by arming a number of local coastal boats to examine the coast of Newfoundland and Labrador for any suspicious activity. SS *Fogato*, SS *Cabot*, and SS *Petrel* were armed and parts of their crew were Naval reservists from HMS *Calypso*.[19] Naval authorities in St. John's agreed on joint areas of surveillance. While the Newfoundland patrols would monitor Labrador, the East Coast, and the eastern half of the southern coast of Newfoundland, Canadian ships would monitor the western half of the South Coast and the Strait of Belle Isle.

In 1917 those Newfoundland reservists who had been serving with the 10th Cruiser Squadron returned to HMS *Briton* in St. John's to await posting to another ship. (The former HMS *Calypso*, it had been renamed in March 1916.) As the Royal Canadian Navy

The Mersey-class trawler, *John Cormack*, of the Auxiliary Patrol.

David Parsons collection.

was short of crews to man the trawlers acquired for service off the East Coast to counter the German submarine threat, 190 Newfoundland reservists were drafted to Halifax and Sydney, Nova Scotia. Nineteen of them were posted to trawlers as skippers. The matter of pay became an issue. Where the Newfoundland reservist was paid at the Royal Navy rate of one shilling three pence a day (about 33 cents), the Canadian seaman was paid 70 cents while at sea. Of course, the Newfoundlanders were willing to put up with the discomfort of serving in the trawlers. But they objected to doing "dirty work" like scraping a ship of rust while their Canadian mates were receiving twice the pay. Fortunately, a wise solution avoided a "mutiny" and the Newfoundlanders were paid the Canadian rate while serving out of their new base in HMCS *Niobe*.[20]

The Halifax explosion of 6 December 1917 marked a new datum in Canada's consciousness.[21] And reservists from Newfoundland were there. Indeed, one lad then serving with the Royal Canadian Navy aboard HMCS *Musquash*, Boy Stewart Pieroway, was killed. He was just 16. For weeks after the city had been razed, reservists from Newfoundland were engaged in rescue work, helping the injured, recovering the bodies from wrecked houses, helping to find shelter and food for those victims of the disaster. Acts of quiet heroism prevailed. In one graphic case, divers had descended a ladder leading to the harbour floor to inspect the base of a crane when the explosion struck. The pressure wave sucked the water away from the dock that held their air pumps, leaving the heavy-suited

The "Newfoundland Navy": SS *Fogato*.

303

The Rooms Provincial Archives of Newfoundland, E 34-35.

The Rooms Provincial Archives of Newfoundland, NA-39-97.

Memorial University College, 1923.

divers wallowing in the muddy harbour floor 5.5 metres below without air, and sweeping the attending crew off the dock. Able Seaman Walter George Critch of the Newfoundland Division was one of the six men working the air pump under Chief Petty Officer John T. Gammon. Bruised and dazed, and with debris from the blast falling dangerously all about them, Critch restored the pump, while Gammon scrambled down to the divers in the muck below, untangled the air lines, and helped the encumbered divers back up to the dock just as the water came pounding back again. For their bravery in saving lives under hazardous conditions Gammon was appointed a member of the Order of the British Empire (Military Division), and Critch was awarded the Meritorious Service Medal.

After the Armistice in November 1918, the Newfoundlanders began returning home to HMS *Briton* for demobilization and civilian life. In 1919 the next entry of reservists to train on HMS *Briton* was cancelled. The Admiralty was reducing the navy. Yet the paymaster was probably the busiest man, figuring out the pay and gratuities for each person. Prize money, the time-honoured method of rewarding sailors, was paid to all seaman of the Royal Navy who served at sea. It was calculated on the value of the ships captured or sunk. A share for each man was calculated, plus a bonus if that man was in the ship that sunk or captured an enemy ship. As late as 1930, efforts were being made to contact men to whom money was owed.

As early as 1912 the question had arisen about relocating HMS *Calypso*. After all, it was said, the space at the wharf could be more profitably used by the Reid Newfoundland Company. Now that the war was over, people pursued this old idea. Then, in 1922 when the Admiralty was reducing the size of the fleet, HMS *Briton* was sold to the commercial firm of A.H. Murray and Company, as a hulk for coal and salt. This marked the end of the Royal Naval Reserve in Newfoundland. In the 1920s, and again in the Royal Commission's Amulree Report of 1934, the question of reviving the reserve arose.[22] Feeling the effects of the Great Depression on its budget, the Admiralty was not interested. For the next 25 years, the hulk lay at anchor in St. John's harbour. In 1954, its usefulness at an end, it was towed to Lewisporte harbour on the Northeast coast. Finally, it was taken to Embree where it rests, forgotten.

The Newfoundland Division RNR panel on the war memorial at Beaumont-Hamel, France.

Courtesy Richard Gimblett.

Yet other memorials do remain. For instance, Fort Waldegrave has been guarding the entrance to St. John's harbour since the 1700s. Named after Governor William Waldegrave (1797–1800), it had been operated off and on until 1870 when the imperial forces withdrew from Newfoundland. In August 1914, it was again guarding the harbour, with a 12-pounder gun from HMS *Calypso*. From June 1916 the garrison consisted of members of the Legion of Frontiersmen, commanded by Lieutenant E. Vere-Holloway. From time to time, seamen from *Calypso* used the gun for training. After the war, the battery fell into disrepair — until 2005 when it was refurbished as a memorial to the men who had served there during the First World War.[23]

During that war, 1,996 men served in the Newfoundland Division of the Royal Naval Reserve. One hundred ninety-two gave their lives. For many, the sea was their grave, and their names are inscribed on the memorial plaque at Beaumont-Hamel Memorial Park in France. The last casualty of war was Seaman F.J. Price, drowned in August 1919 while sweeping mines off the Belgian coast. He is buried in Ostende Military Cemetery, Belgium.[24] Twenty-seven Newfoundland reservists received citations for bravery. One received a Distinguished Service Cross, 11 received the Distinguished Service Medal, one a Meritorious Service Medal, and 14 were Mentioned-in-Dispatches. There were other Newfoundlanders serving in the Royal Navy, other than the naval reserve, who were decorated for gallantry.

There is no doubt that the newly formed Royal Canadian Navy benefited from the assistance of the trained seamen of the Newfoundland Division of the Royal Naval Reserve. They were the personnel who helped man HMCS *Niobe* in 1914–15, and again in 1917–18 were ready to man the trawler fleet of the RCN. While still a separate dominion at this time, Newfoundland expected to offer timely co-operation to its neighbouring member of the empire. Perhaps the greatest benefit resulting from the service and sacrifice of the men and women of Newfoundland during the First World War was the establishment of Memorial University College in 1925. The college offered courses to prepare the students to continue their education in Canada or the U.K. In 1949, Memorial University College became Memorial University of Newfoundland, now one of the largest universities in the Atlantic region, with faculties in Arts, Science, Engineering, Commerce, Nursing, and Medicine. It stands as a lasting tribute to those who served during the war.

Yet another legacy links the seafaring traditions of Newfoundland with those of "the rest of Canada." When HMS *Charybdis* made St. John's harbour its home from 1902 to 1905, its training officer was Lieutenant Walter Hose of the Royal Navy. He readily recognized the value of Newfoundland's reservists and had a high regard for their skills. Not only that, he had married a girl from St. John's. In 1912, seeing little hope for advancement in the Royal Navy, he transferred to the Royal Canadian Navy, which was then but two years old. His experience with the Newfoundland reservists made him a strong advocate of a reserve in the Canadian navy, and helped establish the Royal Canadian Naval Volunteer Reserve. For this reason, he is regarded as the father of Canada's naval reserve.

HMCS *Cabot*, home of the Naval Reserve in Newfoundland, came into existence in 1949 when Newfoundland joined Canada, and thrives today at a new location not far from where HMS *Calypso* once lay moored.[25]

Notes

1. Glen Kehoe, "Imperial Defence and the Foundation of the Royal Naval Reserve" (B.A. Honours thesis, Memorial University of Newfoundland, 1994).
2. Provincial Archives of Newfoundland and Labrador (PANL), Secretary of State (Colonies), to Governor, 6 December 1900.
3. PANL, GN 2/39.
4. P.T. McGrath, "The Naval Incident," *Canadian Magazine*, April 1903, Vol. 67, 531.
5. PANL, GN1/2/0, Statement by Sir Robert Bond, Prime Minister, 1 July 1902.
6. PANL, GN 1/2/0, Admiralty, to Colonial Secretary, 27 November 1902.
7. P.T. McGrath, "The Newfoundland Naval Reserve," *Newfoundland Quarterly*, (March 1906) (4): 17.
8. Communication to the author from Dr. Doreann MacDermott de Carnicer, daughter of Commander Anthony MacDermott, RN, OBE, KM (1878–1965).
9. PANL, GN 1/10/1, Governor Sir Walter Davidson, to L. Harcourt, Dominion Secretary, 23 November 1914.
10. Shannon Ryan, *Ice Hunters: A History of Newfoundland Sealing to 1914* (St. John's: Breakwater Press, 1994).
11. PANL, GN1/10/1, Commander McDermott to Sir Walter Davidson, 28 November 1914
12. PANL, GN1/10/1, Captain Robert Corbett, RN, to Sir Walter Davidson, Governor of Newfoundland, 27 March 1915.
13. F.G. Bowen, *History of the Royal Naval Reserve* (London: Lloyds, 1926), 129–30.

14. Lieutenant-Commander J.T. Randell (in command of the armed trawler HMT *Tenby Castle*) received the Distinguished Service Cross, while Seamen A. Gregory, L. Green, and M. Pottle received the Distinguished Service Medal. Four others were Mentioned-in-Dispatches: Lieutenant. Stanley Duder, and Able Seamen G. Boucher, A. Collins, and Enos Ryan. In 1939 Randell was appointed naval officer in charge (St. John's). He resigned in 1942 because of ill health and died the next year.

15. Among those killed in action were Seamen William Dawe and Nathan Mugford. Able Seamen Alfred Andrews and William Peddle were Mentioned-in-Dispatches for their bravery that day.

16. H.Y. Wells, "Bombarding the Dardanelles," *Veteran Magazine* (Vol. 4 (4), March 1929), 54; (Vol. 10 (3), May 1935), 36; (Vol. 11 (2), April 1936), 33.

17. For this and the following see W.D. Parsons and E.J. Parsons, *The Best Small-Boat Seamen in the Navy* (St. John's: DRC Publishers, 2008).

18. Michael L. Hadley and Roger Sarty, *Tin-Pots and Pirate Ships* (Montreal: McGill-Queen's University Press, 1991), 131.

19. PANL, GN 2/14, box 2, Home Defence and Patrols (April to December, 1918).

20. PANL, Department of Militia Report, 1919; Chief Accountant, North America, to Paymaster, Department of Militia, St. John's, Newfoundland, 9 December 1919.

21. Hadley and Sarty, *Tin-Pots and Pirate Ships*, 203; John Griffith Armstrong, *The Halifax Explosion and the Royal Canadian Navy* (Vancouver: UBC Press, 2002), 4.

22. Newfoundland Royal Commission 1933 (The Amulree Report), (London: H.M. Stationery Office, 1934).

23. PANL, MG 267, 1914–17, Fort Waldegrave.

24. PANL, G2/5 (414), report of the Newfoundland Militia, 1919.

25. Hector Swain, *Cabot, History of the Naval Reserve in Newfoundland*. (n.p., 1975); Anon. "Sailing through the Narrows: the Naval Reserve in Newfoundland. Celebrating the 50th Anniversary of HMCS Cabot" (St. John's: n.p., 1999).

CHAPTER 3

The Reserve Preserve: How the RCNVR Saved the Navy

Barbara Winters

Canada never really experienced the "roaring twenties." The wealth and glamour of that decade were confined mostly to jazz-age America. In Canada, the brief, happy celebrations of armistice after the 1914–18 war were soon doused by the cold reality of the war's ruinous toll. In the decades that followed that calamity, Canada suffered its way through debt, disease, inflation, and the Great Depression.

From its formation in 1923 to the beginning of the Second World War, the fortunes of the Royal Canadian Naval Volunteer Reserve mirrored those of Canada itself. Born out of tough economic choices, the RCNVR struggled for recognition in the 1920s. It struggled for its existence in the 1930s. Yet the reputation, character and traditions of the service were established in these years. Thankfully, they were as solid and unassuming as Canadians themselves. But the history of the reserve in this period is important not just because these were the formative years of the service, but because, in these decades at least, the RCNVR formed the heart of the naval service in Canada. Indeed, without the Naval Reserve, it is questionable whether a naval service could have existed at all.

The value of Prime Minister Laurier's "tin-pot navy" had triggered heated debate since its inception. With only one ship on each coast and 350 men, it could hardly defend Canada's long coastlines. During the First World War, Britain had been forced to assume direct responsibility for defending the sea approaches to Canada and its shipping lanes. But even with this support, German submarines had managed to lurk off the East Coast, and sink ships. The "tin-pots," it turns out, were too small to defend Canada in times of war and too expensive to expand in times of peace. The solution, argued the British in 1920, was for

Canada to contribute to a single, unified "imperial fleet" under their command and control. Britain would again assume responsibility for Canada's coastal defence, and Canadians would simply have to pay for it.

For England, it was the perfect solution to a series of post-war problems. Its ships and men lay idle, and if Canada paid for this "defence service" it would save the Royal Navy from having to sell off its ships for a fraction of what they were worth. Despite some preliminary discussion, Laurier's successor, Prime Minister Robert Borden, dismissed the idea as unsupportable. Having been denied Canadian contributions to the cost of their fleet, the British then insisted that their admiral of the fleet, Earl Jellicoe, undertake a cross-Canada tour under the guise of providing advice. In reality, however, his tour was an opportunity for England to shape Canada's domestic defence decisions.

Prime Minister Borden intended to craft the country's own defence policies. Faced with the impending arrival of Admiral John "Hell-fire" Jellicoe, a naval committee was created to meticulously examine Canada's present and future naval requirements. The committee consisted of only three men: the deputy minister of naval services, the director of naval services himself, and the assistant to the director. The qualifications of Vice-Admiral Kingsmill as director, and Captain Hose as assistant to the director, were impressive. Both Kingsmill and Hose had begun their careers in the Royal Navy. Walter Hose, in particular, was a sailor's sailor. He had been born on the Indian Ocean aboard a steamer, joined the Royal Navy at 14 and spent 21 years at sea before his first desk assignment. He had proved

A grim metaphor of the future facing the RCN, *Niobe* ended the war as a depot ship hulk in Halifax harbour.

Department of National Defence, CN-6369.

his worth several times over during the war. Both he and Kingsmill were Canadian nationalists, and their goal of a large domestic navy was not born out of envy, but out of a conviction of Canada's potential for becoming a great nation.

In its three short years of existence, the committee explored naval defence matters to such a degree that no less than 37 formal reports were submitted to parliament for consideration. These reports, however, were so fiscally optimistic that they completely miscalculated the mood of the nation. The First World War had done more than simply rob Canada of the bloom of its youth; it had made its politicians wary of wars in general, and leery of imperialist squabbles in particular. Curiously, the committee missed or ignored this enormous sea change in attitude. This crucial oversight imperilled their whole enterprise. Indeed, the political response to the committee's final proposal was the near elimination of the naval service itself.

Just consider what the very young, 50-year old nation had been through. Six hundred thousand Canadian men had served in the war; over 60,660 had lost their lives. Thousands more had been injured, permanently disfigured or disabled. Halifax, a major city at the time, had been levelled by the 1917 explosion, and had never properly recovered. Unbearable delays forced war-weary soldiers to wait up to a year and a half before they could get home. Some of the riots that broke out among the stranded were so violent that men were killed. When they did come home, the soldiers brought the Spanish influenza with them. Almost as many Canadians died from the flu as all the battlefield deaths combined. Worse still, the disease hit the young hardest; six out of 10 mortalities were adults between the ages of 20 and 40.

Then there was the cost of the war. Inflation had risen to outrageous levels. In 1916, it was eight percent; one year later, it had risen to a staggering 18 percent. Wages, however, remained at their 1913 levels. One year into the war, military spending alone equalled the government's entire expenditure for the previous year. By 1918, the outlay was more than $2.5 million *a day* (over $30 million in 2008 dollars). In response, the government turned to personal income tax, corporate tax, and borrowing through wartime bond issues. However, bonds only increased the country's debt load. And by the end of the war, the government was paying $164 million a year on interest alone — more than $2 billion in today's dollars. It spent a further $76 million a year in soldier's pensions — almost $1 billion in today's dollars. This was more than the country's entire pre-war budget. Sales tax was introduced, and rose to a peak of six percent by 1926.

Imperial War Museum, Q-055499.

British Admiral Lord Jellicoe, seen here during the action against the German High Seas Fleet in the Battle of Jutland, 1917, toured the Dominions in 1919 to offer professional advice on their postwar fleet development.

Library and Archives Canada, PA-064568.

Commodore (first class) Walter Hose in his official photo as chief of the naval staff.

On the political front, conscription had splintered the thin veneer of Anglo-French relations, causing riots and a political crisis. Borden's efforts to win the 1917 election fractured the country along regional, cultural, linguistic, and class lines. A few women had won the vote, but other Canadians — recent immigrants associated with enemy countries — had seen this right rescinded.

Financially, militarily, and politically, the cost of the war had been too great. Canada turned inward as disgust over the ravages of the war began to set in. At the first assembly of the League of Nations on 16 January 1920, the Canadian delegate rose to chastise the Europeans and to make clear the cost of their folly. As the records of the debate reported: "Fifty thousand Canadians under the soil of France and Flanders is what Canada has paid for European statesmanship trying to settle European problems."

In any event, who was the enemy? "There is no world menace," declared a Liberal member when debating the defence expenditures of 1920. And again: "the Minister says that this expenditure is needed for the defence of Canada — defence against whom? There is no answer; there is no answer to be made."

The only enemy, it seemed to some, was the enemy within. With the economy faltering, and inflation and taxes hitting the working class hard, class tensions were simmering. Much of the dissent came from ex-servicemen. Significantly, the police were listening. The Royal Northwest Mounted Police (RNWMP), the forerunner of the Royal Canadian Mounted Police (RCMP), was handling domestic intelligence at the time. Their intelligence reports in the month before the 1919 Winnipeg general strike noted that unions were "fanning grievance [by] pressing their views that it was a "capitalists' war" telling the men that they should get easy posts after their exertions etc." The main source of danger would come when the one year post-war service gratuity ran out, and the men were "cast to their own resources," a situation the police viewed as "exceedingly dangerous."[1]

Vice-Admiral Kingsmill apparently shared this view. Alarmed by the secret reports of the RNWMP, Kingsmill wrote to his fellow committee member, the deputy minister:

> In view of a disturbance at any moment at Victoria, Vancouver etc. we have not sufficient naval force to protect the dockyard and government stores nor the magazine at Cole [sic] Island ... a considerable naval strength is necessary if the government finds itself compelled to cope with an attempt at revolution.[2]

This then, is the environment in which the Naval Committee drafted recommendations for the future of the navy. In the three years in which the committee existed, Canada was rocked by a financial crisis so severe that only the Great Depression would best it. The country lay stressed by violent labour and linguistic unrest, and was laid low by a pandemic that killed 60,000 young and healthy adults. The Naval Committee ignored the big issues: lack of a foreign enemy, increased world isolationism, and growing pacifism. Yet it blithely proposed that the navy should grow in both strength and permanency. Canadian naval defence, they wrote, should be ushered into a new age by a program of expansion until the fleet consisted of seven cruisers, 12 destroyers, six submarines, 18 patrol craft, and three parent ships with a proposed complement of 8,500 officers and men. The total estimated cost for shipbuilding alone was $57,740,000. It was, according to the committee, "a good basis for future development."[3]

Reality burst through the door in December 1921, when Mackenzie King was elected prime minister. His government ushered in a new and uncomplicated approach to defence. "It is the public will, not force, that makes for enduring peace, and peace can always be kept, whatever the grounds of controversy, between people who wish to keep it." Public opinion supported this view. Writing on 9 September 1927, a few years after the Liberal win, Victoria's *The Daily Colonist* editorialized:

> *Few people in British Columbia, and not many in Canada, sustain any interest in questions of naval or military activity or "preparedness" in either of these fields of national effort. Neither by intuition nor imminent necessity are*

The first lodgings of many RCNVR companies often were quite primitive, such as this one in Prince Rupert, seen "dressed overall" in 1928.

Directorate of History & Heritage, Chatham PRF.

from "civvy street," who were taught their seafaring skills. Two months later, the first steps were taken to put plans into effect. Units were established — on paper at least — in Charlottetown, Saint John, Quebec, Montreal, Ottawa, Toronto, Hamilton, Winnipeg, Saskatoon, Calgary, Edmonton, and Vancouver. Because of the presence of the RCN "regular force" in both Esquimalt and Halifax, no reserve units were created in either city. The design of the RCNVR was patterned on the RNVR. The period of service for officers was "at pleasure," while the term of enrolment for men was a period of three years. But both officers and men could request a discharge at any time.

All members were required to attend naval training for a minimum of 14 days a year either in Halifax or Esquimalt. Facilities in which parades could be held were scarce, and equipment almost non-existent; the men had to be dedicated, for the financial rewards were few. Ratings were paid 25 cents a drill night for a maximum of 30 nights. Often, men paid for their own manuals, shared them, or simply did without. Full training days did not include meals. Unlike today's members, however, a marriage allowance was paid when the men went into active service (training). The maximum amount of voluntary service remained the same throughout the interwar period: two weeks of training for first-year ratings and four weeks for others.

The destroyer HMCS *Vancouver* passing through the Panama Canal on her way to spring exercises in the Caribbean in the late-1920s.

Department of National Defence, CN-5098.

The RCNVR units had no permanent homes. Given the budgetary constraints, the buildings they used had to come cheap. Usually, the quality of the structure matched the rent paid. Pipes leaked, heating was poor, space was at a premium, and supplies virtually non-existent. The units generally had no administrative or training areas, men studied by drawing up chairs in open areas. There were no phones, no staff, no stores, and no support.

The severe lack of funding forced the Vancouver Half-Company to train aboard a private yacht rather than a military vessel. And while the unit's commanding officer went to great expense to provide his company with the training they needed, his methods were often unconventional. Consider his description of a training weekend:

> *The ... weekend cruise of the month was made to Ganges Harbour, Salt Spring Island. The ship was brought to anchor in the harbour and three very pleasant days were spent in training work. As this was the opening of the deer season, the C.O. went ashore and shot a deer. The venison was much enjoyed by all hands. On the return an excellent breeze carried the ship, under full sail, across the Gulf of Georgia and much experience was gained by the men in handling the ship under press of sail. When the ship was safely back at her moorings in Vancouver all hands expressed their regret that the pleasant voyage had come to an end.*[8]

Significantly, inadequate funding meant that some reserve companies were forced to provide their own vessels. For cities such as Vancouver with access to a schooner, all training was confined to mastering the elements of sailing rather than steaming. More to the point, contemporaries must have found it difficult to see beyond the apparent frivolity of such a weekend to the skills that were being acquired.

The reserve therefore faced a problem common to all organizations in their infancy — the lack of recognition by other, more established, institutions. In Vancouver, the problem was so pressing that it had to be reported to Ottawa. The commanding officer of the Half-Company reported that the RCNVR was not recognized "by certain authorities, in particular the Mayor, the Harbour Commission, and *[not even] the Military*" itself [emphasis added].[9] The reply came from no less than the deputy minister himself who pointed out to the Harbour Commission that the unit "was an integral part of the Naval Service of Canada, and as such, forms part of the defence forces of the Crown."[10] Internal memos to the army and regular RCN were no doubt similarly dispatched. It is not particularly surprising that the question of recognition arose. Canada had never before enjoyed a proper, national naval reserve, and its role was in any event sketchy and ill-defined. Indeed, the naval secretary felt that the primary duty of the reserve was simply "the education and familiarisation of Canadians with the presence of a naval force."

Taking in "Ammunition" at Bermuda: H.M.C.S. Champlain, *1932*, sketch by Wendy Trethewey.

Department of National Defence, HS020787r57.

The issue of recognition by the public was not insignificant. As noted above, Naval Headquarters considered it to be the *only* important role of the reserve during this period. But press clippings from the time reveal the ambiguity and distrust Canadians still felt toward military matters. On the creation of the reserve unit in Vancouver, *The Vancouver Sun* of 5 July 1924 could offer nothing better than a grudging remark:

> *Following the example of many Canadian inland towns, Vancouver has at last formed a half-company of the Royal Canadian Naval Volunteer Reserve.... Whatever views he may have on militarism, conscription, disarmament and kindred subjects, every citizen honours the young man who gives freely of his own time and energy to the performance of what he conceives to be a high public duty.*

Military service, as the article reveals, was no longer the only — or even proper — proof of civic loyalty. If Naval Service Headquarters had any doubt that Canadians did not welcome the idea of a strong military, and even less a strong navy, that proof lay in the difficulty the service had in recruiting commanding officers. One month after the post had

The rifle team of the Halifax Half-Company, 1930, including (back row third from left) Chief Petty Officer Instructor Charles Parnall and (front row centre) Lieutenant Joseph P. Connolly, a close friend of future Minister of the Naval Service Angus L. Macdonald.

Department of National Defence, CN-6724.

been advertised, not a single application had been received despite the assistance of both the Naval Officers Association and the Navy League.

The new Naval Reserve might strive to be a Canadian force that was local in presence and national in organization, but it was essentially British in character. This is not surprising, for several reasons. First, the reserve was based on the British system. Canada was, after all, a dominion and a proud member of the Commonwealth. Both the RCNR and the RCNVR, like the RCN, were subject to British Admiralty law. British mess rules and regulations applied, as did Royal Navy habits of mind.[11] Second, most of the men who enlisted were of British heritage anyway. Again, this is not particularly surprising since most immigrants to Canada until the late 1940s were from England and men from that maritime nation were more likely to find naval service compelling. Third, financial difficulties reinforced the intermingling of the reservists with the Royal Navy. Reserve sailors sent to the West Coast for training might occasionally sail with the British aboard His Majesty's Ships *Hood, Repulse, Norfolk*, and *Danae*. (*Hood* and *Repulse*, for example, had visited the West Coast in 1924.) Canadian ships and crew were too tightly stretched to provide adequate shipboard experience. Dockyard facilities were shared equally with the RCNR and the RNR who were frequently stationed in Canada to make up shortfalls in naval staffing. Advanced naval training was conducted in England, as the expertise simply did not exist in Canada. Finally, senior officers in the naval service had been drawn from the Royal Navy. RCN officers (who in turn would assist in training RCNVR officers) studied in England as they progressed through the naval system. Even if RCNVR officers were not offered the opportunity to study at Greenwich, they still absorbed the culture, attitudes, and behaviours of the Royal Navy.

The qualifications required for appointment as commanding officer of a reserve division are revealing: patriotism, a keen interest in naval affairs, a position in the town that enabled the candidate to command the support of the men of his company and "stir up interest" in the formation of the company, and sufficient spare time to devote to organizing the company.[12] Officers worked for free on drill nights. They received pay only for their two-week annual training periods. They bought their own uniforms. Indeed, they were expected to purchase: "a frock coat, a Mess Dress Jacket, Evening Waistcoats (blue and white), a Cocked Hat, Epaulettes, a full dress belt, boots and shoes as necessary for above, and their white uniforms."[13] They often bought their own equipment and did their paper work at home on their own time. In other words, most officers, commanding officers in particular, were of a certain class.

In the case of Vancouver and Toronto, the men who headed up the first reserves were not just wealthy — they were millionaires. Unable to find or fund an adequate training facility, the commanding officer of the Vancouver Half-Company, Lieutenant-Commander J.W. Hobbs, manoeuvred to have his company train at his yacht club. When the only vessel delivered to the unit for training proved inadequate — it was a 8.2-metre whaler — he simply went out and spent $1,000 of his own money to purchase the schooner *Naden*. Most commanding officers were not so fortunate as to have such easy wealth, but all were extremely dedicated to the service. Much of their work was not compensated, and regardless of their personal circumstances most incurred expenses that they never claimed.

Esquimalt Naval Museum, VR2002.160.001.

Reservists often would get "big ship time" when larger vessels of the Royal Navy visited Canada, such as HMS *Hood* seen here in Vancouver harbour, 1924.

In 1927 Commander Woodhouse remarked that so long as the RCN was comprised of British ships and British men, it would be impossible for the Canadians to see any point in the essential idea of a Canadian navy operated by Canadians. With its British traditions, laws, ranks, culture, and traditions, the RCNVR did little to change that. Moreover, as the 1920s drew to a close, the status of the RCNVR was still tenuous. The lack of adequate funding had hampered any meaningful training; no naval reserve exercises had taken place, and the much-touted "education of the public regarding the importance of a naval force" remained as elusive as ever.

The 1930s are forever remembered for two things: the Great Depression, and the slow but inexorable slide to war. Still struggling with the war debt of 1914–18, Canadians found no relief from the government. Its finances were almost as desperate as the decade before. Military funding remained at its shoestring, post-war levels. In 1930, the strength of the Naval Reserve had to be reduced from 1,500 to 1,000 officers and men, just to be able to continue meeting its payroll.

By the time the depression hit hardest, most of the wealthy commanding officers had gone. Those reservists who remained continued on, in part because of the camaraderie it offered, and in part because of civic pride. They were dedicated and loyal. Sadly, they were also desperate for the paltry pay it offered. Across the country, units were vandalized by people seeking meagre supplies. Under the guise of deterring theft, some members began sleeping at their reserve units.

The poverty of some of the men could lead to abuses. In Vancouver, one retired Royal Navy officer secured an arrangement whereby eight members of the unit would crew on his yacht, without pay, during the summer racing months. In return, he would "train them in the art of seamanship."[14] Though the men had to work for free, they were nonetheless fed, and for the yachting season at least, were given a "home." The offer must have appealed to a great number of unemployed men. When the retired officer was later denied use of the reserve facilities to store his effects, his dedication to the service vanished and his "training" sessions ceased.

The situation got progressively worse. By 1933 the very existence of the naval service became threatened. Faced with a desperate economic situation, Canada's Treasury Board cut $3.5 million from the total defence budget. Fully $2 million of this amount was to be cut from the naval service. This left the navy only $422,000 out of the $2,422,000 it had been promised at the beginning of the year. The new budget was one-sixth of the original. As Commodore Hose pointed out, since one-sixth of the year had already passed, no funds were left. The navy would therefore have to be disbanded.[15]

Commodore Hose sought support from Chief of the General Staff, General A.G.L. McNaughton. He was not successful. "Fearful that any reduction in the proposed cuts in

A meeting of the Defence Council, 13 August 1930. Left to right: Brigadier A.C. Caldwell, Commodore W.J. Hose, Deputy Minister G.J. Desbarats, Minister of National Defence the Hon. J.L. Ralston, Major-General A.G.L. McNaughton, Brigadier A.H. Bell, and Group Captain J.L. Gordon.

Library and Archives Canada, PA-062488.

the naval service would simply be transferred to the army and air force budgets, General McNaughton ... proved quite prepared to throw the naval service to the wolves, if some of the remainder could be saved." He then appealed to the minister of national defence and successfully arranged a hearing before the Treasury Board. At the meeting Commodore Hose put the stark facts before the board: the navy was not in a state of sea-going or fighting efficiency, and it could not withstand further impairment. Any cut greater than $200,000 would make it uneconomical to run a navy at all. When asked what he would do if he were issued an edict to reduce his budget by $600,000, the commodore placed both his career and the fate of the navy on the line. He answered: "I regret that I should have to state that I had been told to do the impossible, and that I could not possibly accept any responsibility for the proper conduct of the Service."[16]

When pressed whether that meant he would resign, Commodore Hose said yes. Mindful of his authority, he diverted attention from his honest response by stressing another point: it was impossible to lay up ships for the duration of budgetary constraint, since both the men and their vessels needed to be constantly exercising at sea. He also drew attention to the growing tensions between Japan and the United States. Although Canada's military had always been a defensive force, he noted, "un-neutral acts" on Canada's Pacific coast were a real possibility. Acting Prime Minister George Perley agreed, and proposed that the board accept a reduction of only $200,000 from the naval service budget. The board unanimously concurred.

Commodore Hose's actions had been both unorthodox and desperate. Yet they demonstrate the enormous battle for survival that the naval service has faced over the years. An expensive service to establish and maintain, it never received proper funding in the first three decades of its existence. The army, relatively well-established, and the air force, modern and alluring, were content to see it eliminated if it meant more funding for their own services. If the distribution of cutbacks in the 1933 budget is any indication of relative value, the government clearly agreed. The actions of Commodore Hose and the commitment of his officers in both the RCN and RCNVR demonstrate outstanding leadership and commitment. They struggled throughout the decade against a welter of obstacles: impossibly low levels of financing, a lack of support from the other services, aging ships, and virtually no infrastructure. Moreover, all this created an East-West divide as travel, even for training, was curtailed and personnel were sent to the nearest coast. Reservists had little contact with their peers on the opposite side of the country. Differences in approach and training began to appear, and the effect was a near-splintering of command. In 1937, the director of the naval service thought the problem serious enough to comment that "efforts are being made to eradicate as far as possible the splitting of the RCNVR as a whole into two sections consisting of Eastern and Western Divisions. [...] it is the intention that the RCNVR shall always be considered as one unit."[17]

To encourage a unified *esprit de corps*, Commander of Naval Divisions, Commander E.R. Mainguy, created a monthly national newsletter. While reminding each company that they were part of a national force, the letter provided news on the activities of each unit, and served as a sort of self-help manual. Solutions to problems caused by the severe shortage of funding were published along with gentle words of encouragement for others to similarly

Courtesy HMCS Carleton.

The Ottawa Half-Company,
November 1931.

"use their initiative."[18] These small, but effective, measures by Commander Mainguy continued to bolster the morale of the Naval Reserve during a time of severe restraint and personal financial hardship.

Despite the setbacks, the professionalization of the RCNVR continued as its role was expanded and refined. In 1930, the Department of National Defence had published a revised set of regulations. Established at last were the terms and conditions for entry, service, promotions, pay, trades, training, compensation, uniforms, kit, discharge, and retirement. The RCNVR was clearly a young man's organization; mandatory retirement was required for all sub-lieutenants at age 35, for lieutenants at 45, and for lieutenant-commanders at 50. There were only four officer occupations: naval, medical, accounting, and engineering. Ratings were divided into three classifications — seamen, technical, and logistics — each with its own ranking system.[19]

Slowly, the RCNVR began to evolve as a separate organization. Perhaps most readily distinctive were the wavy stripes that officers in the RCNVR wore on their sleeves to distinguish them from their RCN "regular force" brothers. They even provided the motif of the reservists' remarkably durable and robust theme song: "Roll Along, Wavy Navy, Roll Along." Inspired by Jimmy Kennedy's 1934 hit "Roll Along, Covered Wagon," and made famous by Harry Roy's orchestra in England, the original portrayed a youthful cowboy heading home to his ranch. Having rejected the attractions of the "city ladies" in favour of "that girl of mine," he moans a homespun truth. But in 1936, two young Canadian sailors adapted both tune and lyrics to the realities of their own Canadian sea-going world, and gave it an upbeat lift.[20] The result, the unofficial anthem of the Naval Reserve in Canada, abounds in ebullient self-irony that has appealed to generations of reservists ever since: "oh, we joined for the Glory of it all," and "for the chance to go to sea," and finally, "for the payment and the fun."

> *Roll along, Wavy Navy, roll along!*
> *Roll along, Wavy Navy, roll along!*
> *When they say "O there they are!"*
> *It's the RCNVR —*
> *Roll along, Wavy Navy, roll along!*
>
> *Oh we joined for the Glory of it all!*
> *Oh we joined for the Glory of it all!*

But the good old RCN
Made us change our minds again —
Roll along, Wavy Navy, roll along!

Oh we joined for the chance to go to sea,
Yes we joined for the chance to go to sea,
But the first two years or more
We spent parading on the shore —
Roll along, Wavy Navy, roll along!

And when at last they sent us out to sea —
Yes when at last they sent us out to sea,
There were several things we saw
That were not brought up before —
Roll along Wavy Navy, roll along!

Oh we joined for the payment and the fun,
Yes we joined for the payment and the fun,
But of pay there has been none,
And the fun is yet to come —
Roll along Wavy Navy, roll along!

Now before we pull up hook and sail away,
Yes before we pull up hook and sail away,
If you want some good advice
Before you join think once or twice —
Roll along, Wavy Navy, roll along!

Throughout the 1930s, Canadian reliance on the British Admiralty for training, for support, for supplies, and often for men grew, rather than diminished. Yet one saw some signs of change: the first wireless telegraph (W/T) training got underway, although according to Commodore Jeffry Brock funding was so scarce that a good deal of the equipment was bought (once again) by the officers themselves. In 1937, the navy approved Good Conduct medals for the RCNVR. Despite its increased professionalization, the Naval Reserve presence in Canada remained limited. In 1939 the staffing levels of the RCNVR had not risen beyond that which was originally authorized. When war broke out, the RCNVR comprised but 180 officers and 1,511 ratings.

The legacy of the Naval Reserve in the interwar period is an ambiguous one. The reserves clearly had saved the naval service from its complete breakup in the early 1920s. But had they created a national sense of pride in naval matters? By participating in fairs and exhibitions, by marching in parades and Armistice Day ceremonies, each reserve unit reminded Canadians that a naval service did, in fact, exist in Canada, no matter how battered and bedraggled.

Department of National Defence, PMR80-647.

The Winnipeg Company marches through the city, 1932.

The post–First World War Naval Commission had failed to notice the simple fact that its budget was controlled by parliament — and parliament answered to the public. Kingsmill, Hose, and others looked at the social upheavals of the day, and thought of reasons for the military to grow. Their political masters, Borden and King, by contrast, remembered the folly of wars, and sought to eliminate them. Hose and his followers had the Admiralty bred in their bones and the reserve they created reflected this. Canadians had wanted nothing to do with Europe and its wars, and the navy they were offered was made of the elements that had inflicted such a savage toll on their country only a few years earlier.

By failing to make the navy and its reserve truly Canadian rather than a pale imitation of the British Admiralty, naval leaders failed to capture the public's attention. The RCNVR never really succeeded in educating the public because most of the public did not care for its overt British overtones. By the dawn of the Second World War the RCNVR was no larger than its original complement. Its yacht-based training was obsolete, and its units were converted to recruiting centres. In the end, the Royal Navy had to send instructors over to train the wartime recruits.

Notes

1. Library and Archives Canada (LAC), Record Group (RG) 24, Vol. 3985, File NSC 1055–2-21 Vol. 3.

2. Cited in letter from A.B. Perry, RNWMP HQ, Regina, to Major-General W. Gwatkin, Chief of General Staff, 11 June 1919. LAC, RG 24 Vol. 3985, File NSC 1055–2-21, Vol. 3.

3. For this and the following, see James George Eayrs, *In Defence of Canada: From the Great War to the Great Depression* (Toronto: University of Toronto Press, 1965), 144.

4. Website of CFB Esquimalt Naval and Military Museum, *www.navalandmilitarymuseum.org/ resource_pages/beginnings/hose.html* (accessed 18 June, 2010).

5. In 1923–24, for example, Canadians spent $1.46 per capita on defence. Britons spent $23.04; France somewhat more than that; Australians $3.30. The Americans spent around $7.

6. Directorate of History and Heritage (DHH), NDHQ, File: NS 1141–31, Vol. 1, RCNVR — Org.

7. See Lieutenant Peter Ward, "The Naval Reserve in Canada," *Canadian Shipping and Maritime Engineering News* (March 1962), 93.

8. LAC RG 24, Acc 83–84/167, Vol. 553, File 1700–47, Vol. 1, *Monthly News Letter*, the Vancouver Half Company, 10 October 1925.

9. LAC RG 24, Acc 83–84/167, Vol. 553, File 1700–170/47, Vol. 1, Eveleigh Eager, Naval Secretary, to the Senior Naval Officer, 6 July 1927.

10. *Ibid.*, Letter from G.J. Desbarats, Deputy Minister, to The Secretary, Harbour Commission, Vancouver, B.C., 6 July 1927.

11. For example, during a mess dinner "it is forbidden to: smoke, mention a woman's name, speak a foreign language, use profane language, behave in an unseemly manner, leave the table or sit down at it without the President's permission, receive or send a signal or other written or spoken communication from or to anyone not at the table without the President's permission. For committing any of the offences it is customary for the Offender of be fined one round of port." DHH, NDHQ, File NS 114-1-31, Vol. 1, RCNVR — Organization.

12. LAC, RG 24, Acc 83–84/167, Vol. 553, File 1700–170/47, Vol. 1, Memorandum from A. Woodhouse, Naval Secretary to Senior Naval Officer, Esquimalt, dated 9 February 1923.

13. DHH, File RCNVR 1700–905, Naval Service Headquarters, letter dated 19 June 1936.

14. This was the same Commander B.L. Johnson (Retired) who had been offered the position of the half-company's first commanding officer but had insisted his rank be equivalent to that of the senior naval officer in Esquimalt.

15. For this and the following see D.C. Watt ("The Day They Nearly Sank the Navy," *The Atlantic Advocate*, June 1962) who describes how Commodore Walter Hose "set forth the need to defend Canada's trade on the seas and carried through the battle that saved the Navy."

16. Eayrs, *In Defence of Canada*, 280.

17. DHH, file NS 114–1-31, Vol. 1, RNCVR — Organization, Newsletter No. 27, 1 October 1937.

18. DHH, File: NS 114–1-31, Vol. 1, RNCVR — Organization.

19. Ian Holloway, *Self-reliance Through Service: The History of Her Majesty's Canadian Ship Scotian* (Hantsport, NS: Lancelot Press, 1988), 117.

20. The sailors were Gunner (later Rear-Admiral) Patrick Budge and Sub-Lieutenant Rufus Pope while serving in HMCS *Saguenay*. Promoted to commodore in 1953 Budge served as chief of staff to the commanding officer naval divisions in Hamilton, Ontario.

CHAPTER 4

The People's Navy: Myth, Reality, and Life in Canada's Naval Reserves, 1939–45

Richard Mayne

War and its aftermath spawned a multitude of myths and yarns about the Navy and the Naval Reserve. Given wartime secrecy and propaganda, and the isolation of some Canadian communities, how could it have been otherwise? Stories of adventurous voyages, combat against a wily and dangerous foe, rapid mobilization of civilians who swelled the regular force to almost 50 times its pre-war size — all this with the requisite whiff of gun smoke — quickly took on the aura of fact. Of course, even once the real story was known, the Naval Reserve still bristled with rousing adventure, grand achievements, and colourful personalities. But the reality was now different.

In the spring of 1943, a small Toronto-based magazine declared that the Canadian Naval Service was in the process of a major transformation. The demands of war had led to a huge influx of reservists, most of whom had joined directly from Canadian society for the duration of "hostilities only." And this, the magazine went on to explain, had effectively changed the service into a "People's Navy." The message was clear: the days of elitist pre-war permanent force members treating the RCN as their own exclusive Old Boys' Club were over. Two other services were also doing their part to bring victory in the war: the Royal

Canadian Naval Reserve, and the Royal Canadian Naval Volunteer Reserve. Where the RCNR put their merchant marine experience to good use fighting German U-boats, members of the RCNVR had started out as amateurs, with perhaps limited pre-war training or experience as yachtsmen. Their simple reality was this: Canada was depending on its citizen sailors for its survival.

But this was by no means the only myth about naval reserves to emerge from the Second World War. Legends regarding the infamous "prairie sailor," the "Sheep Dog Navy" — or the idea that the reserves were sent to sea in place of the regulars — all gained strength over the years. Only through the process of exploring these myths, most notably the legend that the RCNR and RCNVR collectively constituted a "People's Navy," is it possible to gain a larger insight into what it was like to be a reservist in the Canadian Navy between 1939 and 1945.

Four days after the release of a preparatory mobilization order, cryptic coded instructions hidden in a message sent to Naval Reserve units across Canada turned the unthinkable into reality: as of 1 September 1939 the Naval Reserve found itself on a war footing. A mere 48 hours later, in a remarkable display of preparedness, the first draft of reservists was on

Recruits at HMCS *York*, February 1942, perform close-order drills in front of a mock up of a King George V-class battleship.

Library and Archives Canada, PA-204587.

"Hostilities only" naval recruits parade through Esquimalt, 1940.

Esquimalt Naval Museum, VR99.3.267.29.

its way to Halifax. That this had been accomplished so seamlessly seven days before hostilities had broken out between Canada and Germany was impressive. Director of Naval Personnel, Captain Harold Grant, RCN, was quick to congratulate the reserves for having carried out its mobilization so close to the intended plan. But as efficient as their mobilization was, Grant was even more impressed by the reservists themselves and the way they had volunteered for active service in droves. "It is to the everlasting credit of the RCNVR," Grant wrote in 1940, that they "tore themselves away from their homes [and] families, in twenty-four hours, even *before Canada [had] officially declared war*."[1]

Other Canadian citizens were equally keen to do their part. Applications to join the Volunteer Reserve — or VR as the RCNVR was affectionately known — were on the increase throughout 1939. Those numbers skyrocketed once recruiting advertisements began to appear in local newspapers after the commencement of hostilities. Canadian men between 18 and 32 who were British subjects and physically fit with at least a grade eight education were invited to serve their country through the RCNVR.[2] The pool of potential recruits was large (particularly since recruiters were not known for checking birth certificates to confirm age). The divisions, as the reserve units were often called, were responsible for recruiting and enlistment, and were inundated with over 5,000 applications within the first six weeks of the war.[3] In fact, the desire of Canadians to join the RCNVR was so strong that the divisions could not handle the demand. With unit quotas easily filled, many applicants were placed on a list for future call-up or referred to the other armed services.

That so many Canadians were selecting the navy over the army and air force strongly suggests that the RCNVR was indeed a people's navy. Yet a closer examination of those recruited reveals that certain groups and areas of the country were heavily under-represented. It also exposes significant facts about the social composition of the reserve itself. For example, reservists tended to be more educated than their professionally trained RCN counterparts. Officers in the reserve had generally gone to university, and a slight majority of the ratings had at least attended high school. Those in the Volunteer Reserve were also more likely to have been born in Canada. VR officers had come largely from the professions, such as lawyers, journalists, engineers, doctors, and accountants, or some other type of white-collar job. Of course, RCNR officers differed from their RCNVR brethren by having been masters and mates from the merchant marine who were five times more likely to have emigrated from Britain. VR ratings, on the other hand, tended to join from the trades, unskilled labour, service sector, and agricultural worker industries; by contrast, their RCNR counterparts had generally left positions as crewmen in merchant ships for temporary duty with the navy.[4]

Although the RCNVR came much closer to reflecting the national mosaic than either the RCN or RCNR, there were important differences. Minority groups tended to be excluded. For example, black Canadians were under-represented in the VR, for they were not allowed to join the navy until 1943. Aboriginal Canadians were also discouraged from enlisting, while Canadians of Japanese descent were excluded altogether. Recruiting policies identified other groups such as German and Italian Canadians, or those with family in occupied territories, as "undesirable." Hence the enlistment averages for these ethnic communities into the VR was also below national levels. The fact that the navy operated exclusively in English presented a significant barrier to unilingual francophones who either saw little point in joining or else experienced high washout rates during training.[5] Consequently, despite having a larger proportion of French-Canadians and Roman Catholics than either the RCN or RCNR, the RCNVR was nonetheless a predominately Protestant, English, and white service.

They were also a male service. Of course, the Wrens or Women's Royal Canadian Naval Service did come into being on 31 July 1942. This marked "the first time women were admitted to the Canadian navy in any capacity save that of nurse."[6] Though just as much a part of the navy as the RCNVR, the Wrens remained essentially separate and apart from it. They were a service within a service, and therefore not officially part of the Naval Reserve. Like the reserves, however, the WRCNS were also composed of volunteers who were serving for the duration of "hostilities only," and therefore form part of the "people's navy." Though women found opportunities for naval service after the Second World War, and continued to be regarded as Wrens, the WRCNS was formally disbanded in August 1946.

Typical of naval relationships of the day, the model for the Canadian Wrens was provided by Britain's Women's Royal Naval Service (WRNS). Three senior WRNS officers came to Canada to set the organization in motion. In August 1943, however, Adelaide Sinclair was appointed as the first Canadian director of the WRCNS. She was a remarkable person: she held a master's degree in political economy, had served on the Wartime Price Control Board, received the OBE for her naval leadership, and became

Department of National Defence, CT-254.

This beautiful study of HMCS *Arrowhead* captures the "Corvette Navy" image usually associated with the wartime RCNVR.

the first woman to reach the rank of naval captain. Veterans speak of their service with the Wrens as offering a range of experience unavailable to them before the war: "liberation" from the constraints of parents and family, travel, a wider sense of independence in establishing new relationships, and new experiences through easy fellowship with their peers of both sexes. It was, many reported, the "high time" of their lives. As recruits, they were first posted to Galt, Ontario, for basic training in a former girl's detention facility reconverted to HMCS *Conestoga*. Former Wrens still chuckle over the story that the *Conestoga* building had once been a "Home for Wayward Girls." Like, the "Wavy Navy" itself, the Wrens had their own memorable characters. Many, for example, recall their master-at-arms, Phyllis "Sandy" Sanderson, standing with her "Great Dane" (he was large, but not a Dane) on *Conestoga*'s parade square, calling out: "On the Double!" or "Nip to it, Matilda!"[7] Or the feisty Jenny Pike who in the post-war years refused to have the Wren contingent march at the rear of the Remembrance Day parade as they had been ordered: "We are women veterans, we will *not* march at the back, we're going to join the men where we belong." And we did."[8] These women, like many others, form part of the Wrens' lore about the particular style that women brought to the navy.

a medical board and swearing an oath of loyalty to the King during their attestation, new recruits were then taken on divisional strength and sent to the supply depot. Here they were issued with a uniform, various pieces of kit, and a hammock. Unfortunately, not everyone received these accoutrements in the earliest days of the war. The VR was growing too fast. It had almost doubled its size between August and December 1939, and had surpassed the total strength of the regular force by the following February.[14] The divisions simply could not cope with such numbers, and according to the commanding officer at HMCS *York* in Toronto, it did not take long before they "degenerated into a chaotic, hand-to-mouth existence." Frugal pre-war spending had taken its toll on *York*, and all the other Naval Reserve divisions. For, as this officer observed, "We had absolutely nothing — we started completely from scratch. We had no uniforms in stores, or any sort of equipment whatsoever, except for a few old Lee Enfield rifles and the twelve-pounder gun."[15]

Money to upgrade and provision the divisions would eventually come. But it was patriotic citizens who responded to the immediate need. Take, for example, the willingness of the T. Eaton Company to provide free uniforms for *York*, or the Montreal businessman who hired a band to help teach reservists to march at HMCS *Donnacona*. These were all early

The Crows Nest was a popular refuge for officers stationed in St John's, Newfoundland.

LADIES NIGHT AT THE 'CROWS NEST' (SEA GOING OFFICERS CLUB)

Courtesy The Crows Nest / Gary Green.

signs of a people supporting their local naval affiliation. Yet the shortages did lead to some comical moments, such as when an admiral learned that material for uniforms was going to the Wrens rather than to the men. In an attempt to reallocate resources he wrote the memorable (but unfortunate) signal: "WRENS clothing to be held up until the needs of seagoing sailors have been satisfied."[16]

The divisions nevertheless had to learn to adapt to such shortages, particularly since new recruits would remain there until they were drafted to the coast for advanced training. The local division therefore handled initial training — a charitable term describing the process of turning raw civilians into naval recruits. It was a surreal world that, at times, tested the bounds of reality. Strange concepts and vocabulary prevailed — such as new sailors being told that their brick and mortar building was actually a ship, and that "downstairs" was now "down below." These were topped by awkward scenes of young men learning boat drill on lush green lawns, while at the same time struggling to adjust to uniforms and uniformity. Of course, these types of apparent absurdities represented ample fodder for those with a sense of humour. For instance, after learning that the building that housed his division was considered a commissioned ship, one rating from Winnipeg's HMCS *Chippawa* was heard to remark: "Well that's one Canadian ship which will never be sunk."[17]

While each individual unit was responsible for designing its own training syllabus in the early stages of the war, most involved some type of instruction in seamanship, marching, rifle drill, rope work, physical training, and communications. The lack of equipment and a shortage of qualified instructors contributed to the *ad hoc* nature of this training. It was replaced in February 1941 by a more structured eight-week course designed to produce a sailor who would arrive at the coasts adjusted to naval life and prepared for his advanced training. As the war progressed the larger and better-equipped facilities on both coasts became increasingly responsible for almost all aspects of reserve training. They, too, however, had trouble managing the unprecedented influx of reservists. Construction of new establishments certainly helped. But the demands of war placed a tremendous strain on this developing system; the more so since training that had once taken years before the war was now jammed into roughly 90 days,[18] which led to those who passed the course being dubbed "90-day wonders." Worse yet, operational requirements ensured that qualified regular force instructors were in short supply, and those who could be found for training reservists tended to have less experience. This, however, was only the start of a process where, by the end of the war, the reserves would eventually be teaching their own personnel how to specialize in naval trades such as signals, ASDIC, radar, gunnery, torpedo, and electrical and marine engineering.

Like the ratings, reserve officers found training a rushed affair. In fact, in the early and more desperate stages of the war, many RCNR officers did not receive any training at all, and instead were sent directly on operations as skippers, chief skippers, or skipper lieutenants. Starting in 1940, however, they did at least receive a course that covered topics such as naval discipline, tradition, seamanship, navigation, pilotage, signals, regulations, gunnery, and physical training. RCNVR officers, on the other hand, lacked the practical experience of their RCNR counterparts, and required much more attention. Thanks to

Wren signallers at work in a hut at the mouth of St John's harbour.

Library and Archives Canada, PA-128241.

schools such as HMCS *Stone Frigate* in Kingston, HMCS *Royal Roads* in Victoria and Halifax's HMCS *Kings*, over 3,800 executive branch reserve officers were trained throughout the course of the war.[19] Nevertheless, the training that VRs received was far from adequate when compared to pre-war regular force standards. Instead, it was tailored to give them just enough information on ship handling and anti-submarine warfare to at least survive on the bridge of a ship.

What was not taught at the schools had to be learnt in the ships. Both the sea and enemy inflicted many painful lessons. As confusing as training ashore may have been for young men fresh out of school, the office, or off the farm, life on the North Atlantic was worse: long periods of boredom and sea sickness, followed by convoy action and moments of sheer terror. In time, however, reserve sailors would become just as professional as their regular force counterparts, but in the first half of the war they were amateurs — and it showed.

What they lacked in experience was often balanced with colour and personality. Vivid stories from the VR were legendary. They are worth telling not only because they emerged from one of the richest periods of the navy's history, but also because they helped to define the reserve's character as one of innovation and inspiration. Accounts from individuals such as Hal Lawrence who, along with Petty Officer A.J. Powell, leapt off the deck of their corvette HMCS *Oakville* to board *U-94* in a pitching Caribbean Sea, were a recruiting officer's dream. Reminiscent of the days of hand-to-hand combat on the 17th century Spanish Main, Lawrence's actions caught the attention of the media and were circulated across the nation. Lawrence's own words capture the excitement and even humour of his two-man assault on *U-94*:

As I hit the deck of U-94 the belt of my tropical shorts snapped on impact. My pants slid down to my ankles. I stumbled, kicked them off, and rose. Clad only in a pistol, two grenades, a gas-mask, a length of chain, a flashlight, and a life belt, I lurched up on the deck.... Oakville was stopped a half-mile away. Her after gun opened up at us. Luckily it started at the other end of U-94's hull.... The bullets ricocheted off with nasty whinging sounds.... Despite casualties, there were still some thirty able-bodied Germans on board. We were two. We reached the forward gun, by now a tangled mess of steel. A German slid from behind it. With my pistol barrel I knocked him over the side. Twenty-nine to two. Rounding the conning tower we saw two more. We rushed. Both took a long, horrified look at my uniform — or lack of it, and jumped into the water when we were within three feet. [Staring at my nakedness] they must have been thinking along the lines of "Blimey — he's come to bugger us all."[20]

Lawrence and Powell made it inside *U-94.* But unfortunately the U-boat had already taken in enough water that it was beginning to make its final spiral descent to the sea floor. Though *U-94* escaped capture, its loss was still a huge victory for the RCN.

Tales of U-boat actions were always exhilarating. So, too, were the stories of the more exciting personalities within the VR. Take, for example, the dashing motor torpedo boat commander, Tommy Fuller, whose unconventional style was both a blessing and curse for the allied cause. Barred from joining both the Royal Canadian Air Force (RCAF) and the Royal Navy's submarine service because of his "old age" (Fuller was 31 in 1939), this officer enjoyed a career as eccentric as his personality. Three courts martial should have been enough to end any officer's tenure in the navy. Yet Fuller's exploits, such as his giving stores from captured coastal craft in the Aegean to local partisans (not to mention his whopping 135 actions against the Germans) earned him a Distinguished Service Cross and Bar as well as a Mentioned-in-Dispatches.

The North Atlantic convoys also produced their own fair share of heroes within the reserves. The life on these routes helped foster a unique reserve community. Harrowing events — such as the involvement of the corvette HMCS *Chilliwack* in the epic 32-hour "hunt to exhaustion" of *U-744* in March 1944 — were a remarkable point of pride for the VR. It went a long way to erasing the blunders of earlier years. Of course, it was not the VRs' fault that it had had a tough time on the North Atlantic between 1939 and 1943. Inadequate equipment and training as well as manning shortages plagued Canada's navy throughout

Department of National Defence, Z-8471-1.

Landing craft operated by RCNVR crews loaned to the Royal Navy were amongst the participants in the ill-fated raid on Dieppe, 19 August 1942.

The wartime expansion of the RCNVR is marked by the laying of the cornerstone for HMCS *Discovery* at Vancouver in June 1943.

Library and Archives Canada, PA-183345.

its unprecedented 50-fold expansion.[21] The VRs nevertheless found ways to carry on despite these difficulties, and such perseverance helped define them as a community.

Shared experiences at sea were an essential factor that fostered a bond of brotherhood among reservists. Yet the VR was also drawn together by an identity that consistently challenged the social norms that had come to define the regular force. For instance, reservists tended to downplay the distinction between officers and men. Indeed, they were far more likely to ignore some of the more restrictive regulations considered sacred by many regulars. Yet while reservists tended to be more easygoing than the permanent force, when it came to fighting a war at sea they were just as serious about their duties and obligations.

Accepting VRs as equals was a difficult pill for some regulars to swallow. If true, a comment a VR attributed to Rear-Admiral George C. "Jetty" Jones — "no Reserve officer would take command as long as [I am] around"[22] — reflected their views plainly enough. Jones's prediction (if he indeed said it) quickly proved incorrect. With the pool of experienced RCNR officers quickly drying up, the appointment of Lieutenant R.J.C. Pringle as the commanding officer of the minesweeper HMCS *Suderoy V* on 19 March 1941 marked the beginning of a process that would see clearly two-thirds of all the navy's warships under RCNVR command by the end of the war. In some ways, the regulars' original apprehension was somewhat understandable: the idea of handing warships over to former civilians who in peacetime had either been hobby sailors, or had had no knowledge of the sea whatsoever, seemed like legitimate grounds for concern. Even Captain Rollo Mainguy, a great admirer of the reserves, displayed some reluctance when he gave Lieutenant A.G.S. Griffin the first VR corvette command on 29 April 1941. As he told Griffin: "I'm taking a big chance on you and you must not let me down."[23]

Of course, command was not the only professional qualification that the regulars aggressively guarded, as Lieutenant-Commander Louis Audette discovered when he took over the corvette HMCS *Amherst* in 1942. Audette best tells the absurdity of how he finally got his bridge watchkeeping certificate, signifying his competence to take charge of a watch at sea under a commanding officer's authority:

> *I got my WK in the most ridiculous way … On my second ship,* St. Francis, *I still didn't have one. I asked Hugh Pullen to recommend me for it … he's "Old School." He said "No, Louis, I'm sorry. I'm certainly not going to recommend you for your WK. I suggested, "I hope this is not personal?" and he replied, "I just don't think any officer who's only been in the Navy for a couple of years should have a WK. I may be wrong, but I'm not treating you any worse than I am the others." When I was appointed in command of* Amherst, *I was still without a watchkeeping ticket, I went to see Harold Grant, Captain (D) in Newfoundland, and said, "Here I've been in command of this ship for several months and I still haven't a watchkeeping ticket." Harold said, "This is an odd situation! I think as commanding officer of the ship you had better go back and write to me, recommending this fellow Audette for his ticket." I did, and I got it.*[24]

Seeing reservists get quick qualifications that had taken regulars years to earn in peacetime was undoubtedly a sore spot for some permanent force officers. As one such officer recalled:

Courtesy Edward Milton.

The very symbol of the regular force's blue water aspirations, the powerful Tribal-class destroyers were crewed largely by Reservists. This irony is underscored by the present-day berth of HMCS *Haida* as a museum ship at the jetty of HMCS *Star*, the Naval Reserve division in Hamilton, Ontario. (Note the ship is preserved in postwar configuration and colours.)

The majority [of reservists] knew nothing. There was great keenness and high heartedness and so on, but absolute abysmal knowledge ... you arrived there looking like naval officers with stripes on your sleeve, and it was patently obvious that you knew nothing about it.... This was bothersome to us who regarded ourselves as professionals....[25]

The rank braid on the sleeves of the officers in this group photo of HMCS *Haida* at the height of the pre-D-Day actions in the Channel, 5 May 1944, illustrates the point from the previous photograph: other than the captain, Commander H.G. DeWolf, seated in the front row at the right, the clear majority are Reservists.

Unfortunately, such comments from the RCN were not altogether uncommon. But often a quick wit was all that was required to defuse these types of uncomfortable situations, as one permanent force officer found out when picking on the wrong VR officer. "Why is it," the unsuspecting regular asked, "just because you've taken a degree or whatever you call it, in law, you go about referring to each other as 'my learned friend' and 'my learned counsel,' and 'my learned opponent.'" Without missing a beat, the reservist responded: "Oh, it's nothing, quite meaningless. It's like referring to you as a gallant officer."[26] Other reservists had similar verbal torpedoes in their arsenal to counter regular force jibes. For instance,

Department of National Defence, R-1679.

one common poke at the regulars held that the RCNVRs were gentlemen trying to be sailors, the RCNRs were sailors trying to be gentlemen, while the RCN were neither trying to be both.

While most VRs ignored the permanent force's razzing and carried on with winning the war, others believed that the joshing actually contributed to a developing identity whereby the reservists increasingly saw themselves as a separate family in a larger naval community. VRs embraced their civilian backgrounds and, as expressed in their own poetry, songs, and vocabulary, they took tremendous pride in the important contribution they were making both ashore and at sea. That they were able to do so without the type of training the permanent force had received only served to strengthen their distinctiveness.

VRs also differed from their regular force counterparts in their attitudes toward naval discipline. It was not always easy for men fresh from democratic society to adjust to an authoritarian structure where the iron hand of naval discipline came down hard on freethinkers. According to one British officer, this was the product of the VR's "brief training in sea discipline" that made them "natural and outspoken in criticism. They were highly intelligent Canadian civilians in a seafaring role, with initiative and determination to win the war; they were frank, sincere, and sometimes angry …"[27] Indeed, there were some VRs who were upset at what they labelled the regular force's "discrimination" against reservists. For them, no other symbol captured their plight better than the wavy, interlocked, and straight stripes on an officer's uniform that distinguished the RCNVR, RCNR, and RCN. The problem, they argued, was that VRs were branded as amateurs on sight even though by the mid-stages of the war they might have considerable sea time and experience. As a result, they were made to feel like third-class citizens and this was at odds with the Canadian society they had left in order to join the "people's navy."

This rubbed a small group of politically connected VR officers the wrong way. Although their numbers were extremely limited — amounting to no more than a handful of VRs — these officers had considerable power in Canadian society. Thanks to their backgrounds they were able to bypass the usual lines of command, and managed to convince the naval minister that reform was required. Coincidentally, change and recognition for the reserves was already on its way. For instance, as the reserves gained more experience at sea and prestige at home, the regulars — while not necessarily accepting the VRs as true "professionals" — were willing to give them more responsibility and autonomy over their own affairs. This began in November 1941 with the decision to officially grant the Naval Reserve divisions the official status of commissioned ships. The stature of the reserves continued to increase to the point where 13 months later the reserves were given their own separate

Department of National Defence, CT-338.

Canadian Wrens visit a London barrage balloon site, March 1944.

command under Captain Eustace Brock, who was appointed the Commanding Officer Reserve Divisions. For those complaining to the minister of defence for naval services, this was not nearly enough, and he in turn was persuaded by their case. As a result, measures were put in place that sped up VR promotions and granted them "qualified status." This term described the process whereby the regulars would have to share seniority with reservists at sea. To recognize the importance of the reserves to the navy, they were also given a voice on the minister's top advisory body, the Naval Board, by the appointment to it of the chief staff officer reserves in January 1944.

In these instances the concept of a "people's navy" served to convince the minister that a serious gulf between the regular force and the reserves did indeed exist. Two other popular myths from the period — most notably that the regulars sent the reserves to sea in their stead, and that RCNRs and VRs were purposely confined to the corvettes and minesweepers — did the same thing. Neither myth was true, of course. A survey conducted in early 1943 confirmed that the percentage of regulars and VRs serving at sea was virtually identical: 43.8 percent and 44.7 percent respectively. These figures would have surprised a great number of reservists who truly believed in this myth. Reservists often resorted to homespun poetry to express their feelings toward the navy, and the notion that they were the ones slogging it out on the North Atlantic was no exception. In a poem entitled "Swan Song of the Reservist," or "Strange as it Seems I Don't Regret Doing It," one reservist conveyed his frustration at the regular's perceived lack of sea time as follows:

> The War is over and we're in clover
> We leave the job to you
> This is no guff, it's safe enough
> We've shown you what do.
>
> Oh — it's VO [rye whiskey] for the VRs
> And gins for the RCN
> Who stayed ashore throughout the war
> But now sail forth again.
>
> From the VRs and the NRs
> Here's a toast to the RCN
> Comes times of stress and deep duress
> We'll take the strain again.[28]

It was the reserve's preponderance in the navy as a whole, representing some 88.4 percent of the service's total at this time, which was responsible for creating the perception that the VRs and NRs were the only ones going to sea. The reality was otherwise; the reserves and regulars were a team who shared the burden at sea in equal measure.

Differences aside, the regulars did respect the reserves for the major role they played. In a typical piece of shipboard verse, Commander Kenneth Adams, RCN, a regular force skipper and escort commander, playfully extolled the qualities of the reserves whom he

Courtesy Royal Navy Fleet Air Arm Museum, CRSR/43, and Richard Gimblett.

The Royal Canadian Navy's only Victoria Cross was awarded posthumously to RCNVR pilot Lieutenant Robert Hampton Gray (inset), whose aircraft is seen about to launch from the carrier HMS *Rajah* on operations a year earlier in the North Atlantic.

had trained — and whom he admired. Of course, he knew "The Swan Song of the Reservists." Now he wrote "The Response." With mock superiority and an acute sense of irony, he contrasted the fastidious, self-conscious professionalism of the regulars with the jaunty, devil-may-care competence of the reserves. Not only did he recall the yarns and fellowship and the nostalgia of a collaborative effort, but Adams also managed to slip a few jibes of his own into his response:

> *Yes, I recall the stories tall*
> *Made up in times of stress,*
> *Of thrilling days and sailors' ways*
> *Of cleaning up a mess.*
>
> *The war is won and you're the one*
> *Who always could be found.*
> *You steamed your ships on all the trips,*
> *And seldom ran aground.*
>
> *Except now and then, and only when*
> *The land was near at hand.*
> *From all us men in R.C.N.*
> *We hate to lose you now.*

I'm proud as punch of all you bunch
Of sailors old and new.
I wish you well and please don't tell
Of what you owe the few.

Adams's last two sentences were absolutely true: the small core that had formed the pre-war RCN was largely responsible for preparing the VR for life at sea and the hardships of battle.

Dispelling the myth of the "Sheep Dog Navy" — the term that reinforced the belief that the VRs were purposely relegated to the smaller escort ships while the RCN operated the destroyers — further suggests that the reserves and the regular force were far more integrated than previously thought. This legend, like the earlier one, was also rooted in perception. Because of a shortage of regulars, the vast majority of officers on the corvettes and minesweepers were indeed reservists. Thanks to the distinctive lace on their sleeves, this created the impression that VRs and NRs were being segregated to the smaller ships. However, right from the start of the war, reservists actually represented the majority of

The crew of the cruiser *Uganda* were mostly reservists, including these gunners setting shell fuses before the bombardment of Truk, 23 June 1945.

Library and Archives Canada, PA-114920.

officers in destroyer wardrooms as well. Take for example the River-class destroyer HMCS *St. Laurent*. Between September 1939 and March 1940, 61 percent of its wardroom were reserve officers. A larger sample of wardrooms from the destroyers, Prince-class ships, and cruisers, attests that this trend continued throughout the war. Officer complements averaged 75.8 percent reserve in May 1943 and 68.6 percent reserve in May 1945. Moreover, as they gained suitable experience, RCNR and RCNVR officers were also getting command of some of these vessels. The trend began with Lieutenant-Commander D.C. Wallace, RCNR, who assumed command of the Town-class destroyer HMCS *St. Clair* on 24 September 1940, along with the first VR command, that of Lieutenant-Commander Angus G. Boulton, RCNVR, who had the destroyer *Ottawa* from 21 July to 18 August 1941. (He later commanded the destroyer HMCS *Annapolis* from 4 December 1942 to 2 March 1944.) The trend continued to the point where 36 RCNR and VR officers would find themselves in command of seven Town-class and eight River-class destroyers.

While the officers' statistics are telling, it is actually the figures for the ratings that best dismantle the myth of the Sheep Dog Navy. That the crew of the corvette HMCS *Wetaskiwin* was 81.6 percent reserve in 1941 is not surprising. But that number is far more significant when compared to the ratings in the destroyer HMCS *Skeena* who in July 1944 were 86.6 percent reserve. In fact, nominal lists from other destroyers show that RCNRs and RCNVRs often made up over 80 percent of a ship's complement. What is even more revealing, however, is that a similar survey of minesweepers, corvettes, and frigates shows that, while some were almost entirely reserve, many were composed of between 10 and 20 percent regulars. That this compares favourably to the destroyers was no accident. It was the result of deliberate policy. The limited number of experienced permanent force members was purposefully parceled out to as much of the fleet as possible to help develop VRs fresh from training. Hence, rather than portraying a deeply divided navy (as the "sheep dog" myth tends to do) these statistics strongly suggest that the regulars and reserves came together to collectively serve their nation as a "people's navy." Each one gave the other the necessary skills to make an effective contribution to the country's defence.[29]

At its peak strength, approximately 78,000 (or 84 percent) of the naval service's 96,000 personnel were VRs. Together, they served their country in every theatre from Alaska to Iceland, out to Burma and back again. Moreover, they did so in many diverse postings, ranging from aircraft carriers to motor torpedo boats and landing craft. Nor did they serve solely as sailors. Others gave distinguished service as beach commandos, typists, pilots, naval accountants, doctors, and many other non-traditional naval roles. And when it was all over, the vast majority went full circle by returning to the Naval Reserve division where they had joined so that they could be demobilized and reintegrated into Canadian society. Significantly, the Naval Reserve took the lead in reviving a modern equivalent of the Women's Royal Canadian Naval Service. In 1951 — four years before the regular force admitted women — the reserve permitted a small contingent of 500 to join the 20 Naval Reserve divisions across the country. So successful was the initiative that *The Ottawa Citizen* announced one year later on 24 September 1952, "Wren force being doubled."

But no matter whether the naval volunteers from the RCNR, RCNVR, and WRCNS went back to civilian life, to part-time service with a Naval Reserve division, or even joined

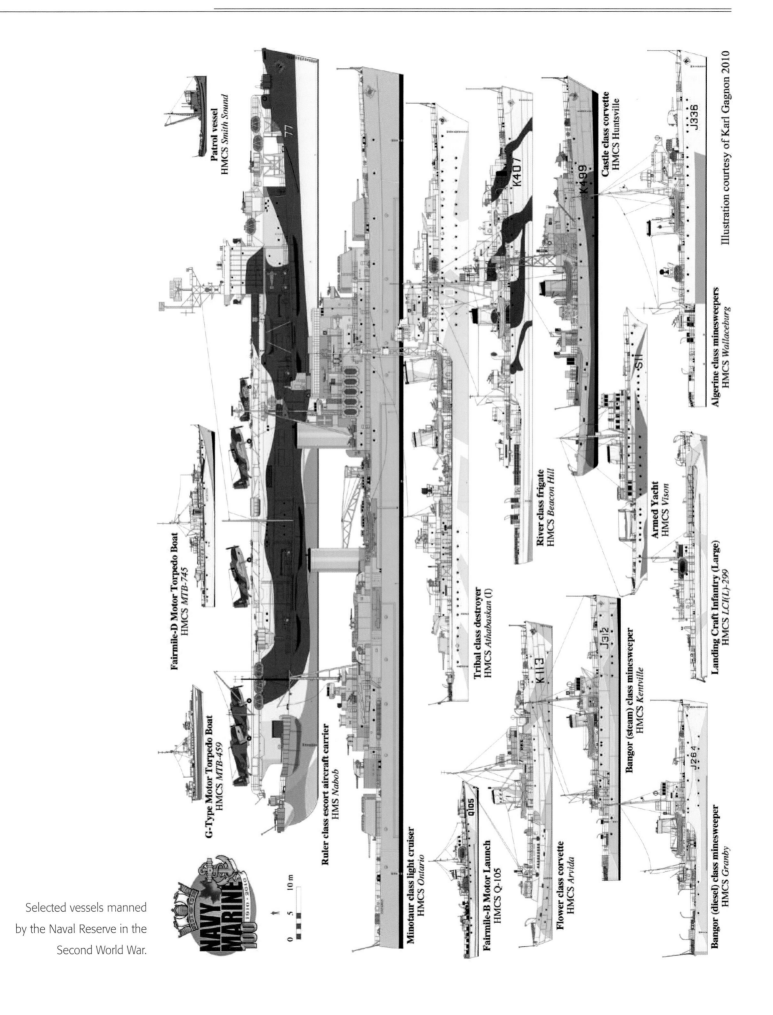

Patrol vessel
HMCS *Smith Sound*

Fairmile-D Motor Torpedo Boat
HMCS *MTB-745*

G-Type Motor Torpedo Boat
HMCS *MTB-459*

Ruler class escort aircraft carrier
HMS *Nabob*

Minotaur class light cruiser
HMCS *Ontario*

Tribal class destroyer
HMCS *Athabaskan (I)*

River class frigate
HMCS *Beacon Hill*

Castle class corvette
HMCS Huntsville

Algerine class minesweepers
HMCS *Wallaceburg*

Armed Yacht
HMCS *Vison*

Landing Craft Infantry (Large)
HMCS *LCI(L)-299*

Bangor (steam) class minesweeper
HMCS *Kentville*

Flower class corvette
HMCS *Arvida*

Fairmile-B Motor Launch
HMCS Q-105

Bangor (diesel) class minesweeper
HMCS *Granby*

Illustration courtesy of Karl Gagnon 2010

Selected vessels manned
by the Naval Reserve in the
Second World War.

0 5 10 m

the regulars (as a number did), every single one of them played a key role in securing victory for the Allies. That they did so in the name of Canada — and alongside their permanent force colleagues — is all the proof needed to confidently proclaim that they were an essential part of what was, and always had been, a "people's navy."

Notes

1. Directorate of History and Heritage (DHH), 81/520/1700–905, Vol. 2, Box 119, file 3, Cuthbert Taylor (DNP) memo, 11 March 1940; Mckee, *Volunteers for Sea Service*, 40.

2. Brad Thompson, *HMCS Griffon: A Naval History* (Thunder Bay, ON: Privately Printed, 1985), 15. Until spring of 1942 the only education requirement was grade eight. From 1942 onwards, the navy adopted testing procedures based on the army's model that judged an individual's ability to learn.

3. DHH, 81/520/1700–905, Interview with E. Brock, 25 October 1944.

4. David Zimmerman, "The Social Background of the Wartime Navy: Some Statistical Data," in Michael L. Hadley, Rob Huebert, and Fred Crickard, eds., *A Nation's Navy: In Quest of Canadian Naval Identity* (Kingston: McGill-Queen's University Press, 1996), 256–79.

5. Gilbert Norman Tucker, *The Naval Service of Canada: Its Official History, Vol. 2* (Ottawa: The King's Printer, 1952), 270–71.

6. Barbara Winters, "The Wrens of the Second World War: Their Place in the History of Canadian Servicewomen," in Hadley et al, *A Nation's Navy*, 280–96. See also Barbara Dundas, *A History of Women in the Canadian Military Art* (Montreal: Art Global, 2000), 60–64.

7. Doris Grierson Hope, "A Wren Remembers: Recollections of the Women's Royal Canadian Naval Service (W.R.C.N.S.)." Website of CFB Esquimalt Naval and Military Museum: *www.navalandmilitarymuseum.org/resource_pages/pavingtheway/dorishope.html* (accessed June 24, 2010).

8. Barbara Fosdick, "Picturing Victory: Jenny Pike, Photographer, WRCNS," Website of CFB Esquimalt Naval and Military Museum. *www.navalandmilitarymuseum.org/resource_pages/pavingtheway/pike.html* (accessed June 24, 2010).

9. Barbara Dundas, *A History of Women in the Canadian Military*, 60, 64; Tucker, *The Naval Service of Canada (II)*, 317–22.

10. Thompson, *HMCS Griffon*, 16.

11. Tucker, *Naval Service of Canada (II)*, 322.

12. DHH, 81/520/1700–905, Box 118, file 21, Public Relations Office, 5 September 1941.

13. Robert Williamson, *HMCS Star: A Naval Reserve History* (Hamilton: Superior Printery, 1991), 28.

14. DHH, 81/520/1700–905, Box 118, file 21.

15. J.R. Anderson, "An RCNVR Division Mobilizes — August to October, 1939," in Mack Lynch, ed., *Salty Dips*, Vol. 1 (Ottawa: NOAC, 1983), 15.

16. James Lamb, *The Corvette Navy: True Stories from Canada's Atlantic War* (Toronto: Macmillan, 1977), 142.

17. Mark Neilson, *Winnipeg's Navy: The History of the Naval Reserve in Winnipeg* (Winnipeg: Privately Printed, 2003), 69.

18. Joseph Schull, *The Far Distant Ships: An Official Account of Canadian Naval Operations in the Second World War* (Ottawa: Queen's Printer, 1952) 26.

19. LAC, MG 31, E 18, 14–5, HMCS *Stone Frigate*.

20. Hal Lawrence. *A Bloody War: One Man's Memories of the Canadian Navy 1939–45* (Toronto: McClelland and Stewart, 1979), 100–01.

21. For an excellent account of the RCN's training deficiencies see William Glover, "Officer Training and the Quest for Operational Efficiency in the Royal Canadian Navy, 1939–1945" (Ph.D. diss., King's College, London, 1998).

22. Cited in Richard Mayne, "George C Jones: The political career of a naval officer," in *The Admirals*, ed. Michael Whitby, Peter Haydon, and Richard Gimblett (Toronto: Dundurn Press, 2006), 138.

23. Anthony Griffin, *Footfalls in Memory* (Toronto: Privately Printed, 1998), 89.

24. Louis Audette, "Une Mer Cruelle," in Mack Lynch, ed., *Salty Dips*, Vol. 2 (Ottawa: NOAC, 1985), 68.

25. DHH, 85/476, Rear-Admiral Michael Grote-Sterling, interviewed by Hal Lawrence, Victoria, BC, 8 January 1985.

26. Richard Mayne, *Betrayed: Scandal, Politics and Canadian Naval Leadership* (Vancouver: UBC Press, 2006), 39.

27. *Ibid.*, 178.

28. Cited in *Salty Dips*, Mack Lynch, ed., Vol. 2, 212. The reference to drinks (VO and gin) underscores presumed social differences between the two branches of the service, regular force and reserve. VO (Canadian rye whiskey) is portrayed as the liquor of choice for "Canadians," while gin was the choice of the "English" gentleman officer. This is one of many examples of Canadianization versus "Englishness" in the navy.

29. All these statistics are the process of an exhaustive study conducted by the author on the nominal lists of over 140 ships, held at the Library and Archives of Canada.

CHAPTER 5

From "Wavy Navy" to "Jolly Green Giants," 1945–68

Michael L. Hadley

The legacy of the war years determined the character of the Naval Reserve well into the 1970s. The wartime navy's achievements, ethos, and mythology formed part of its continuing identity and image. Most of the "hostilities only" personnel who had helped swell Canada's naval forces from a meagre pre-war level of 3,900 to over 90,000 by 1945 returned to their civilian occupations. In the words of one veteran of the Battle of the Atlantic: "I turned and ran down the ladder into a waiting boat. And I left behind me a ship and a fleet, a host of friends and a way of life that I would never see again. The corvette navy was dead, and I walked away into the strange civilian world of peace."[1] For many, that world of peace included further volunteer service in the Naval Reserve. As so-called "Saturday night sailors" they would drill one evening a week, take their two-weeks annual training, parade publicly on official occasions such as church parades and Remembrance Day, and represent the navy to civilian society.

Reservists regarded their "stone frigates" — a colloquial term for their drill halls — as ships, and indeed named them as such. Like seagoing units of the fleet, these reserve units in cities and towns across Canada bore the designation HMCS — His/Her Majesty's Canadian Ship. And when "going aboard" (one never simply entered the building), one stepped onto and saluted the "quarter deck" (foyer), saw commemorative plaques and photographs on "the bulkheads" (walls), walked briskly along "passageways" (corridors) to the Seamen's Mess or the Chief's and Petty Officers' Mess (lounges), or perhaps went "up top" (upstairs) to "the Wardroom" (officers' lounge). On official business, one might find the captain in his "cabin" (office). On formal occasions like Ceremonial Divisions, platoons of reservists "turned out in their No. 1's" (dressed in their best uniform) and paraded proudly, war medals clinking as they marched to the stirring strains of their city's naval band. Traditional melodies like "Heart of Oak" evoked the Canadian Navy's rich association with its parent, Great Britain's Royal Navy. Others, like "Roll Along Wavy Navy" (see chapter 3) celebrated what had become the Canadian devil-may-care, "can do" spirit of getting on with even the toughest job whatever the shortcomings in professional training: "If they ask us who we are/we're the RCNVR/Roll along Wavy Navy, Roll Along."[2] This, in naval parlance, celebrated the "gung ho" attitude of the Royal Canadian Naval Volunteer Reserve, the VRs who had joined the navy directly from "civvy street." With typical self-irony, another popular song captured the self-same spirit: "Then here's to the lads of the Maple Leaf Squadron/At hunting the U-boat it's seldom they fail/Though they've come from the mine and the farm and the workshop/The bank and the college and maybe from jail."

Life in the Naval Reserve offered not only its challenges in a unique culture, but opportunities for elegance. For example, Trafalgar Day, commemorating Admiral Horatio Nelson's stunning defeat of the French fleet in 1805, provided the occasion for the annual Trafalgar Day Ball. This was a grand formal event that attracted large numbers from throughout the civilian community as well. Like other social events, it highlighted the close links between sailors and society. Formal dining in the wardroom (later practised by ranks other than officers) inculcated a graciousness in relationships, often with echoes of the past. Thus officers and guests might promenade to table to the lilting air of "The Roast Beef of Olde England." Commander Freddy Grubb's *Rules for Mess Etiquette* set the tone by stressing civility and "good manners" after the fashion of English gentlemen. These "Mess Dinners," as they were called, could, however, become delightfully rambunctious when diners wilfully misconstrued "Grubb's rules."[3] Yet "ours is a Way of Life," Grubb had observed, "not an adherence to a series of arbitrary rules. We obey the rules ... because we want to. It is our self-discipline as individuals and as a group that makes us worthy to lead men." In many ways, the Naval Reserve in these years kept Canada's seafaring tradition alive.

But these traditions would soon change. The "Englishness" of the Royal Canadian Navy had begun to rankle during the early 1940s. This characteristic finds early expression in Alan Easton's memoir *50 North: An Atlantic Battleground* (1963). Famed even in his own day as an especially competent reservist and wartime skipper, Easton felt deeply in tune with the navy in which he served. He expressed what others in the wartime navy had acutely felt: an awareness that during the Battle of the Atlantic the Canadian Navy had

The anticipated "come as you are" nature of atomic warfare seemed to make the recent experience of a reserve redundant.

Department of National Defence, RNC-1165.

finally come of age on its own terms. Admiral Nelson, he reflected, belonged to the British, and Canadians had no direct right to him. "Our tradition," Easton had written, "is probably being made right now." Indeed, the navy would have to adopt the Canadian way of doing business. The Mainguy Report (1949) on several post-war mutinies that had taken place in the fleet was a reminder of what would befall Canadians who disregarded such advice.

The immediate post-war period was, of course, a time of demobilization. A navy that had undergone severe growing pains between 1939 and 1945 now experienced the reverse: painful downsizing. The government began disposing of its "war assets." After all, the war had been won, and the ships that had once pulsed with life and had beaten the enemy now seemed a liability. Men

Department of National Defence, COND-5854.

RCN(R) officers attend the ABCD (Atomic, Biological, Chemical Defence) School to learn what nuclear weapons can do to warships.

and women could be released from service, and with them their hard-won skills and experience. Unless, of course, they could be retained as reservists, ready to be mobilized in the event of some future national emergency. Precisely this situation had been faced during the interwar years 1919–38 by the man known as the "father of the Naval Reserve," Captain Walter Hose. Reductions of personnel and equipment in all the armed services in those years had threatened the very existence of the whole Canadian Navy. Thus (as recounted previously in this volume) in 1923 he had created the Royal Canadian Naval Volunteer Reserve as a means of sustaining a nationwide grassroots basis for the naval concept. As it turned out, the existence of reserve units right across the country had provided a critical infrastructure that made it possible to recruit and mobilize for the Second World War on a massive level. Though the navy's existence after 1945 was far from threatened, it nonetheless faced challenging issues of how to reduce its fleet to peacetime levels while maintaining its expertise. The Naval Reserve was a key to the process. But for this process to work, the general public had to be convinced that the navy was a cause for national pride, and a national institution that shaped our identity as a people.

Public relations about the navy in the late forties focused on preserving its past glories and trying to envision the future — a future in which reservists would play an important role. Although some of this PR was official, novelists and memoirists played their part as well. Take, for example, William Sclater's *Haida* (1947). Advertising blurbs dubbed it "a story of the hard-fighting Tribal-class destroyers of the Royal Canadian Navy on the Murmansk convoy and in the English Channel and the Bay of Biscay." These Tribals were virtual "pocket cruisers," hence different from the "corvette navy" more commonly associated with the reservists. Yet, as a reservoir of national values it served as a magnet for the memories that contributed to naval lore. Indeed, the author himself saw the ship as "a symbol of our times."

Reservists trained aboard Tribal-class destroyers, as well as in cruisers and frigates, throughout the 1940s and 1950s. In writing his novel *Storm Below* (1947), landlubber Hugh Garner perhaps unwittingly introduced the theme of "unity in diversity" that would increasingly characterize post-war Canada and its reserves despite regional misunderstandings. His description of the reservist crew of his fictional corvette shows reservists bristling with potential interpersonal conflict and geographical bias. Reservists had indeed been drawn from every region in Canada — as they would throughout their history. They were posted wherever they were needed, primarily with regard to their expertise or phase of training. Once arriving on site they set about becoming a cohesive crew. That, too, was part of the post-war reservist picture. Garner dished up somewhat of a stew pot of a crew, each one of them a cultural stereotype. There were "plough jockeys" from the prairies, an ex-patriot Anglo-Canadian from British Columbia with a hyphenated name, a rough diamond called "Cowboy," and an arrogant Torontonian. The sole member from Quebec was a character called Frenchy Turgeon, whose fractured English marked him out as an outsider from the beginning. Drawn inexorably into a deeper compassionate understanding of themselves and their microscopic world, this unlikely menagerie in the novel actually does become an efficient fighting ship. Unlikely as it seems, this yarn hints at the role of the Naval Reserve in later years in contributing to national unity. For as the Naval Reserve grew, it developed closer and more understanding relationships with francophone Canadians — although it would not be until the 1980s that four francophone reserve divisions would be created in Quebec as a means of integrating francophones into this distinctive national institution known as the Canadian Navy.

But perhaps no single volume of this period had greater influence on the lore, mythology, and hopes of these early years than Joseph Schull's *The Far Distant Ships* (1950). It influenced the popular imagination. Commissioned to write what was touted as the "official operational history," Schull told the very story that the naval staff wanted: big-ship heroism and adventure, epic battles, the smells of gunpowder, and the mastery of fear. The memories of now elderly ex-reservists suggest that *The Far Distant Ships* was an effective recruiting tool. It appealed to all the tough-minded romanticism of which Canadian youth thought themselves capable. Certainly, university students applying for entry into the University Naval Training Division were well advised to know "their Schull," for the interview board was bound to test them on their grasp of Canadian naval history. And at the time, Schull's book was about all there was.[4]

Founded in 1943, the University Naval Training Division had supplied over 500 officers to Canada's wartime forces. Reorganized and expanded in 1947, they were known by the regular force as the "Untidies," a name suggested by their acronym UNTD. But untidy they were not. This unique, nation-wide officer-training corps provided a broad spectrum of university students — hundreds of them each year — with the opportunity to undergo professional training with the regular force. Between the years 1953–57, for example, almost 1,700 entered the UNTD, and over the life of the plan some 7,000 enrolled. They received pay for the time served, and a naval commission on graduation from university. Half a year at a civilian university, and half a year with the navy was an attractive mix. Typically, one calendar year of volunteer reserve service — balanced between campus and navy —

Library and Archives Canada, O-1405-5.

"Hard hat" diving operations by Reservists of HMCS *Chippawa* during the Red River flood of May 1950.

covered the costs of subsistence, books, and tuition. Based on university campuses and in reserve units across the country, the UNTD offered francophone students the first opportunities to join the navy in large numbers. By requiring aspiring officers to achieve university graduation before receiving a commission, the UNTD plan pioneered officer education for the whole force. In time, producing well-trained officers who were also well educated became the standard for the naval service.

UNTD trainees enjoyed the added attraction of travelling across Canada by train to summer training in Halifax and Esquimalt, sea experience aboard famed warships like the cruisers HMC Ships *Ontario* and *Quebec*, the Tribal-class destroyers, and Prestonian-class frigates. The training program was intense and demanding. It involved theory and practice in a wide range of subjects: seamanship, pilotage, and celestial navigation; naval gunnery and communications; fleet tactics, practical weapons training, and torpedo–anti-submarine practice, carried out both in tactical trainers and at sea. Sea training took the UNTD cadets on deep-sea cruises to Pearl Harbor, operations along the West Coast from Alaska to San Diego, and on the East Coast from Labrador to New York and San Juan, Puerto Rico, and European ports. Some of these naval cadets undertook flying training with the fleet air arm in Harvard trainers. These aircraft were the most advanced trainers in the Canadian

summer khaki. The only upbeat to the pervasive dark humour was the reservists' boast: throughout the dismal years of Hellyer's ungainly, and ultimately failed, experiment, they had been the ones who had kept "navy blue" alive in the armed forces. Those reservists who staunchly weathered these lean years would eventually experience a naval renaissance of sorts in the 1970s. And in the 1980s they would eventually wear blue once again. But the colour would actually be black, and the uniform fashioned after the pattern of the U.S. Navy. A new identity had been forged.

Notes

1. James Lamb, *The Corvette Navy: True Stories from Canada's Atlantic War* (Toronto: Macmillan, 1977), 174.
2. See my "The Popular Image of the Canadian Navy," in Michael L. Hadley, Rob Huebert, and Fred Crickard, eds., *A Nation's Navy: In Quest of Canadian Naval Identity* (Kingston: McGill-Queen's University Press, 1996), 35–56.
3. Commander F.E. (Freddy) Grubb, RCN, had written his "rules" (as they were known by generations of naval officers) to document the way in which officers of the Royal Canadian Navy of the 1930s through early 1950s actually behaved. Entitled "Some Naval Customs and Social Practices" the undated lecture notes (32-page legal-size mimeograph) are now a collector's item. He had first presented them (in all likelihood in the early 1950's) as a divisional course, that is, a course for junior officers outlining elements of the culture into which they were entering. The "rules" were descriptive (saying what actually was the custom of the Naval Service) and not prescriptive (saying what must be). As he concluded in part: "any well-bred civilian, merely by following the rules [of civility, courteousness, and good manners] under which he was brought up, could get by in the Navy without much comment, and it would take him short time to learn the few special cases that exist."
4. See Marc Milner, "The Historiography of the Canadian Navy: The State of the Art," in Hadley, et al, *A Nation's Navy*, 23–34.
5. See, for example, Michael A. Hennessy, "Fleet Replacement and the Crisis of Identity," in Hadley, et al, *A Nation's Navy*, 131–53.
6. For a thorough discussion of the regular force background of the following, see Marc Milner, *Canada's Navy: The First Century* (Toronto, Buffalo, London: University of Toronto Press, 1999), 199–280.
7. *Ibid.*, 216.
8. Only in the late 1960s did the Naval Reserve, as a sea-going component of the regular force, face the threat of having to adopt militia-style roles such as aid to civil power. Enunciated as official policy, this radical shift in role demoralized large numbers of experienced naval reservists who now found themselves facing the possibility of having to serve as infantrymen. This was put briefly to the test during the "October Crisis" of 1970 when the militia (with some reserve sailors) was called out with the army to deal with apprehended insurrection. The "October Crisis" had been triggered by high profile kidnappings and murder perpetrated by the *Front de Libération du Québec*, also known as the FLQ.

CHAPTER 6

The Quest for Relevance, 1968–90

Ian Holloway

The story of the Naval Reserve in the last two and a half decades of the Cold War mirrors the story in the first two and a half. It was an organization in search of a mission. This was in large measure because the whole of Canadian defence policy was to a significant degree detached from reality in the 1970s and 1980s. The official statement of Canada's defence posture was contained in the post-unification white paper, *Defence in the 70s*. The document suffered from many flaws, not least of which was its virtual de facto abdication of Canada's commitment to the principle of collective security in Europe that lay at the foundation of the NATO treaty. But as far as the Naval Reserve was concerned, *Defence in the 70s* contained a particularly significant omission. For, unlike the naval reserve forces of many of our allies — including Great Britain, the U.S., and Australia — Canada's Naval Reserve was not given a formal role in the defence structure. But herein lies the paradox: in the middle and closing stages of the Cold War, it was arguably the Naval Reserve that provided Canada's greatest contribution to NATO's objective of European survivability. The reserve did so through its leadership role in the Naval Control of Shipping Organization.

As the last chapter made plain, the 1960s had not been kind to the Naval Reserve. Again, as we have seen previously, the Pearson government really had little idea what kind of a navy it wanted, except that it should be "distinctively Canadian" and cost as little as possible. Considered in hindsight, though — for it hardly seemed this way at the time — it was perhaps a blessing to have been left to toil away in relative obscurity. What the Naval Reserve did for much of the 1970s and 1980s was to chart its own course. Ultimately, it

The reserve was chock-full of "characters." Each division had a number of members, generally senior petty officers or passed-over (unpromoted) lieutenant-commanders, whose quirks of dress or affectations of behaviour added to the charm of belonging to the organization. Because of these sorts of things, a tremendous amount of cohesiveness existed among naval reservists. As one observer of the time put it, a Naval Reserve division in some respects bore a closer resemblance to an army regiment than to a naval establishment.

The reserve's institutional isolation from the regular navy in the post-unification years served to breed a curious sort of reverse snobbery. In the years following unification, the Naval Reserve thought of itself as the custodian of naval tradition. This expressed itself in a variety of subtle — and not so subtle — ways: whether through the regular (though illicit) appearances of the White Ensign, or the punctiliousness with which form was observed in the Mess, or something as simple as the wearing of gaiters by the parade gunnery instructor (or, indeed, the continued use of the title "gunnery instructor" itself). It is easy to poke fun at this, but it was a role that the reserve took seriously.

Until the mid-1980s, most of the Naval Reserve's activity had limited military value. Instead, the emphasis was on breeding *esprit de corps*. In 1973, for instance, to commemorate the 50th anniversary of the establishment of the RCNVR, the Naval Reserve mounted a three week, 1,400-mile sailing expedition from Yellowknife down the Mackenzie River to Tuktoyaktuk on the Beaufort Sea. The expedition sailed in two 8.2-metre naval whalers (with the White Ensign, of course, flown astern). Concurrently, Navel Reserve crews sailed two gate vessels, *Porte Saint Jean* and *Porte Saint Louis*, into the Northwest Passage in the eastern Arctic. That same year, the Royal Navy's 10th Minesweeping Squadron (operated largely by Royal Naval Reserve personnel) visited Halifax for a grand party to celebrate the RCNVR's golden anniversary. To top off the anniversary celebrations, HMCS *Star* in Hamilton held the first of the annual national Naval Reserve regattas in October of 1973. The national regattas lasted into the early 1980s. For a couple of years, they were supplemented by winter-based events, including a curling bonspiel and a sports tabloid during the Quebec Winter Carnival. Another source of morale-building was the annual competition for the so-called "Silver Destroyer," a trophy instituted in 1952 by Vice-Admiral Harold Grant, a former chief of the naval staff. A sterling silver–plated model of a St. Laurent-class destroyer escort, the trophy was awarded each year to the most proficient Naval Reserve division. Competition for the Silver Destroyer was keen, and there was a good deal of regret among old hands when it stopped being awarded in the 1990s. None of this did much for the defence of Canada, but it was all great fun.

What some might call the "country club" tone of the Naval Reserve was also reflected in the operational tasking so successfully carried out by the reserve in the 1970s and 1980s. Three years

Diversity in action during a firefighting exercise aboard HMCS *Fort Steele* in 1977. In many respects the Naval Reserve led the regular force in getting women and members of the ethnic communities to sea.

Department of National Defence, IHC77-335.

after the Golden Anniversary celebrations, almost the entire Naval Reserve was mobilized in support of the 1976 Montreal Olympics. Some reservists were employed at the main Olympic site in Montreal, but a large contingent — who dubbed themselves "Davies' Navy" after their officer-in-charge, Commander Hal Davies — served at the Canadian Olympic Regatta (CORK) facility in Kingston. This image of the Naval Reserve — as an auxiliary organization with Gilbert and Sullivan overtones — was reinforced by the reserve's involvement in the Tattoos. The first of the modern Canadian military tattoos had taken place in 1967, during Canada's centennial year. The Tattoo was a tri-service affair, and it toured the country from coast to coast. In 1980, to commemorate the navy's 70th anniversary, the navy established another nationally touring Tattoo, this one with a decidedly naval flavour. While the 1980 Tattoo involved representatives from all branches of the navy (and, indeed, all branches of the Canadian Forces), a disproportionately large share of the touring company (and the support team) was drawn from the Naval Reserve. To be sure, there were always reservists who were given the opportunity to serve in regular fleet units. And during the early 1970s, a number of reservists served with the army on U.N. peacekeeping duties in the Middle East. Moreover, the so-called "support trades" — cooks, storesmen, medical assistants, and clerks — were regularly employed in regular force billets. Yet in no way could it be said that in the aftermath of the seriously flawed Hellyer experiment the Canadian Naval Reserve was fulfilling any definable role in Canada's defence structure.

In 1971, the primary source of recruits for the Naval Reserve and, therefore, the complexion of the reserve, changed dramatically. It was in that year that the government introduced the Summer Youth Employment Program, or SYEP. Called a number of names over the years, it was known to most as "the summer program." Funded jointly by the secretary of state and the department of national defence, each of the reserve components of the Canadian Forces operated its own scheme. The program offered young Canadians the opportunity to undergo eight weeks of general military training during the months of July and August. While they were under no obligation to apply afterward for entry into the reserve force, many did. So much so, that by the mid-1970s, and well into the 1990s, the Naval Reserve had a steady infusion of new recruits each autumn. This proved to be a double-edged sword. On one hand, from top to bottom the Naval Reserve was probably the best-educated element of the Canadian Forces. At a time when it was still possible to join the regular force with only a grade eight education, most naval reservists had university education. And that included those in the non-commissioned ranks, or "lower deck," as

Department of National Defence, ISC86-312.

Diesel Mechanic Leading Wren Henia Malinowski adjusts the engine of YFL-104 *Pogo*, the tender to Ottawa's Naval Reserve Division HMCS *Carleton*, May 1986.

Courtesy Laraine Orthlieb.

When promoted to the rank of commodore to assume the appointment of Senior Naval Reserve Adviser, Laraine Orthlieb became the first female flag officer in the Canadian Forces.

they were called. It was not uncommon to meet, say, a Naval Reserve boatswain who in civilian life was a lab technician or an accountant. Or an able seaman who was a microbiologist. And there was a famous incident (infamous, to the regular navy) in the early 1980s where the captain of HMCS *Preserver* confessed that he preferred the daily weather briefings he received from one of his Naval Reserve leading seamen over those from the Met staff assigned to the ship. (In civilian life the leading seaman was a professional meteorologist.)

This sort of incident — and variations on it — were plentiful, and did wonders for morale within the reserve. At the same time, though, by the late 1970s, the Naval Reserve had become a de facto summertime navy. From May to August, the coasts were flooded with reservists, particularly the West Coast. But during the other three seasons, only a small nucleus of regularly employed reservists remained on active service. (These were the "Permashads," as they were known.) But many of these "permanent shadows" of the regular force who had come to the reserves had actually joined on retirement from the regular force. They were too few even to man any more than two gate vessels. This tended to give the reserve something of a summer camp feel.

Almost all formal training in the Naval Reserve was carried out separately from the regular navy. As has been noted, the summer program provided the principal avenue into the reserve, both for prospective officers as well as for sailors. Those who later aspired to the wardroom applied for entry into the Reserve Officer University Training Plan. This ROUTP program was a kind of successor, a poor country cousin, to the old UNTD scheme of the 1940s and 1950s. For seagoing officers, the path to "trained" status involved three full summers of training before one earned a BWK, or bridge watchkeeping certificate. This marked the officer as qualified to take charge of a ship both at sea and in harbour. Apart from a few weeks in the first summer, the afloat component of this training was conducted in a combination of gate vessels and other minor (and unarmed) craft. But minor craft or not, the BWK was a prize that only a completely dedicated candidate could win. Regardless of branch, the first summer's training was for the most part common to all trainees. Thereafter, officers in the other branches took their summer training courses in shore-based establishments. In the support branches, this chiefly meant army bases.

For members of the lower deck, the training scheme was slightly more simplified. The summer following the summer program consisted of a further period of general military training. For most of the 1970s and 1980s this was of six weeks duration, followed by an initial trade's course of between three and four weeks in length. A few really lucky individuals might gild the lily with some sea time that second summer. For a few *extremely* fortunate souls, this sea time might even be in a destroyer. While the reservist completed his or her university studies, the following summers would consist of more advanced trade courses, periods of "on the job training" (OJT) and service in the gate vessels. After a few

years, a sailor might be selected for a junior leadership course (JLC), which was a prerequisite for promotion to the rank of master seaman. Standards in the JLC were high, and the failure rate was generally significant. To be promoted to petty officer, one had to complete a senior leadership course, but by this stage, most people who had originally been selected actually completed the course. Yet, it was all very self-contained and self-referential. And it is impossible to overstate the extent to which the Naval Reserve's training cycle was built around the university calendar. Though it was possible to join the reserve without being a full-time student, it was very difficult to meet training requirements otherwise. And it was a near certainty that the non-student reservist would fall significantly behind his or her peers within a few years. This was hardly conducive to morale. Thus the attrition rate among non-student reservists through the 1970s and 1980s, and into the 1990s, was almost 100 percent within the first couple of years of entry.

All of this might suggest that the Canadian Naval Reserve was little more than a burden on the defence budget in the post-unification period. And in fact, that was not an uncommon sentiment among regular naval officers and defence bureaucrats. But in an odd way, it was this institutional isolationism that allowed the seeds for the professional

A Naval Control of Shipping course visits the Vessel Traffic Management Centre at Chebucto Head, Nova Scotia, August 1975.

Department of National Defence, IH75-157.

renaissance of the Naval Reserve to take root and bloom. Professional historians argue about the so-called "great man" theory of history that sees major figures as catalysts for redirection and change. Of course, it goes without saying that the revival of the Naval Reserve as an organization concerned with actual warfighting, and with real operations, came about as a result of collective will *throughout* the organization — and as a result of the awakening by the defence establishment to the reserve's potential. Nonetheless, two officers in particular deserve a great deal of credit for engendering an increase in professional standards. The first was Lieutenant-Commander Don Arnaud, who in 1977 was appointed officer in charge of HMCS *Patriot*, a Naval Reserve training establishment at Albert Head, outside Esquimalt. (*Patriot* had been the name of one of the navy's first two destroyers in 1920–28, and had later become the name of the Naval Reserve Headquarters on the Great Lakes, 1953–68.) As has been noted, the training syllabi at *Patriot* were largely home-grown affairs. The *Patriot* of the 1970s placed a great deal more emphasis on the purely naval way of doing things, than in any regular force training establishment. This, of course, fed into the reserve's sense that it was the custodian of naval tradition in Canada. But in almost every way, *Patriot* was a tremendous success. Standards were intellectually exacting, and there was a degree of physical toughness to the training that engendered a sense of accomplishment for all who went through it. However, perhaps the most enduring benefit of the *Patriot* experiment, which lasted only six years or so before the establishment was largely closed, was that it gave rise to a sense of organizational confidence in the Naval Reserve. The reserve had always had competent officers and sailors; *Patriot* showed that it could also act as a competent organization.

The second of the "great men" whose efforts helped breathe new professional life into the Naval Reserve was Lieutenant-Commander Ernie Moffatt. Moffatt was in fact a regular force officer who was appointed staff officer (training) at Naval Reserve Headquarters in 1980. Moffatt had joined the navy in the 1950s as an ordinary seaman, and trained as an armourer's mate. He had, in the old naval expression, gone up to the wardroom "through the hawsepipe." Moffatt was no stranger to the Naval Reserve. Before going to reserve headquarters, he had commanded the Reserve Training Unit (Atlantic), the formation to which the East Coast gate vessels and HMCS *Fort Steele* belonged. So he knew the organization that he was joining. On his appointment to headquarters, he enlisted a team of ex-RCN chief petty officers, who proceeded to rewrite Naval Reserve training specifications. Together, Arnaud and Moffatt helped inject a degree of warlike seriousness into reserve culture, a feature that had largely been missing since the Korean War.

The 1970s and 1980s were a time of increasing opportunities for female members of the reserve. At the dawn of the 1970s, the principal employment of Wrens was in the clerical, medical, supply, and cookery branches. But by the end of the 1980s, there were female officers serving as bridge watchkeeping officers at sea and female ratings serving in operational billets in NATO headquarters. And most amazingly of all, the senior appointment in the entire Naval Reserve was held by a female. In 1989 naval captain Laraine Orthlieb of Edmonton was promoted to the rank of commodore, and made senior naval reserve adviser to the commander of the navy. She was the first female naval flag officer in the Commonwealth.

Department of National Defence, IOC85-256.

Reserves frequently preserved naval tradition by performing the annual "Gun Run" display with naval "field pieces" once used in shore landings. Here, in a throw-back to the image in chapter 9, they perform the annual "Gun Run" display at Maple Leaf Gardens, Toronto, 01 August 1985.

The nucleus of the expansion of the role of female members of the reserve was a small, elite group of Wrens employed in the communications branch, known as "communications support," or "comm supps" for short. There were never more than 100 trained comm supps in the reserve at any one time, but they were all well-trained, and extremely highly regarded by members of the regular force. They gave women what one might call "operational credibility" in the Cold War–era navy. Thanks to them, beginning in the latter years of the 1970s, women began to be admitted to hitherto exclusively male occupations. At the same time, and as a precursor to their appointment to regular force fleet units, Wrens began to be posted to gate vessels. One retired Naval Reserve captain recalls a particularly memorable milestone when skippering a gate vessel in 1978–79. Outbound from Esquimalt late one night, he made his night rounds after having cleared harbour. To his surprise, he found the engine room "manned" completely by women.

In 1985 the navy embarked on a concerted effort to raise its profile among francophone Canadians. This was known as the "Naval Presence in Quebec" project, or NPQ (more on this in chapter 8). But given that it was practically impossible to shift any regular fleet units away from the coasts, the main driving force behind the project was the Naval Reserve. The Naval Presence project involved the move of Naval Reserve Headquarters from Halifax to Quebec City, and the commissioning of four new Naval Reserve divisions in Chicoutimi, Sept-Îles, Trois-Rivières, and Rimouski. These were named, respectively, NCSM (*Navire canadien de Sa Majesté*) *Champlain*, *Jolliet*, *Radisson*, and *d'Iberville*. After a period, some reserve training was moved to Quebec as well. It was housed in a new establishment known as Canadian Forces Fleet School Quebec. It is fair to say — though politically incorrect to do so — that initially, the project was deeply unpopular in the lower deck (non-commissioned ranks) of the Naval Reserve, at least outside the two already existing Quebec divisions. At a time when reservists were beginning to think in operational terms, it seemed positively retrograde physically to remove the reserve further from the regular navy. As one wag asked: why was it permissible to have an establishment known as NCSM *Montcalm* (the Quebec City division), but not an HMCS *Wolfe?* At the same time, however, the naval component of the Conference of Defence Associations did support the move. Significantly, that naval component consisted almost entirely of officers of the Naval Reserve. Even today, there remain some linguistic challenges associated with NPQ since, two official languages or not, the functional language of most naval operations among our allies remains English. But it is equally fair to say that NPQ represented an important step in making Canada's naval service seem real to francophones. Moreover, the relative ease with which the Naval Reserve in the end adjusted to its new identity as a Quebec-based organization is something that could probably usefully be studied elsewhere in government.

The one area of real operational commitment that the Naval Reserve maintained throughout the period was the Naval Control of Shipping Organization. The Naval Reserve

The Commander Maritime Command, Rear-Admiral Douglas Seaman Boyle, conducts the annual inspection of the operations room of HMCS *Scotian*. From left to right: Petty Officer 2nd Class Fred Devlin, Commander Bruce Waterfield, Admiral Boyle, Lieutenant-Commander John Palmer, Commander Rowland Marshall (CO *Scotian*), Commander L.A. Cormier, and Lieutenant Barbara Morris.

Department of National Defence, HS74-1451.

inherited this naturally enough, as it had grown out of the Convoy Organization that had been the mainstay of the RCNVRs work during the Second World War. As it developed under NATO during the Cold War, NCS came to be recognized as a Naval Reserve area of specialty. The NCS Training Centre in Halifax thus came to be a sort of operational home ground for the Naval Reserve. An NCS specialization existed for officers and to mirror this, in 1981 a distinct trade, the shipping control operator, was established for members of the lower deck. In the days before women were regularly able to serve at sea, NCS was one of the few places where female members of the Naval Reserve could serve in an operational capacity.

As the 1970s progressed, and through the 1980s, the Naval Reserve took to NCS with increasing gusto. On the West Coast, for example, neighbourly relations between Victoria's HMCS *Malahat* and its U.S. naval reserve counterpart in Seattle triggered an, at first, unofficial international exercise called Operation Spring Thaw. This initiative took advantage of the "Winter Weekend Gate Vessel" program that formed a highlight of winter training. The idea behind the Winter Weekends was for inland divisions to fly to the nearest coast for sea training. Of course, this tended to favour the West Coast because of its milder weather. Nonetheless, each weekend saw one division or another reaching the nearest coast and heading to sea. Thus, for example, reservists from Winnipeg's HMCS *Chippawa* would typically board an air force Hercules transport aircraft late on a Friday afternoon, fly directly to Victoria, and then board naval buses for the dockyard. There, after sea-safety checks by the regular force, they would man the gate vessels and put to sea, returning to harbour by Sunday, and then home by air force transport that evening.

Operation Spring Thaw piggy-backed on this system by exploiting the Easter weekend. Leading up to the long weekend, American and Canadian NCS officers prepared the sailing orders for the passage Esquimalt-Port Angeles (U.S.) and return. The gate vessels (and sundry Canadian minor vessels and American craft) formed the convoy under regular force escort (minesweepers under the guise of destroyers). A retired senior Canadian naval officer served as convoy commodore. Role-playing aimed at creating all the wartime scenarios: intelligence briefings, conference of "merchant masters," opposed entry ("minefields" in the American port of arrival), shipboard firefighting and damage control, and of course simulated attacks by submarine. And all the while reservists not immediately engaged in the convoy exercise were training in their usual shipboard duties. Elsewhere, other large scale exercises were held annually. Some were Canadian-only affairs; others involved allied naval reserve forces, which allowed the reserve to hone and develop its skill level. By the end of the 1980s, Canada's Naval

Department of National Defence, IOC90-18-10.

A long way from home, HMCS *Porte Saint Jean* enters Toronto harbour for training with HMCS *York*, November 1990. Note the new wrap-around bridge.

Control of Shipping Organization was widely recognized within NATO as being very much on the leading edge. And Canadian NCS officers and senior ratings were regularly sought out to serve in planning, directing, and training staffs in American and British-run NCS exercises. This was a time when the "resupply of Europe" was still a keystone policy of Cold War strategy.

A natural, though long-overlooked, sibling to the NCS organization that came to life again in the 1980s was the Convoy Commodore Organization. By the mid-1980s NATO had realized that what had been forgotten was the science of actually shepherding merchant ships across the ocean in the face of hostile naval and air forces. Ironically, this occurred while its procedures for organizing the movement of mercantile shipping in time of conflict had become highly sophisticated, and while the regular navies continued to refine anti-submarine warfare tactics. So, beginning in the late 1980s, NATO began to try to relearn tactics for successfully convoying groups of ships with different characteristics that were unused to sailing in company. The Canadian leader of the Convoy Commodore Organization was another of the Naval Reserve's "great men," naval Captain Rex Guy. Guy had actually begun his nautical career as an officer in the Merchant Navy, serving in convoys (in high-risk oil tankers, no less) during the Second World War. After the War, he joined the RCN and, upon his retirement from the regular force, transferred to the Naval Reserve to take the helm of the program to revitalize the Convoy Commodore Organization. Rex Guy had a forceful personality. Indeed, there were few people who served under him who did not at one point or another experience the lash of his tongue. Yet he inspired tremendous loyalty and affection from all who knew him. The fact that Canada became one of NATO's acknowledged leaders in convoying procedures was in no small measure a result of his efforts. Guy's brief was to train a cohort of convoy commodores. For the most part these were retired regular force flag officers. But to assist him in this, he assembled a small group of reservists. They were chiefly officers from the MARS and NCS branches, and senior sailors from the signalman trade. Together, they formed a cadre of convoy expertise for the nuclear age. It now seems ironic that all of this took place just as the Cold War was in its waning years, but the level of professionalism and commitment among the convoy commodore team in the late 1980s and early 1990s was really extraordinarily high.

The success of the Convoy Commodore Organization extended beyond its narrow professional confines. The organization linked the Naval Reserve's operational expertise through the NCS organization, with the day-to-day work of the seagoing regular navy. It all came to a symbolic head in 1993 in a major NATO exercise involving major

This group of officers in the wardroom of HMCS *Porte de la Reine*, June 1988, show the change of rig back into distinctive naval uniforms.

Department of National Defence, ISC90-2072.

operations forces," namely counterinsurgency.[2] For reservists the new vision has meant getting over their own biases, and overcoming a bias from their regular force partners that suggests reservists are not really qualified to do a job. Importantly, it has also meant beating down the "militia myth," which maintains it is unnecessary to sustain highly trained armed forces. Part-time soldiers and sailors, the flawed argument runs, have always been the best line of defence in an emergency, as the country can simply draw on their innate talents and patriotism, no special training needed. This attitude leads to poor preparation in peacetime.

By contrast, the policy concept called Transformation underscores the professionalism of reserve forces (and the need for them to grow more professional). Transformation has coloured the Naval Reserve in many ways. It has impacted upon command, equipment, purpose, self-worth, and on its ability to make a meaningful contribution to the seaward defence of Canada. Yet, despite the potential for colour and zest, its current mission statement reads rather blandly: "to provide to Maritime Command trained personnel to man its combat and support elements to enable Canada to meet its objectives in time of peace, crisis or war." This statement differs little from the purpose of the reserve during either the Second World War or the Cold War. Arguably, the actual capacity of the reserve to meet the navy's hopes and expectations has increased exponentially, yet the mission statement reveals none of this. It captures neither the subtle shifts within its various roles and missions, nor the process that developed as the reserve matured. To that process we now turn.

The 1987 white paper on defence, *Challenge and Commitment*, had called for a balanced navy based on one or two principal classes of ships capable of responding to whatever realities the NATO alliance faced. But even if the plan were totally implemented, the navy would not be able to respond to all of Canada's sovereignty concerns. Of nine maritime initiatives, little survived, and much of what survived fell — in theory — to the Naval Reserve. Faced with Soviet maritime power, the white paper foresaw acquiring our own nuclear-powered submarines. Of course, we never did get nuclear submarines, and the cancellation of replacements for diesel-electric subs kept the old Oberon class in the water long past their usable life. In the fullness of time this resulted in the acquisition of the four "slightly used" Upholder-class submarines, whose full introduction to service remains a continuing challenge. The white paper specified a second flight of Canadian patrol frigates and cancelled a third. It authorized a new ship-borne aircraft (NSA) that, after many false starts, may be on the horizon. (NSA is actually a helicopter borne in a destroyer or frigate that vastly increases the ability of the ship to prosecute operations.) New maritime patrol aircraft (MPA) — a land-based aircraft with very sophisticated sensor suites that deal with surface and sub-surface surveillance — were

In anticipation of the new role, an officer of the Royal Naval Reserve (left) explains minesweeping equipment to a Canadian reservist aboard a British vessel, July 1989. Note the Canadian officer's uniform now cut in the "American" style, which retained one vestige of the "green" uniform of unification: the "scrambled eggs" on the brim of a lieutenant-commander's cap. As was the case with the "old" Canadian navy, the British officer of that rank will have to await a promotion before he wears such a "brass hat."

Department of National Defence, ISC89-429.

With the end of the Cold War came many opportunities for naval peacekeeping and the application of reservist small vessel skill-sets, such as those of Lieutenant Carl Tremblay, here as a U.N. naval observer in an ex-Soviet Stenka-class patrol boat along the Cambodian Coast in the Gulf of Thailand during Operation Marquis, June–October 1993.

Courtesy Carl Tremblay.

also in the cards. And the ancient Tracker, designed as a carrier-borne aircraft, was to be re-engineered and given a new role in mid-range surveillance. (The Tracker was scrapped when the white paper lost relevance, and was never replaced.) The 1987 white paper envisaged all kinds of futuristic hardware: SURTASS ships (surveillance towed-array sensor system) and — a harbinger of things to come — an Arctic fixed sonar system to detect the passage of submarine vessels.

It was here that the Naval Reserve entered the defence picture. For, as the 1987 white paper recognized, Canada no longer had any mine countermeasures (MCM) capability. That meant that the country was at serious risk from a low-tech but determined enemy; one with a delivery vehicle (perhaps a small boat) and access to mines. The response to such a threat was the maritime coastal defence vessel (MCDV) program. These vessels would be ships, modern and capable of operating in a dangerous MCM/Coastal Defence environment. But they would be built to commercial rather than naval standards. They would be all steel (an odd thing for something that would have to sweep magnetic mines) and operated by the Naval Reserve. The entire Canadian Forces would become a "Total Force," and all reserves (army, navy, air, and "others") would be expanded from 23,500 to 90,000. This, it was argued, would facilitate augmentation of the Canadian Forces for multiple commitments, and give the various reserve elements their own specific roles and missions. The Naval Reserve was to commission two more Naval Reserve divisions and create the Maritime Coastal Defence Organization (MCDO). The purpose of this new organization

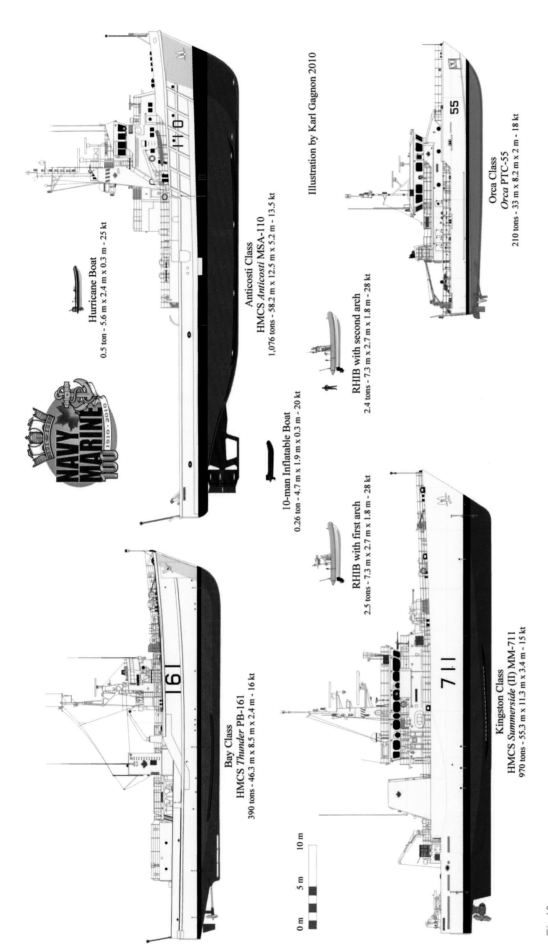

Hurricane Boat
0.5 ton - 5.6 m x 2.4 m x 0.3 m - 25 kt

Anticosti Class
HMCS *Anticosti* MSA-110
1,076 tons - 58.2 m x 12.5 m x 5.2 m - 13.5 kt

Illustration by Karl Gagnon 2010

Orca Class
Orca PTC-55
210 tons - 33 m x 8.2 m x 2 m - 18 kt

10-man Inflatable Boat
0.26 ton - 4.7 m x 1.9 m x 0.3 m - 20 kt

RHIB with second arch
2.4 tons - 7.3 m x 2.7 m x 1.8 m - 28 kt

RHIB with first arch
2.5 tons - 7.3 m x 2.7 m x 1.8 m - 28 kt

Bay Class
HMCS *Thunder* PB-161
390 tons - 46.3 m x 8.5 m x 2.4 m - 16 kt

Kingston Class
HMCS *Summerside* (II) MM-711
970 tons - 55.3 m x 11.3 m x 3.4 m - 15 kt

0 m   5 m   10 m

Selected vessels of the Naval Reserve
in the 1990s and 2000s.

was to consolidate all the marine assets in Canada — Coast Guard and Fisheries, for example — under a centralized naval command in an emergency, and explore more far-reaching involvement with the U.S. for protection around the coastlines of North America.

The MCDO policy was consistent with the white paper's new focus on the defence of Canada, a concept that shifted Canadian defence priorities from mid-Atlantic and the central European front to home waters. However, the "Three Ocean Strategy" — Atlantic, Arctic, and Pacific — emphasized that the maritime security of Canada did not start and stop at home. For, Canada's navy was to have sufficient capability to deny access to its waters in all three oceans within the projected demands of Western security. This is what is known as "sea denial capability." It took account of security concerns elsewhere. For example, it envisaged patrolling the Arctic by nuclear submarine (SSN). Significantly, this marked the first real recognition of maritime security in the North since the voyages of the navy's icebreaker HMCS *Labrador* in the 1950s. These points had not been made in the white papers of 1964 or 1971.[3]

In the meantime, the United States Naval Institute had in 1994 asked the commanders of the world navies what they believed would be the most important naval developments of the next decade.[4] Their responses had significant elements in common: first, the need for balanced, general-purpose forces; second, the importance of technology and of command, control, communications, and intelligence; third, the evolving importance of joint and

Reserve and regular force vessels operating in close company was a common sight by the summer of 2008, when HMCS *Shawinigan* (left) met up with HMCS *Toronto* for Operation Nanook in Frobisher Bay.

Department of National Defence, IS2008-9046.

Courtesy Marta Mulkins.

Lieutenant-Commander Marta Mulkins, the first female commanding officer of a Canadian warship, at home on the bridge of HMCS *Kingston*.

combined operations; forth, the growing importance of national roles in the coastal zones; and fifth, the need to act within a fiscally restrained regime. Already these ideas were coalescing into the concept of Total Force.

Against this background, the Naval Reserve began the official process known as capital "T" Transformation, even though, as we have seen, the 1987 white paper was ultimately overtaken by events. A series of chiefs of the maritime staff actively promoted this process of Transformation. For while the militia was starved and the air reserve squadrons sacrificed to keep their regular force components going, the navy invested in the Naval Reserve. Indeed, it protected the reserve from the worst of the budget cuts that flowed from the end of the Cold War. This investment created a "One Navy" feeling, at least within the Naval Reserve. It seemed readily apparent to reservists that, unlike the past when they had sailed off in antiquated museum pieces, they were actually perceived by the admirals as being as much "their sailors" as any regular force matelot might be. This recognition gave an enormous, but largely unheralded, boost to the feelings of professionalism among reserve sailors.

The focus on a real mission that would see reservists go to sea and do meaningful work of naval and national importance, in proper ships, triggered a discernable shift in the idea of being a reservist. This was reflected in a renewed interest in the professional side of the business of being a seaman. In reserve divisions, part-timers began to prepare for and pass the seagoing command examinations and to get sea time on their watchkeeping tickets. This was an acknowledgment of the potential to go to sea in a real ship and to have a real role. Most of those who strove for sea-going command felt a sentiment like "Well, maybe they will actually let us drive the new ships; and if that is the case I'll be damned if they have an excuse like there aren't enough qualified Reservists." Maybe not an altruistic motivation,

Naval Reserve sailors and militia soldiers place sandbags to protect threatened homes from the Red River flood in May 1997.

Department of National Defence, ISD97-069.

but it was an effective one. This pursuit of knowledge created some conflicts within the Naval Reserve, as young command-qualified officers, smug in their new-found knowledge (I know this to be true, because I was one of them) had little time for the long-serving senior officers who had never qualified in their classifications. The truth was that the service had not provided them with the opportunities that their younger shipmates had, and the navy had been content that they simply show up week after week and keep the land-bound Naval Reserve divisions going. They did that, and we should have honoured them for that. But, with the cruelty of youth, we did not. Of course, sailors of the "gate vessel generation" had been actively lobbying since the 1970s for precisely this sort of critical change. By involvement in the Maritime Defence Association, the naval component of the Conference of Defence Associations, reservists had in fact been representing the interests of the whole navy in the political arena. They had been pressing not only for the patrol frigate program, but also for urgent replacements for their beloved "gates." When these replacements eventually came, they themselves were too old to sail them.

The search for the body of nautical knowledge morphed immediately into the quest for the warfare side of the business. One fed the other. At the same time, MCM and the Maritime Coastal Defence Organization (MCDO) gave a rationale for learning what made a navy tick. It was the first time in a generation that reservists had actually thought about the warfare disciplines. MCDO was relatively short-lived, but its impact was significant. Its successor, Harbour Defence, began as a concept that many saw as little more than applied camping. These first harbour defence units (later called port security units, or PSUs) aimed at protecting out-of-the-way places, and did so in tents, army combat clothing, and field

Department of National Defence SU2004-0123-01.

kitchens. As the doctrine developed, someone eventually realized that we were much more likely to defend a major harbour or anchorage than some "dot" in the middle of nowhere. If one can defend Halifax Harbour, then the middle of nowhere ought to be a breeze. But it evolved into a "Class A" reserve task, that is, a task for the part-time reservist who drilled weekly, on weekends and for some measure of time during the summer. And such Class A reservists made an important contribution to the seaward defence of the nation. Port security became a resource to the fleet that can provide competent personnel, armed and deployed, in support of such events as the Winnipeg Flood, the APEC forum (Asia-Pacific Economic Co-operation), and Operation Port Guard. The latter required the concerted

This 2004 portrait of the ships' company of Ottawa's Division HMCS *Carleton* contrasts greatly with the image in chapter 3.

Department of National Defence, ISD01-9671.

Through the course of recent overseas deployments, such as here during Operation Apollo in the Persian Gulf in November 2001, the Navy has been able to call upon the language skills of reservists from diverse ethnic communities.

effort to man a full port security unit, which had to be worked-up, certified, and then deployed to protect a carrier group of the French Navy. It worked.

As the "gate vessel era" drew to a close, and the coastal defence vessels replaced them, a series of questions loomed large in the Naval Reserve divisions: how to man these new vessels, and what a part-time person could be expected to learn, retain, and actually perform. A considerable slice of the navy's middle management had genuine concerns about what part-timers could reasonably be expected to do. The full-time gate vessel crews answered this doubt. These were the reservists who became the cadre for operating the minesweeping auxiliary vessels (MSAs) — HMC Ships *Moresby* and *Anticosti* — and then the first MCDVs. *Anticosti* (ex-*Jean Tide*) and *Moresby* (ex *Joyce Tide*) had come to the navy as second-hand, offshore supply vessels. Some 58.2 metres in length and displacing 976 tonnes, they were of significant size to train a core of sailors to use mechanical minesweeping gear. The navy had procured them to make the transition from gate vessel to the fully modern MCDV.

In the final analysis, the transition was much smoother than expected. The first ships were crewed and commanded by reservists who took time away from their professional practices or employment, and who performed extremely well. Significantly, however, doubts about what a part-timer could be expected to do have resurfaced with consideration of the Arctic offshore patrol vessel (AOPV). This challenge, too, will be met and overcome in exactly the same way.

The last gate vessels were decommissioned in December 1996 in Esquimalt; at the same time, and on the same day, HMCS *Ottawa*, the last of the patrol frigates (CPF) and HMCS *Nanaimo*, the first West Coast maritime coastal defence vessel, joined the Pacific Fleet. The end of the "gate vessel era" saw highly professional MCDV ships' companies

While the major surface fleet was engaged overseas, it was the reserve fleet that led the Navy back into the Arctic.

Courtesy Shaun Perry.

sailing with rules of engagement (ROE), loaded weapons, and real tasks. These "rules" are orders to the commander of a ship or unit authorizing self-protection measures, and setting forth levels of force that may be used. Like any other warship, MCDVs sail with the ROEs tailored to the mission and level of risk. MCDVs have deployed to Europe, Hawaii, and the Caribbean. They have operated with our allies, who have high praise for what the Naval Reserve of Canada can bring to the table in an international setting.

As successive Canadian governments discovered the Arctic dimension, they realized that we could neither prevent nor regulate access to the Canadian Arctic or to the Exclusive Economic Zone that we claim. The first Canadian warships into Hudson Bay in nearly 40 years were MCDVs. When those ships were alongside in Churchill, Manitoba, in 2005, they were closer to Victoria than to their homeport of Halifax. Getting to Churchill required them to steam well over 2,400 nautical miles and every mile was in waters we claimed as territorial. The North will see much more of the Naval Reserve in the future.

Among the most influential and sustained of all reservists at the time was Commodore Ray Zuliani. He went on to become a rear-admiral and chief of reserves and cadets. Under his leadership, the Naval Reserves' basic training and classification training became systematized and compatible with the training offered to a regular force officer or non-commissioned officer. The two solitudes, permanent force and reserve, became interchangeable parts. This training regime has had a number of consequences. These include the ability of a member to move from one part to the other without more training. The most important consequence has been the training of regular and reservist together, with the training itself provided by both regular and reservist instructors. When you train with someone to the same standard and in the same way, then barriers topple, friendships develop, and understanding is born. This has been an immense benefit to the idea of a Total Force Navy. This common training extends to levels well beyond that of new entry, and now includes such diverse disciplines as professional military education and leadership training.[5] It also has allowed at least one reserve classification to move from a "reserve only" Cold War discipline into a very necessary and demanding classification called naval control of shipping. NCS has always been a vital requirement for the safe and timely arrival of merchant vessels; it is still required today. Naval control of shipping is now much more. This is because the new intelligence classification is one that has had

With the re-organization of the Naval Reserve roles and trades more closely aligned with those of the regular force, one of the few remaining unique qualifications is the Port Inspection Diver, a specialty that came into even higher demand after the terror attacks of 9/11.

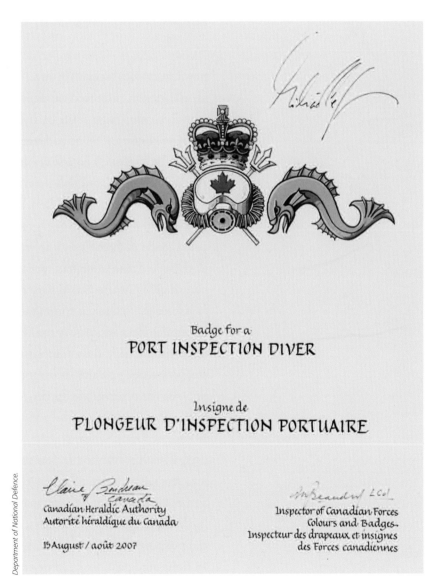

Badge for a
PORT INSPECTION DIVER

Insigne de
PLONGEUR D'INSPECTION PORTUAIRE

Canadian Heraldic Authority
Autorité héraldique du Canada

15 August / août 2007

Inspector of Canadian Forces
Colours and Badges
Inspecteur des drapeaux et insignes
des Forces canadiennes

Department of National Defence.

Leading Seaman Benjamin Neil (left), a boatswain from Ottawa's HMCS *Carleton*, and Ordinary Seaman Dustin Burdett, boatswain from HMCS *Discovery* in Vancouver, conduct a security patrol for the Vancouver 2010 Winter Games.

Department of National Defence, IS2010-0011-10.

naval reservists serve all around the globe, in conflicts far from the sea, and gives the navy an additional, enhanced capability.[6]

Given this high level of integration, then, who should command this new Naval Reserve? Before 1992 it had been commanded by a regular force naval officer in the rank of naval captain. Of course, a Naval Reserve commodore served as Senior Naval Reserve Adviser (SNRA), but this position was "advisory only." Under the inspired leadership of Commodore Laraine Orthlieb, at the time SNRA — the first woman to reach that rank and station — the "advisory" position changed into a command appointment. With moral courage she endured much to make this a reality. It is not too much of a stretch to suggest that the regular force has reacted much more positively to the notion of a reservist as commander of the Naval Reserve than it ever did to the SNRA. Significantly, as soon as a reservist had taken command, the position of deputy commander fell in turn to a series of regular force officers. A number of these officers have gone on to more senior appointments in the navy, thus demonstrating that service with the reserve is not a sinecure, but a stepping stone upward for competent senior officers.[7] This has been a very happy event not only for the reserve, but for the regular force officers who are "going places," and who have been exposed to the reserve with all its warts and its magic. The issue of command gave rise to the need for a senior reserve presence from among the senior non-commissioned officers. This has resulted in formation chief petty officers who have integrated completely into the navy's cadre of senior chief petty officers, and who have given selfless leadership and inspiration to the reserve sailor.

What we do repeatedly for a long time becomes a habit, and habits that serve an essential purpose as either part of the ethos of a group or which bolster a sense of linkage to an honoured past can become traditions. Across Canada the Naval Reserve embodies the traditions of Canada's navy. In cities like Edmonton, Saskatoon and Thunder Bay, in mid-winter the Naval Ball or the Sweethearts' Mess Dinner bring a little sparkle of navy blue (really black with the current uniform) and gold to an otherwise drab winterscape. The social side of the Naval Reserve, particularly its role in linking communities away from the sea to the Canadian fleet, is important. In years past when there was not as much professional work to cram into "navy nights," the social side loomed larger. Nonetheless, gatherings in a social setting remain necessary today.

Years ago, I took a reporter to sea for a week or so in a gate vessel crewed by the reserve division HMCS *Nonsuch*. The story he eventually published was not that great really, focusing on the delicious fare produced in the galley (our cook, who prepared fabulous meals, is currently a commander and until recently commanded *Nonsuch*). But comments by the reporter that failed to make it into print expressed his utter amazement that lawyers, engineers, students, trades people, and homemakers could do things "naval" a long ways from adult supervision and do it as well as anyone else. However good the food, he missed the best story, and he did not bring the best story to his readers! In short, sea spray over the bow, rough weather, overcoming the mechanical breakdowns to which ancient equipment was prone, and standing watches in a working ship with other "interested persons" instead of spending spring break skiing — all these experiences leave overriding and indelible memories with those who were permitted the opportunity to enjoy them.

Many significant issues remain that challenge and complicate the scene for the Naval Reserve. Not the least of these are what size the Naval Reserve should be, and what will be the impact of the large numbers of middle managers who have recently transferred from the reserve into the regular force; one wonders how the Arctic offshore patrol vessel (AOPV)

Courtesy Mark Shepherd.

With the transformation of the Canadian Forces in recent years, naval reservists have found themselves engaged in very non-traditional employment, such as Lieutenant Mark Shepherd seen here at the graduation of Afghan National Police he helped to train.

will be handled, and what other tasks will be allocated to the reserve. The list goes on. It's a certainty, however, that those challenges will be managed, and managed well.[8] The Naval Reserve will continue to be the navy's mobilization base, as well as the footprint of a navy that stretches right across this country. The new Orca-class patrol vessel will take the Naval Reserve back to the future. It will offer the Naval Reserve divisions a chance to go to sea as a unit in the way they used to crew the gate vessels, to keep skills alive and to develop those shared experiences that give them organizational cohesion — but this time with an operational purpose for each sailing.[9] A problem remains with the two distinct styles of reserve service: the so-called Class A and Class B. Class A sailors serve one evening a week, on weekend training, and up to 14 days consecutively. They are the backbone of the Naval Reserve, and the group from which all other reserve sailors come. Class B sailors, by contrast, serve for from 14 consecutive days to up to three years by contract. A dynamic tension exists between these two classes of reservist. The challenge at all levels of the Naval Reserve is to manage this interface. In short, the reserve must bridge the Class A and B divide.

The Naval Reserve today is by far the most cost-effective reserve in Canada.[10] It is the only formation in the Canadian Forces that spans all 10 provinces, is commanded by a reservist, and is reasonably balanced by gender and language. (The ratio stands at 24

HMC Ships *Kingston*, *Glace Bay*, *Shawinigan*, *Summerside*, *Moncton*, and *Goose Bay* perform manoeuvres off the coast of Nova Scotia in August 2007.

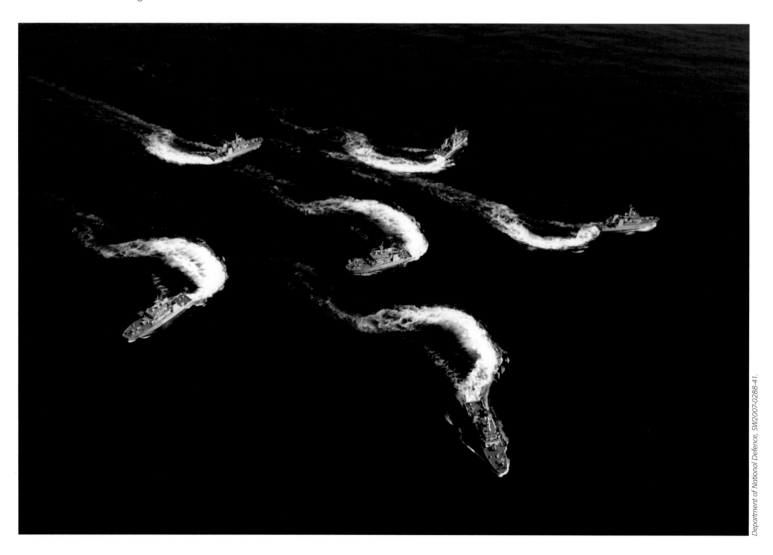

Department of National Defence, SW2007-0288-41.

percent francophone, and 31 percent female.) The regular force navy accepts it as an equal partner. The formation is at strength, and daily takes on more of the load of a "One-Navy." It is a formation whose transformation actually predated, by a long chalk, the transformation-talk of defence bureaucrats. The Naval Reserve will continue to evolve, and that evolution will be considerate of the needs of the country, the Canadian Forces, the Naval Service, and the reservists themselves. Surely, that must suffice.

Notes

1. Sir John Sinclair, *Thoughts on the Naval Strength of the British Empire*, [1782] Second Edition (London: T. Cadell, 1795), 13.

2. Elinor Sloan, *Military Transformation: Key Aspects and Canadian Approaches* (Calgary: Canadian Defence and Foreign Affairs Institute, December 2007).

3. R.B. Byers, "The 1987 Defence White Paper: An Analysis," *Canadian Defence Quarterly* (Autumn, 1987), 16.

4. Peter W. Cairns, "Points of Departure: Towards the Next Forty Years," in Michael L. Hadley, Rob Huebert, and Fred Crickard, eds., *A Nation's Navy: In Quest of Canadian Naval Identity* (Kingston: McGill-Queen's University Press, 1996), 351–58.

5. Professional Military Education (PME) is the intellectual part of military education; it is the command and staff college portion and focuses on the operational and strategic levels of war. The leadership training for officers, junior non-commissioned members (NCMs) and senior NCMs in the navy is the same, and frequently taught to regulars and reservists together.

6. While still in the rank of naval captain, Vice-Admiral Ron Buck embarked a young NCS officer (then-naval Lieutenant Kim Kubeck) in a task group (TG) under his command. Her role as an NCS officer was to develop a surface picture and "deconflict" (i.e., exclude) the neutral merchant shipping from the exercise. This means accessing non-classified information on the internet and information from other sources to identify merchant ships at sea during exercises or operations and to decide whether to "take them in or out of the combat equation." This worked so well, that when Admiral Buck was the chief of maritime staff he created an intelligence classification for the Naval Reserve that retains the NCS skills. These officers are in high demand across the Canadian Forces today.

7. The following were incumbents as naval captains: Vice-Admiral J.Y. Forcier, Rear-Admiral Roger Girouard, and Commodore Viateur Tremblay. As well, the post allowed senior francophones the opportunity to serve in their home province and in their mother tongue.

8. Recently, large numbers of officers and NCMs, some very senior, have transferred from the reserve to the regular force. This cross-pollination has a number of excellent outcomes. But the fact remains that the gaps created by these departures make it much harder to administer the Naval Reserve and to operate ships.

9. The *Orca* is a small ship designed to replace 50-year-old wooden-hulled vessels at the end of their service life.

10. The Naval Reserve budget for 2008 stood at $82 million, compared to the Army Reserve budget of $1.4 billion. Even by taking a big slice out of the budgets of the naval formations on each coast and assigning them to the Naval Reserve, the cost of getting trained sailors, ships' companies, and port security units out the door are miniscule by comparison.

CHAPTER 8

The Naval Presence in Quebec

Hugues Létourneau

Quebec is first and foremost a maritime province. This idea will surprise those accustomed to limiting the term to New Brunswick, Nova Scotia and Prince Edward Island as the sole maritime provinces, not to forget Newfoundland and Labrador, also on the East Coast, and British Columbia on the West Coast. Yet Quebec has 12,746 kilometres of coastline, and the St. Lawrence River — Quebec's economic and emotional centre — is a salt-water body from Les Escoumins down. Whatever the reason, average Quebecers almost never use the term "maritime" when describing their vision of Quebec. Arguably, they have little knowledge of the province's deep maritime character or its naval character. Of course, the army is a different matter. The widespread fame of the Canadian army in Quebec, particularly that of the Royal 22nd Regiment (Le Royal 22e Régiment) is a case in point. This is so even though its exploits have taken place far from Canadian soil. Great naval events, by contrast, have taken place right in Quebec's own backyard — and remain largely unknown. It would seem that "naval blindness," the indifference to navies in our culture, is just as pronounced in Quebec as in the rest of Canada.[1]

Quebec has a maritime tradition dating back centuries, to well before the Conquest. With its forests and a strong workforce, for example, New France had been an important shipbuilder for France, and had impressive naval shipyards, particularly on the St. Charles River and at Place Royale. Again, all Quebec students learn about the exploits of Pierre Lemoyne d'Iberville who in 1689 captured three ships of Britain's Royal Navy in Hudson Bay. Snapshots along the path of history illustrate the impact of maritime affairs on Quebec. In 1825 Davie Shipbuilding was founded on the St. Lawrence across from Quebec City. It built a wide range of watercraft from sailing vessels to steel ships. During the Second World War, 35 warships were built there for the Canadian Navy. It went on to build modern destroyers and oil rigs in the 1970s and 1980s. Adding to this shipbuilding saga was the

Courtesy Richard Gimblett.

The combined British, French, and American fleets, anchored in the St. Lawrence River below Quebec for the Tercentenary celebrations in 1908, vividly portray the strategic importance of the city.

story of Canadian Vickers, a Canadian division of the British shipbuilding and weapons manufacturing conglomerate, which established itself in Montreal in 1911 in anticipation of obtaining contracts to build ships for the Royal Canadian Navy. In 1915, Vickers naval shipyard built under British licence the first submarines to cross the Atlantic under their own power.[2] In 1937 Marine Industries Limited opened its naval shipyard in Sorel. A successful shipyard, it merged in 1986 with Davie to form MIL–Davie Shipbuilding. In the years 1993–95 the new firm built three Halifax-class patrol frigates: HMC Ships *Ville de Québec*, *Regina*, and *Calgary*.

The navy can be said to have "sprinkled" Quebec with naval installations in the 20th century. Aware in 1939 of the importance of the St. Lawrence River as a trade artery, the navy created naval control of shipping centres in Quebec City and Montreal. These centres formed part of the NOIC (naval-officer-in-charge) organizations in those cities, and focused on the security of shipping. Another naval control of shipping centre was established at Bic Island, a convoy marshalling area near Rimouski. That was in 1942, the year the navy built a maintenance base in Rimouski for ASDIC (sonar), the top-secret underwater detection device the navy used to detect enemy submarines. Rimouski also became the site in 1944 of the Department of Transport's new *Institut maritime*, a training centre for civilian seamen. From 1940 onward, the navy conducted patrols from headquarters at Rivière-du-Loup, from l'Île-aux-Coudres in Charlevoix to the westernmost point of Anticosti Island. The flotilla comprised the ships *Ambler*, *Anna Mildred*, *Cleopatra*, and *Eileen*. In 1941, the navy opened a training centre for DEMS (defensively equipped merchant ships) at Hôtel Place Viger, in Montreal.[3] It was one of the largest such schools in the British Empire, and stayed in business until the end of the war. That same year, as the navy was undergoing massive expansion, it set up a vital communications school in Saint-Hyacinthe. It was a major centre:

> *At its peak, the student population reached about 2,600 and during its almost five years of service St. Hyacinthe trained 9,600 sailors, Wrens, and signal officers in the many skills of naval communications. At the time it was considered to be the biggest signals school in the British Empire.[4]*

Closed in 1946, the sole physical hint of a time so rich in history, and marked by such upheaval, is the "Avenue de la Marine" in the city of Saint-Hyacinthe.

The war years were always triggering new initiatives. In 1941–42, the navy built the Gaspé naval base HMCS *Fort Ramsay* to guard the entrances to the Gulf of St. Lawrence and the river itself. Here it operated a degaussing gear range station to detect electrical anomalies in ships leaving or entering the Port of Quebec. Of the four armed yachts that first formed its core — HMC Ships *Racoon, Reindeer, Lynx,* and *Vison* — one, *Racoon,* was destroyed with all its crew by German submarine *U-165* near the island of Anticosti.[5] Ultimately, this gulf escort force comprised 19 ships: seven corvettes, five Bangor mine-sweepers, six Fairmile motor launches, and a single armed yacht. Before the base closed at the end of the war, over 2,000 men were stationed there. Convoy escort operations, heavy Allied deep-sea shipping, and anti-submarine warfare characterized the war years off Quebec's shores. All these initiatives and events are but tiny pixels of activity in the larger portrait of Quebec's maritime and naval affairs.

Perhaps no other single naval event had greater impact on the popular imagination of Quebec than the Battle of the St. Lawrence of 1942. When German submarines penetrated defences to within 250 kilometres of Quebec City, they made people realize that the war had really come to Canada. Within sight and smell of Gaspé shores, the U-boats sank warships and merchant vessels, and those living along the coast witnessed bodies of the shipwrecked washed up on shore. Newspaper headlines in French and English screamed the startling truth that the St. Lawrence had become a naval battleground. After this, nobody could ever be in any doubt whatsoever that Quebec was a maritime province, with the enemy striking deep within its heartland. But, remarkably, that memory quickly faded. The events of those days remained largely forgotten until rekindled in the mid-1980s by books and monographs, and later by museum exhibits in Rimouski and Quebec City, and finally by a commemorative historical conference in Rimouski in 2003 co-sponsored by these museums.[6]

If Quebecers have forgotten great naval events in their home waters, they have also forgotten great naval sports victories: the day in 1944 when a team from the Naval Reserve

Courtesy Accueil Port Québec, VL2008-0108-121.

A century later, Canadian, French, American, British, and Irish ships gathered for the *"Rendez-vous naval de Québec 400"* in May 2008 along the Lower City waterfront complex that includes Naval Reserve Headquarters, the Fleet School Québec, and the present-day HMCS *Montcalm.*

won the Grey Cup. Today the Canadian Football League is restricted to professional teams. That was not the case in the 1940s, however. At that time the umbrella organization was the Canadian Rugby Football Union (CRFU) and several of its players were amateurs. At that time as well, it was much easier than it is today to create a team, join a football association and compete. However, during the Second World War, with many players serving in the armed forces and no longer available, several CRFU teams were simply put on hold. In 1944, seamen from HMCS *Donnacona* and HMCS *St. Hyacinthe* formed a team they christened the Donnacona-St. Hyacinthe Combine, better known as "the Combines." Aided by circumstance and by luck, the Combines found themselves, by default, in the final game against the Hamilton Wildcats, a civilian team. (The Quebecers had been soundly defeated 12–1 in semi-finals by the Toronto Navy Bulldogs, but as the Bulldogs were not members of the CRFU they could go no further in the competition.) Thus, despite the obvious superiority of the Ontario team, the Quebec seamen won. It was a "miraculous" Grey Cup victory, they said in the football world — defeating their opponents 7–6. The 1944 plaque on the Cup is inscribed "Montreal Navy," a testament to the efforts of the seamen of the RCNVR. The event was almost forgotten, even at *Donnacona*, the unit that had won the Grey Cup. However, during the 50th anniversary celebrations of this Naval Reserve division, *Donnacona* had the Grey Cup brought home to reconnect with its history. In 1995 — 51 years after the 1944 victory — the team was inducted into the Canadian Forces Sports Hall of Fame.

Meanwhile, motivated by the Cold War and the conflict in Korea during the 1950s, the navy underwent its largest expansion in peacetime.[7] At HMCS *Hochelaga*, the big naval

The Naval Reserve created a reenactment group of the *Compagnies Franches de la Marine* in 1992.

Courtesy HMCS Montcalm, CFM 2008.

supply depot in La Salle, a Montreal suburb, the navy decided to open a training school in naval logistics. Founded on 1 October 1955, "*Hochelaga*… had a twofold function: it was responsible for the storage of all manner of naval supplies, which it shipped to other establishments on demand, and it provided training installations for the Supply and Secretariat branch of the RCN. In addition to several hundred Naval personnel on staff or following courses, some 550 civilians were employed on the base."[8]

However, the downsizing of the Canadian Forces in the late 1960s, together with the unification of the armed forces in 1968, signalled the end of HMCS *Hochelaga*.[9] Logistics training was included under a joint forces umbrella at the Canadian Forces School of Administration and Logistics at Canadian Forces Base Borden. *Hochelaga* closed its doors in 1970 and the land was sold to a trucking company.

But if we look at maritime and naval history since the founding of the Royal Canadian Navy in 1910 there appears a striking phenomenon: while the naval presence in Quebec is much greater than now believed, the francophone presence in Canada's navy was minimal until the 1980s. Despite the earliest vision of the founder of the Naval Reserve in 1923, Commodore Walter Hose, who foresaw a national reserve force, significantly little evidence suggests that his vision included francophone Canadians. Nonetheless, he had decided to save Canada's regular force navy from financial collapse by creating instead a network of Naval Reserve divisions in Canada's main cities. These included two in Quebec: Montreal and Quebec City.[10] However modestly, the creation in Quebec City of a new unit — symbolically named *Montcalm* after the French general who confronted an English opponent, General Wolfe, on the Plains of Abraham — assured that there would be at least one place where French would be the dominant language. As one writer recently expressed it: "the creation of *Montcalm* represented the return, although initially somewhat timid, of a "French" navy [*marine à caractère français*] in the former French capital of North America."[11] His use of the term *à caractère français* is revealing. For several decades the Quebec capital would be the only place in the navy where French was used routinely. Elsewhere, life was different. French-speaking Canadians wishing to make a career in the navy faced the dual challenge of learning their naval trade and learning English. Those who succeeded faced a third challenge: assimilation. These challenges remain today.

As the new co-ordinator of official languages at Canadian Forces Base Halifax in 1980, I was told that 14 percent of all personnel based in Halifax were francophones. But really, what kind of francophones were they? Having worked tooth and nail to learn English, the majority had literally "kissed French goodbye" and adopted the dominant language, English. Most had wives who spoke only English, and their children spoke no French. These francophone Quebecers had simply moved on. My attempts at offering official bilingual options, though well-intentioned, received only a lukewarm reception. For example, a Québécois master seaman who had already learned to function in his community in English had no interest in learning from me, the coordinator,

Louis-Joseph-Maurice Gauvreau joined the RCN at the age of fifteen in 1910, was the first French-Canadian officer to command a Royal Navy warship (HMS *Truant* in 1918, at the end of the First World War), and during the Second World War served as Naval Officer in Charge (NOIC) at Québec.

Courtesy HMCS Montcalm.

The 1926–27 Royal Canadian Naval Volunteer Reserve Hockey Club, comprised mostly of members of the Québec Half-Company. From left to right: (top row) Lucien Martel (defence), Lorenzo Simard (defence), Paul S. Laberge (defence), Rémi Bouchard (right wing), Noël Pelletier (referee); (middle row) Léo Demers (offence), F. Arthur Price (goal), Robert Larochelle (Captain / center); (front row) Albert Lepage (offence), Henri Dumas (left wing).

Courtesy HMCS Montcalm.

that he could file his income tax return in French, or speak with a francophone clerk at the vehicle registration office. Like a good number of francophones outside Quebec, he had become indifferent to French. And besides, a significant number of anglophones were actually hostile toward the language. Does that mean that for the Quebec francophone there is "no joy" or no future outside of Quebec (*hors du Québec, point de salut*)? Basically, yes. There is no getting around the fact that even in a theoretically bilingual city like Ottawa, the offices of the chief of the maritime staff operate exclusively in English.[12]

Like most federal institutions before the *Official Languages Act* of 1969, the military disproportionately reflected Canada's Anglo-Saxon majority. Operational units of the Royal Canadian Navy were based in Halifax and Esquimalt, where the British influence was especially pronounced. The "English" character of the Royal Canadian Navy offered little hope or encouragement to francophone Canadians. All its ships, bases, and units operated in English only. In an effort to integrate unilingual francophones into a navy that recognized English only, an English instruction program had been created in 1941 within HMCS *Montcalm* in Quebec City. The success rate was not high, however. No doubt the navy quickly realized that Quebec City, which was predominately French-speaking, was not the best place in which to improve one's English skills. The program shifted to the reserve division HMCS *Prevost* in London, Ontario.[13]

In time, however, francophone Quebecers did join in increasing numbers. A few even broke through the "glass ceiling" to attain the rank of rear-admiral: V.G. Brodeur (1942), M.J.R.O. Cossette (1945), J.Y. Forcier (2003), J.J. Gauvin (2004), R. Girouard (2005), and D. Rouleau (2007) — note the significant 58-year gap between Cossette and Forcier. By

2005 that profile had changed for the Naval Reserve as well, for of the 3,850 naval reservists in Canada, fully one quarter are Quebecers. Yet of all those reservists who attained the most senior positions of senior naval reserve adviser or commander naval reserve (COM-NAVRES) only one — Jean-Claude Michaud — was a francophone.

When the government of Pierre Trudeau took office, the navy had to make an attempt to create a symbolic operational environment in which francophones could work in their language. In 1968, the navy designated the Halifax-based destroyer HMCS *Ottawa* as a francophone ship.[14] It was replaced in that role five years later by HMCS *Skeena*. The navy tried to put together a core group of francophones on a second ship (HMCS *Algonquin*), but quickly realized it did not have enough people to staff both ships at the same time.

It was here that the Naval Reserve came into play. Toward the end of the 1990s it was linked to the newly designed class of ship called maritime coastal defence vessels; francophones clipped the redundant term "maritime" and called them *navires de défense côtière*. It was hoped that the Naval Reserve could help form a francophone crew, with Quebecers making up close to one quarter of its members, for at least one of the these new vessels. But, for many reasons, this proved impossible. In fact, even by 2008 the designated "French" warship — the patrol frigate HMCS *Ville de Québec* — found that francophones barely exceeded 65 percent of the total crew.

It was not until the late 1980s that the French designation NCSM (*Navire canadien de Sa Majesté*) acquired the same official status as its English equivalent HMCS (Her/His Majesty's Canadian Ship). Analyses showed that there was a proportionally much higher attrition rate among francophone seamen than among their English-language compatriots.[15] Demographic reality could not be denied, and because the Quebec presence in the navy was still a problem, one wondered whether the question could be reversed: could the naval presence *in Quebec* be increased?

Of course, reservists from Montreal and Quebec City had been training since the founding of their divisions in 1923. It was in 1941 that the unit known as RCNVR Quebec was renamed as the Naval Reserve division HMCS *Montcalm*. In 1943 the Montreal divisions HMC Ships *Cartier* and *Montreal* merged to become HMCS *Donnacona*. Although the severe budget cuts of 1964 caused the navy to close five Naval Reserve divisions (HMC Ships *Chatham*, *Nonsuch*, *Queen*, *Prevost*, and *Queen Charlotte*) in English-speaking Canada, Quebec — with only two divisions in any case — was spared.

Victor-Gabriel Brodeur was the first francophone Quebecker to reach the rank of rear-admiral; in addition to being the son of the first naval minister, he was among the first naval cadets to be trained aboard CGS *Canada*, and as Walter Hose's staff officer had the task of setting up the naval reserves in 1923.

Courtesy Nigel Brodeur.

Although these units still constituted but a minor Quebec presence, the half-companies that would eventually be named HMCS *Donnacona* and HMCS *Montcalm* were actively involved in their respective cities. Like reserve divisions elsewhere in the country, both of them played an important social role. The officers were professionals or businessmen, and rubbed shoulders with — or themselves were members of — the social elite in their respective cities. In Montreal, the annual *Donnacona* naval ball was covered in the society pages of the city's dailies (though these were primarily anglophone). The event lasted until the late 1960s. Leading dignitaries often attended, and in 1948 they included not only the Governor General of Canada, but the minister of national defence and the chief of the naval staff.[16] One of the unit's officers, Captain Allan Ross Webster, even sat in the House of Commons as a Conservative member while at the same time serving as commanding officer (1956–58). Yet, despite the work of these units, the naval presence in Quebec remained relatively unknown.

During its rapid expansion in the 1950s, the navy established a naval air squadron in Quebec, one of five in the Naval Reserve flying Harvard aircraft. Squadron VC 923 enjoyed a brief existence from June 1955 to March 1959. In 1952, as well, it established a naval recruitment centre in Quebec City to enrol more Quebecers. Named HMCS *d'Iberville*, after the French victor over the Royal Navy ships in Hudson Bay in 1689, it was situated in a building annexed to the one housing the reserve division HMCS *Montcalm*. The recruiting centre operated from 1952 to 1962. However, all other naval units in Quebec — *Donnacona*, *Hochelaga*, and *St. Hyacinthe* — were actually unilingual English-speaking units. Significantly, Montreal's HMCS *Donnacona* reflected disproportionately the influence of that city's anglophone minority. French was a long way from being recognized. Not until the late 1980s did *Donnacona* became mainly francophone.

Fairmile motor launches at HMCS *Fort Ramsay* in the spring of 1945.

Department of National Defence, CN-6585.

But fresh winds were blowing in the 1980s. As a young lieutenant assigned to Maritime Command Headquarters in Halifax at that time, I was asked by my superiors one day to look at the plans and installations of the Port of Quebec to determine whether it would be possible to assign a squadron of destroyers there permanently. This was the first time that I would hear the beginnings of an initiative known as the "Naval Presence in Quebec." At first glance, a task like this seemed complicated. But in reality, it was straightforward: there were no wharves, cranes, or icebreakers for the winter, and so on. In short, there was no support infrastructure. But with money, I concluded, almost anything was possible. However, the fact remained that Halifax, with its large natural port on the Atlantic Ocean, was by far a more logical location than any city in Quebec. This was plain geographic and economic reality. It was smarter and more cost effective to locate the navy's main operational units in Nova Scotia than in Quebec, and so the idea of a Quebec squadron was permanently shelved.

What then could be done to make francophone Canadians feel more at home in their navy? The answer was to look beyond ships — to land installations. It was not until the early 1980s that a real effort was made to increase the naval presence in francophone Quebec. Gilles Lamontagne, Quebec City's former mayor and at the time minister of

national defence under Pierre Trudeau, was the architect of the initiative dubbed "Naval Presence in Quebec," or NPQ. This plan had three phases and would take just over 12 years to become a reality. The first phase was to move Naval Reserve Headquarters from Halifax to Quebec City in 1984; the second was to create four new Naval Reserve divisions in the cities of Chicoutimi (now Saguenay), Rimouski, Sept-Îles, and Trois-Rivières; and the third was to build a fleet school in Quebec City.[17] The fleet school would be similar to the fleet schools in Halifax and Esquimalt, and would train francophone seamen for the regular and reserve forces in their own language.

These plans became reality, although Lamontagne, a Liberal, retired from active political life in 1984. That fall, Canada elected a Conservative government led by Brian Mulroney. Concerned about maintaining the inroads they had made in Quebec, the Conservatives went ahead with Lamontagne's initiative, particularly in the last few years of their second term when Marcel Masse was minister of defence. In 1984, Naval Reserve Headquarters indeed moved from Halifax to Quebec City. In 1986 the navy opened a new Quebec division: HMCS *Champlain* in Chicoutimi. Then followed in 1987 HMC Ships *d'Iberville* in Rimouski and *Radisson* in Trois-Rivières. In 1989 it opened HMCS *Jolliet* in Sept-Îles. Quebec now has six Naval Reserve divisions. (There are seven in Ontario, seven in the Western provinces, and four in Atlantic Canada.) In 1992 Jean-Claude Michaud, a former commanding officer of *Montcalm*, was promoted to the rank of commodore, and appointed senior naval reserve adviser (SNRA). He was the first Quebecer to hold this position.[18] When the Fleet School building opened at Pointe-à-Carcy in 1995 it also housed HMCS *Montcalm*, which had been located since 1947 on long-outdated facilities beside the Grande Allée armoury.[19]

All these plans and initiatives triggered wide-ranging discussion in both naval and professional circles, for on the face of it this seemed an attempt to balance social engineering against the operational requirements of the Canadian Navy. As historian Marc Milner concluded: "In fact, the decision to move the Naval Reserve Headquarters to Quebec City was political: the navy needed a base where francophones could live and work in a French milieu."[20] His point is well taken, of course. But the "political" decision was the correct one under the circumstances. Reflecting on the *"présence navale au Québec"* Gilles Lamontagne observed:

> I had two objectives: first, make sure that our Quebec seamen had a place in
> the navy that belonged to them, and second, integrate Anglophones with their
> Francophone compatriots, in a French environment. It was good for morale,
> and good for Canadian unity. The creation of a real naval presence in Quebec
> is one of the proudest achievements in my entire career.[21]

Department of National Defence, BNC86-1603-15.

Former and serving naval reserve personnel gathered for the commissioning of HMCS *Champlain* in Chicoutimi, 15 August 1986.

In 1992, the minister of national defence, Marcel Masse, announced at a press conference that a seventh reserve division — HMCS *Salaberry* — would be established in the community of Salaberry-de-Valleyfield (which residents simply call Valleyfield) in the Montérégie, one hour from Montreal.[22] While awaiting a permanent location for the future reserve division, the new commanding officer and his team (there was no crew) hung the naval jack in offices in a mall. The rationale for such a move must have struck many observers as rather odd. For my part, as commanding officer of HMCS *Donnacona* in downtown Montreal at the time, I wondered how a small community without a university could possibly support a new naval unit.

Anyone familiar with the procedures for establishing a new reserve division would have known that the road would be a long one. The experience of the 1980s with HMC Ships *Champlain*, *d'Iberville*, *Radisson*, and *Jolliet* was eloquent proof that a division could not create an infrastructure overnight. The experience of *Jolliet* in Sept-Îles was particularly instructive. Naval Reserve divisions usually count many university students among their numbers — seamen and officers alike. Consequently, a reserve division like *Jolliet*, located in a small city with no university, is at a distinct disadvantage: the young people leave to attend school elsewhere and generally do not return. In terms of management, this means starting at zero, both for petty officers and officers. Ideally, the command teams of reserve divisions tend to draw their expertise from personnel in the unit who live in the city where the unit is located. Normally, they advance through the various staff positions as they

Jean-Claude Michaud was the first — and to date only — francophone to reach the rank of commodore in the naval reserve. Here, as first commander of the formation, he welcomes the Right Honourable Jean Chrétien, Prime Minister of Canada, to the official opening of the Pointe à Carcy Naval Complex on 15 May 1995.

defence establishment, as well as a local asset in internal emergencies. Even a brief reading of the preceding chapters reveals the extent of personal dedication to an ideal. At the onset of two major wars the ranks of a few, virtually unpaid, volunteers expanded hugely to become a significant force. They formed the major component of "the Navy" of popular lore, with the regulars teaching them the rudiments in too few weeks or months. At first, as we have seen, this training consisted largely of on-the-job training. In subsequent periods of peace, these often unnoticed volunteers persevered and "hung in there," as the saying went. They did so frequently unappreciated by their government and the populace at large. If I might adapt the RCAF's motto *Per Ardua ad Astra*, it was, in the case of the Naval Reserve, *Per Ardua a Mare* — the hard way to the sea.

Canada is bounded by three oceans: two long, open coasts on the east and the west, and a northern ocean that is becoming even longer and more open as the Arctic ice recedes. As well, the St. Lawrence Seaway cuts one-third of the way into the continent, bearing deep-sea traffic between its major lakes and the Atlantic Ocean. There should be no doubt that we Canadians are a maritime nation. Though we may not have a large merchant fleet, our existence and prosperity depend greatly on those seas, whether our commerce is carried in Canadian hulls or not. And neither should there be any doubt that freedom of the sea depends on our naval presence.

Significantly, a naval presence is not just warships at sea, but an awareness by the tax-paying public that these warships are necessary. Otherwise, the country is at the beck and call of others: mighty countries like the U.S., China, India, and Japan, or minor opponents that are increasing in abilities and range of influence. The 9/11 attack on New York emphasized that threats can come from the most minor of countries or factions — and for often misunderstood reasons.

And just as they did in the early Great Depression days when Commodore Walter Hose promoted his vision, it is still the reserves, spread across the inland towns and cities, that continue to represent the navy in Canadian communities, and that volunteer, as available, for more active naval duties. Reservists are the navy's small toehold away from either coast. They are the back-stop to cover some of the navy's ongoing requirements: in plans for control of merchant shipping, for countermeasures against sea mines, for communications, medical support, and seagoing operations. It does not suffice merely to promote and advertise the navy on government websites. We still need citizen seafarers in our communities ashore to give credence to a naval presence.

Yet, sometimes these often remote Naval Reserve outposts have been misunderstood — even by their government, and occasionally by the senior leadership. In the early 1960s, at the height of the threatening Cold War, the word went out that the local naval forces, like

Courtesy Fraser McKee.

What the properly dressed RCNVR officer of the 1930s should wear when in "full dress." Not bad for a stock salesman, and out of his own pocket — Lieutenant-Commander G.W. Sheldon, commanding officer of the Toronto Company (later HMCS *York*), circa 1937.

the army, were to be prepared to provide aid to the civil power. It struck many reservists at the time that the government had shifted emphasis: no longer helping fill out the navy in an emergency, they now had become foot soldiers and First Aid workers. Locations outside their cities were identified, and — according to official scenarios — those naval reservists who had "survived" any hostile attack were to decamp there at once to provide a rescue force as best they could. The plan had obviously nothing "naval" about it, and from the viewpoint of the locals, the reserves had become blue-clad infantrymen. This policy had a serious effect on recruiting and retention. If soldiering was indeed what was primarily required of them, then why not go off and join the Calgary Highlanders, or Les Voltigeurs de Québec, or the Queen's Own Rifles? Meanwhile, tales abounded of plucky gate vessels taking the seas in all kinds of weather, of towing a stricken vessel in a howling gale, crafting a storm-tossed entry into unknown ports, and otherwise doing what sailors are meant to be doing. Fortunately, policy planners recognized their error in emphasis, and although those plans still remained on the books, the Naval Reserve was again welcomed back into the larger naval family.

HMCS *York* parades in the Automotive Building of the Canadian National Exhibition (CNE) in June 1944.

Courtesy Fraser McKee.

September 1970: Following the change to green uniforms with unification, the chiefs and petty officers of HMCS *York* "commit to the deep" of Lake Ontario their old RCN rank and trade badges.

Courtesy Fraser McKee.

Other seemingly innocent steps, even practical ones, caused the reserves to suspect that the administrators in Naval Headquarters, in Kingsmill's terms, "simply didn't understand." The problem was usually a failure to pass information down the chain of command about the changes being implemented. For a while Naval Reserve Headquarters was effectively moved from close to the fleet headquarters in Halifax to as far away from the sea as Hamilton, Ontario, in HMCS *Patriot*. Then again later, the headquarters shifted to Quebec City. But this was in the days before accepted electronic interconnection, and many commanding officers of reserve units nursed a suspicion that they were being shuffled off out of the way and were losing contact with the main force. Reserve commanders located near Halifax had lost the ability to chat with their counterparts over lunch or at a Friday end-of-the-week "Weepers." They seemed to have lost the ability to test ideas or quietly smooth over perceived problems on an informal basis, thus keeping the operation flowing smoothly. The Quebec Naval Reserve Headquarters has remained, and it works well. It was simply a matter of everyone "getting on board" with the new concept.

As the accounts in this volume have illustrated, the Naval Reserve has retained its tremendous pride of service, whether appreciated by others or not. Increasingly, it has proven to be a foundation on which the larger navy can rely; it is the extensive naval root system in the soil of the country. The ethos of the Naval Reserve finds fitting expression in "The Laws of the Navy" (1896), a poem written by Rear-Admiral Ronald A. Hopwood, RN, when he was a captain. Widely known in Anglo-American naval circles, it captures the relationships and moral laws of the naval service, and continues to speak to future generations. As

Hopwood wrote in part:

> *Now these are the laws of the Navy,*
> *Unwritten and varied they be;*
> *And he who is wise will observe them,*
> *Going down in his ship to the sea.* [....]
>
> *On the strength of one link in the cable*
> *Dependeth the might of the chain.*
> *Who knows when thou mayest be tested?*
> *So live that thou bearest the strain.*

For most of the Canadian Navy's 100 years, the "far distant ships" of the Naval Reserve have carried on with their basic concept of being both the inland voice and the backup for the regular force navy. In many ways, the new generation of sailors differs little from the earliest volunteers. On occasion "there may be 'too much Nelson,' for the times have changed since then." That is how Hopwood expressed it in his poem "Our Fathers" (1913), a year before the First World War. But it is a tradition of service stretching back to Samuel de Champlain that provides a good part of the pride of service upon which the future dedications and skills must be built. Hopwood's "Our Fathers," a work that hearkens back to great seafaring role models like Hawkins, Frobisher, and Drake, speaks of sailors who had been forged "on the anvil of their duty." As Hopwood wrote:

A damage control exercise onboard a gate vessel during the "green" era.

Department of National Defence, ETC88-1415-18.

Naval Reservists on port security patrol for the 2010 Winter Olympics in Vancouver.

Department of National Defence, ET2009-0014-32.

We can seek the God of Battles on our knees, and humbly pray
That the work we leave behind us, when our earthly race is run,
May be half as well completed as our Fathers' work was done.

This is not just a story of ships and reserve half-companies, nor even of a few leaders who had a sustainable vision. But, in the words of the Latin motto of the Naval Officers Association of Canada, it is about all those who claim ...

Maria Obtinuimus — We Hold to the Seas

Vessels of the Naval Reserve of Canada

Carl Gagnon

Whard is a Naval Reserve vessel?

A simple question perhaps, but the answer is far from straightforward. The attempt to reach a satisfactory definition led to this journey of exploration through the backwaters of our history.

Is it a vessel that is crewed mainly by reservists? If that were the case, most Canadian warships of the Second World War would fit this criterion, and this appendix would be huge and largely repetitive, as other publications already cover these vessels (the standard reference is Macpherson and Barrie, *The Ships of Canada's Naval Forces*). However, the vessels operated by sailors of the RCN in the 1950s and 1960s while conducting training of the Royal Canadian Navy Reserve on the Great Lakes would not appear on the list. Neither would the current Kingston-class vessels be discussed, as members of their permanent crew are not always reservists — even though there is no doubt in the mind of any member of today's Canadian Forces that these vessels define the idea of "reserve vessel" in the last part of the 20th century and into the early 21st century.

Is it that they support only the Naval Reserves? Again the Kingstons would not make the list, since they have served, among other tasks, as training platforms for permanent as well as reserve naval personnel until the recent arrival of the Orca class, and they are performing operational defence tasks just like their larger regular naval counterparts. Moreover, some tenders to Naval Reserve divisions (NRD) were operated by permanent staff and supported the training of both groups of sailors.

Is it that the vessels are not commissioned and are only tenders to some larger units such as an NRD or a squadron-like organization? If so, most naval reservists of the 1970s through the 1990s would not be pleased, as they learned and maintained their skills on the unaffiliated vessels of the Porte class or HMCS *Fort Steele*.

Is it that the vessels are under the control of the Naval Reserve? Only the present-day unit tenders truly fall in that category, and still there are exceptions, as some of these have been used for national operations when required.

The answer to the opening question, therefore, can be simple or complex, depending on the perspective of the person who chooses to address it. Because the definition varies throughout the history of our navy, this survey will take a broadly-inclusive approach, in providing a comprehensive listing of the vessels that have been related to the Naval Reserve, along with an understanding of what these vessels accomplished.

A couple of caveats are worth noting. This appendix will not study the period before the establishment of the Royal Canadian Naval Volunteer Reserve companies or half-companies, as its predecessor, the Royal Naval Canadian Volunteer Reserve, was organized to respond primarily to the immediate world situation, did not take deep roots in the geographic regions from which its companies recruited, and quickly disappeared after the First World War. Neither, as suggested earlier, will it cover the operational fighting vessels of the RCN in the Second World War, ranging from motor torpedo boats through to aircraft carriers that are well covered already in other easily accessible sources, even though, as Richard Mayne observed (in chapter 4), they were largely crewed by reservists.

An additional goal here is to record in one place as much general information on these vessels as possible, to serve hopefully as a guide to deeper research efforts before the details are lost to memory. These vessels largely have been overlooked, ignored, or barely mentioned by most works to date on Canadian warships. More worrying is that many of these vessels are unknown to the active personnel of the formations they served, as evident from the generally fruitless attempts to gain information on them from their respective divisions for this compilation. They served the Naval Reserve well and deserve to be remembered.

A note on the various sources that were used to gather the information for this appendix will be of interest to some readers. Books generally available to the public include the already mentioned *Ships of Canada's Naval Forces 1910–2002* and the especially helpful *Canadian Warship Names* by David J. Freeman. A few Naval Reserve divisions have privately published unit histories, but these are inconsistent in their approach and most do not provide much detail with regard to their tenders. The bulk of the information, therefore, is to be found in the archives of the Directorate of History and Heritage of the Department of National Defence, in particular the files of the 81/520/8000 series and various unit annual historical reports. Regrettably, it seems that the original maintenance files of the individual tenders put together at the office of the director general of maritime equipment program management (DGMEPM) are not readily accessible to researchers, making the tracing of vessel details more difficult.

The largest group of vessels of the Naval Reserve has been the unit tenders. A tender is defined for our purposes as a small vessel attendant on a larger one (or, in this instance, a "stone frigate") for carrying stores and libertymen, and for various training functions;

following this definition, we shall see that size can be debated, and that the tender is dependent upon its parent vessel for administrative support. Tenders have been a constant through the history of the Canadian Naval Reserve and continue to be today. Regattas or war canoe races were organized throughout the fleet and squadrons, and NRDs were no strangers to this tradition. Indeed, wooden whalers, cutters, and sail-rigged boats seem to have been the first reserve vessels, as a naval cutter was part of the standard equipment provided to newly formed units, along with rifles and a naval field gun. Relatively small and easy to maintain, these boats were used for seamanship training, boatwork evolutions, and to keep sailors' interest alive. Over time they were replaced in line with updates to the fleet's standard equipment, so that fibreglass whalers, dispatch boats, and sailing boats were assigned to NRDs in the late-1960s. The most recent example is the introduction of rigid hull inflatable boats (RHIB) and the smaller RHIB-like Hurricanes. Zodiac-type boats in various sizes are also common in both the Canadian Navy and Naval Reserve, as they are easy to store, maintain and use. These boats are particularly popular with divers as their low freeboard makes for comfortable access to the boat.

Some divisions kept and maintained whalers past their naval retirement in the late-1980s, either because the RHIBs and Hurricanes did not reach them for some time or so as to have something on hand that could be used by anyone with a small boat qualification; exceptions were taken on a case-by-case basis and with the warning that the boats and engines were to be maintained at no extra cost to the Crown. Still, through the 1990s, the RHIB-Hurricane combination became standard equipment for all divisions, and with the further expansion of the Naval Reserve role to include filling gaps in harbour defence units, the RHIBs were modified with an arch to host equipment in support of this tasking. The initial design was badly balanced, so a new arch was developed incorporating the earlier observations, and also a communications suite and radar set allowing the boats to perform as a mini-escort. The RHIBs are normally held at each NRD through the year, but

Department of National Defence, ET2009-0014-30.

RHIBs: the three to the left with the latest arch, the one to the right with the original.

they can be concentrated as required for the duration of an emergency or for an operation; the 1997 flooding of the Red River in Manitoba or the 2010 Vancouver Winter Olympic Games are good examples.

Class: Rigid-hull inflatable boat (RHIB)	**LOA:** 7.3 m	**Beam:** 2.7 m
	Crew: 3	**Maximal Speed:** 28 kt
Draft: 1.8 m	**Displacement:** 2.1 tonnes	**Armament:** None

Local citizens and organizations assisted some of the original companies by loaning vessels for summer training, but these were not naval vessels; for example, the Charlottetown Half-Company received support as early as 1923 in the form of a private yacht for training, and the Saint John Half-Company was loaned a schooner and the Marine and Fisheries Department cutter *Monarchy* before the Second World War. In 1938, the Toronto Company bought a 11.0-metre gaff-rigged sword-fishing schooner that one officer and three ratings sailed from Halifax for use in "sea training" at the division.

The first generation of "large" tenders to NRDs became reality by necessity. During the Second World War, some RCNVR companies were offered or took over some civilian motor vessels to help with training; these vessels came in all sizes and shapes. The acquisitions varied from unit to unit with conditions differing from gift to loan to requisition, typically for the duration of the war; owners looked favourably upon the second option, as fuel was rationed and therefore unavailable for boating, leaving private vessels unable to be utilized. Many were loaned for $1 a year and by doing so the owners got the benefit of having their boats maintained and run. These tenders provided the new hostilities-only entries their first taste of sea time and provided the unit some visibility to the local population. The Toronto Division listed a number of yachts among its assets: the 25.9-metre *Haidee* from November 1939 to July 1941 when it was transferred first to HMCS *Star*, and, in 1942, to HMCS *Hunter* for the rest of the war; the 45.7-metre *Pathfinder* from May to November 1941 before being transferred to HMCS *Star* for the rest of the war; the 68.9-metre *Venetia* from September 1941 to September 1945; and the 7.3-metre *Eyolfur* from February 1944 to April 1945. In July 1941, HMCS *Cataraqui* took over the 42.1-metre steam yacht *Magedona* from George Fulford of Brockville, Ontario, to be used as a training ship after being overhauled. HMCS *Star* had the 9.5-metre motor vessel *Whisper*, ex-*Nancy*, from July 1944 to August 1945. HMCS *Prevost* operated one tender during the conflict, the 17.1-metre yacht *Shirl* from August 1943 to January 1946. Early in the war, the executive officer of HMCS *Discovery* loaned his 13.7-metre cruiser for $1 a year and for use by the division. The Montreal divisions also had tenders: HMCS *Montreal* had the 34.8-metre yacht *Montreal II* and another named *Jellicoe* until both were transferred to HMCS *Donnacona*, where *Montreal II* was rechristened to *Donnacona II* in October 1943. They served from April 1940 to June 1942 and August 1941 to November 1946, respectively (no information could be found about a tender for the division HMCS *Cartier*). HMCS *Montcalm* could count on the 25.9-metre yacht *Millicette* from May 1941 to November 1945. HMCS *Carleton* operated the 11.6-metre motor yacht *Attaboy*, owned by then-Lieutenant Thomas Fuller, from June 1941 until September 1943, when it was

Department of National Defence, CN-3627.

Yacht *Venetia*.

returned to its owner. HMCS *Griffon* also had the use of a privately owned 13.7-metre ketch (name unknown) from 15 July 1943 for training two afternoons a week, and later on that month a 6.1-metre rigged dinghy was donated to it for instruction in sailing. In June 1944, HMCS *Scotian* had the use of the 19.5-metre *Diving Tender No. 3* that had a complement of 15. After the end of the war in late-1945 most of these tenders either were returned to their original owners or were disposed of through sales. It should also be noted that, when the navy took over the training and administration of the sea cadet corps of the Navy League in the second half of 1941 (the cadets were viewed as a source of possible

Library and Archives Canada, PA-142595.

HMCS *Montreal II* presented by Joseph Simard and Samuel Bronfman for use as a navy training vessel.

future recruits), many divisions' tenders also provided sea training to cadets. In this connection, with the big yacht *Oriole IV* (the future HMCS *Oriole* [480]), providing sea training to the local Toronto branch of the Navy League, and with HMCS *York* responsible for the operation of the Georgian Bay Sea Cadet summer camp, the next natural step was for the navy (through the division) to take over the yacht for the duration of hostilities. It was chartered on the $1-a-year basis until it was returned to the Navy League in September 1946.

With the return of peace, the RCN demobilized tens of thousands of hostilities-only reservists and turned its energies to concentrate on its future "blue water navy" aspirations, in which plans for the reserve were simply to strengthen the permanent navy if and when required. There are no indications that the RCN had plans to delegate any missions to its reserve, or to build and operate a standard class of vessels for the RCNR as part of the reconstitution of that organization in 1947. Some of the wartime assets, however, were distributed to certain NRDs in the form of Ville harbour tugs (wartime-construction, or "old," as opposed to tugboats from the 1950s), a separate class of 14.0-metre harbourcraft, and other vessels that are discussed next.

The 14.0-metre harbourcraft (H.C.) had the advantages of relative standardization and recent construction. Many were listed for the Naval Reserve, but from the surviving records only a few of them can be teamed with a specific division: HMCS *Chippawa* had *H.C. 314* in January 1946; *Brunswicker* received *H.C. 231* in October 1946; *Scotian*, *H.C. 224* in January 1946; *H.C. 268* went to *Prevost* in 1946 and stayed until mid-1950 when transferred to *Cabot*; *Queen Charlotte* had *H.C. 267* in November 1945, *H.C. 258* in January 1946, *H.C. 212* from June 1946, and *H.C. 256* from September of that year; *Griffon* had *H.C. 221* before it was transferred to Esquimalt in 1946; *H.C. 211* was turned over to *Montcalm* until June 1946 when it was transferred to *Cataraqui*, joining *H.C. 311* and *H.C. 314*; *York* had *H.C. 312* and *H.C. 313* in March and received *H.C. 209* in July 1946; and *H.C. 261* was transferred by rail to HMCS *Hunter* in December 1946.

There also were a number of 7.6-metre diesel cutters assigned to NRDs within the year following the end of the war: *H.C. 222* was first put in the water by *Unicorn* in May 1946 but had served with *Chippawa* during the war; *H.C. 341* went to HMCS *Brunswicker*; *H.C. 282* to *Chippawa*; *H.C. 283* to HMCS *Griffon*; and *H.C. 321* to HMCS *Donnacona*. Another 7.6-metre harbourcraft (name unknown) was assigned to Newfoundland's Corner Brook division, HMCS *Caribou*, and disposed of and returned to Halifax when the division was paid off in 1958, along with two 8.2-metre whalers and one 4.3-metre sailing dinghy.

Another variation was the 8.5-metre motor vessel *H.C. 116*, ex-*Queen Bee*, which after serving as the admiral's barge in Esquimalt during the war was transferred to *Malahat* until December 1952 when it resumed its wartime role. *Scotian* was operating *YMT-177* in 1948 before it was transferred to the control of the commodore, Newfoundland, in late 1949. Some NRDs also received 4.9-metre harbour craft as tenders after the conflict: *H.C. 349* was presented to HMCS *Discovery* and HMCS *Chippawa* got *H.C. 350*. In the months after the end of the war, *Discovery* also operated the 15.9-metre landing craft *L.C.9* and HMCS *Chatham* in Prince Rupert, British Columbia, took over *Y.C.8* in May 1947.

Department of National Defence, HS-0019-2.

H.C. 211.

Class: Harbourcraft/46-feet (14-metre)	**LOA:** 14.0 m	**Displacement:** 5.0 tonnes
	Draft: 0.9 m	**Crew:** 3
Beam: 3.8 m	**Maximal Speed:** 10 kt	**Armament:** None

Plans to provide training for new entries into the RCNR and University Naval Training Divisions were realized with the establishment of the Great Lakes Training Centre (GLTC) at Hamilton, Ontario, in 1952. Two Porte-class vessels, later along with the tug HMCS *Scatari* (514), were based there for summer shipboard training, and fleet warships visited the Lakes almost every summer, including Tribal-class destroyers, Prestonian-class frigates, Bangor-class minesweepers, and even the very modern St. Laurent and Restigouche classes of destroyers. The ships took groups of trainees out for two-week stretches, steaming from the mouth of the St. Lawrence River to the Lakehead. Divisions near the sea had similar arrangements on both coasts.

Class: Scatari	**Type:** Tug	**LOA:** 29.5 m
Beam: 7.4 m	**Draft:** 3.3 m	**Crew:** 14
Displacement: 147.4 tonnes	**Maximal Speed:** 11 kt	**Armament:** None

HMCS *Sault Ste Marie* (176) was the largest tender assigned to a Naval Reserve division. The first Algerine-class minesweeper to be commissioned into the RCN, on 24 June 1943 during the Second World War, like all Canadian Algerines it was built at Port Arthur Shipbuilding Company (Port Arthur later merged with Fort William to form modern-day

for officers and non-commissioned members, and from September to December they were available again for weekend training. With the looming acquisition of the Kingston class, in the late 1980s the three Portes on the West Coast were crewed full-time to act as training platforms for the designated personnel. Listing all the NRDs that signed out these vessels on the coasts or all the locations the ships went during their career would exceed the limits of this appendix. Not being especially comfortable on the open water, they generally kept close to home, although it is worth noting that they did venture north along the Labrador and Ungava coasts in the East and to Alaska in the West, not to mention southward with the crossing of the Panama Canal. They were all paid off in the mid-1990s and sold through the Crown Assets Distribution Centre. *Porte Dauphine* was refurbished and can be seen on the West Coast in its new livery of blue hull and white superstructure as the M.V. *Salmon Transporter*.

HMCS *Porte de la Reine*.

Department of National Defence, ETC88-1413-9.

Class: Porte
LOA: 38.3 m
Draft: 4.0 m
Displacement: 389.2 tonnes

Type: Gate Vessel
Beam: 8.1 m
Crew: 47
Maximal Speed: 11 kt

Armament: none; (original) one 40 mm gun.

After the war, with a large quantity of a good selection of vessels available, and with a recognized need to train and maintain reservist qualifications (even if for no readily identifiable role), it had been possible to standardize the distribution to divisions. By the 1960s, however, those conditions were changing. The RCN did not foresee having a great use for the Naval Reserve, as most war scenarios were for surprise nuclear attacks that would not allow time to call the reserves into service, and budget cutbacks meant fewer resources were available for the operation and maintenance of the reserve fleet, which slowly fell into disrepair.

Gaps in the Naval Reserve's complement of vessels were often plugged by seizing upon an opportunity. One presented itself in the early 1970s, when the Royal Canadian Mounted Police Marine Division was disbanded, leading to the disposal of its vessels. The permanent navy had no use for them, but a number were suitable for turning over to the NRDs to supplement the supply of unit tenders for local training and visibility in the community. These vessels all kept their previous name but were assigned new pennant numbers, and came in three categories. The largest was *Fort Steele*, the only one to be commissioned, thus becoming the smallest vessel to have this honour. Built by Canadian Shipbuilding and Engineering Ltd., in Kingston, Ontario, it was assigned on transfer to the Navy, in 1973, to the Reserve Training Unit (Atlantic) in Halifax, Nova Scotia, for general seamanship. It was commissioned as HMCS *Fort Steele* (140) on 29 November 1975 and operated in the Maritimes and Great Lakes regions. Like the gate vessels, NRDs could sign it out for off-season weekend unit training, and during the summers it carried a full-time crew in support to the main reserve training period. It was paid off on 26 August 1994 and disposed of through the Crown Assets Distribution Centre.

Department of National Defence, IHC86-101-1.

HMCS *Fort Steele.*

Class: Fort Steele	**Type:** Patrol	**LOA:** 36.0 m
Beam: 6.4 m	**Draft:** 2.1 m	**Crew:** 16
Displacement: 80.7 tonnes	**Maximal Speed:** 20 kt	**Armament:** None

The other two batches of vessels from the former RCMP marine division actually encompassed two sub-groups of similar-type vessels: the 65-foot (19.8-metre) and 75-foot (22.9-metre) Detachment vessels, the main distinction being that the second group had two engines and was faster. Given new pennant numbers and CF livery, they were distributed to NRDs in the Maritimes and Great Lakes. The 19.8-metre Detachment vessels were allocated as follows: *Detector* (192) with *Cataraqui*; *Captor* (193) with *Montcalm*; *Acadian* (194) with *Cabot* until 1980, then with *Donnacona*; and *Adversus* (191) with *Brunswicker*. Again, listing all they did and where they went exceeds the mandate of this chapter, but

Department of National Defence, ISC80-1092.

The 65-ft detachment vessel, *Acadian*.

fitted with sleeping arrangements and equipped with communications, radar, and echo sounder, they provided an adequate platform for maintaining qualifications, performing diving operations, and just delivering a first taste of life at sea. A great morale booster, they were particularly active in the Summer Youth Employment Program (SYEP) through the 1980s, while providing community visibility for the Naval Reserve through involvement in providing water safety to local events such as sailing or swimming races, and air shows. Many of these boats supported the Canadian Olympic Regatta at Kingston (CORK) for the Games of 1976, and PBL *Acadian* patrolled the river near Montreal during the Oka Crisis (Operation SALON in 1990).

Class: 65-ft Detachment	**Type:** Patrol Light	**LOA:** 19.8 m
Beam: 4.6 m	**Draft:** 1.7 m	**Crew:** 9
Displacement: 41.3 tonnes	**Maximal Speed:** 10 kt	**Armament:** None

The two 22.9-metre Detachment vessels were *Nicholson* (196) with HMCS *York*, and *Standoff* (199) with HMCS *Cabot*. Another ex-RCMP vessel that made its way to the Naval Reserve at the same time was the 16.76-metre *Sidney* (195); it had a smaller body but a comparable speed of 14 knots and was assigned to HMCS *Discovery*. It was disposed of at the same time as its sisters.

Class: 75-ft Detachment   **Type:** Patrol Light   **LOA:** 22.9 m

Beam: 5.2 m   **Draft:** 1.8 m   **Crew:** 9

Displacement: 63.5 tonnes   **Maximal Speed:** 15 kt   **Armament:** None

Among the miscellaneous vessels acquired by the Naval Reserve was *Crossbow* (197), built in 1954 by Russel Brothers Ltd. of Owen Sound, Ontario. Originally known as *YMU-116*, it served as a tender to HMCS *Cataraqui* as early as 1969. Renamed *Crossbow*, it was assigned to HMCS *Hunter* as a tender in May 1977, replacing the Windsor division's previous tender, the 12.2-metre *Egret* (925), which had been given to the division in 1970. In October 1978, *Crossbow* returned to Kingston to undergo an extensive five-month refit at Canadian Forces Base Kingston. It returned to Windsor the following year completely metamorphosed into a much better training instrument. Throughout its career, it supported the division's training and recruit program (extended to members of HMCS *Prevost* in 1990 and 1992), and conducted ports visits on the Great Lakes for events such as antique boat shows in Wallaceburg, the tall ships visit to Toronto, and the historic crossing of the Niagara organized by the Canadian War Museum in 1992. *Crossbow* was transferred to HMCS *York* in May 1994 but removed from the naval list the following year.

Class: Crossbow   **Type:** Patrol Light   **LOA:** 14.6 m

Beam: 3.7 m   **Draft:** 1.2 m   **Crew:** 9

Displacement: 59.0 tonnes   **Maximal Speed:** 7 kt   **Armament:** None

The vessels studied so far were tenders to NRDs accessible from the sea or the Great Lakes, but tenders were also present in surprising inland locations.

Originally built as a support vessel to the icebreaker HMCS *Labrador*, *Pogo* (104) was built by Marine Industries Ltd. of Sorel, Quebec, and was completed in 1954. When the icebreaker was transferred to the Department of Transport, *Pogo* was retained by the navy for use as a local launch in Halifax harbour. In July 1970, *Pogo* was transferred to HMCS *York* in Toronto to become the unit's tender. In the mid-1970s, one of its pipes burst below the waterline causing it to sink at its mooring. Quickly salvaged by *York's* divers, it was raised, refitted and transferred to Ottawa as HMCS *Carleton's* tender. By the 1980s, it was serving *Carleton* as its principal large training vessel and diving support vessel, although it did not lend herself well to that latter role because of its high freeboard. It was also used in support of the Summer Youth Employment Program. Age and lack of regular maintenance took their toll over the years, and in 1993, as it was being taken out of the water for winter storage, one of the lifting lugs broke and it hit the pavement, cracking its rudder skeg and splitting a number of deck welds. It was acquired by the Canadian War Museum in 1995 and remained part of the collection until 2005, when it was transferred to the Navy League of the Ottawa-Gatineau region who have repaired it with the intention of using it as a training vessel on the Ottawa River.

LOA: 11.0 m   **Beam:** 3.1 m   **Draft:** 1.1 m   **Crew:** 6

Displacement: 6.6 tonnes   **Maximal Speed:** 8.5 kt   **Armament:** None

Courtesy Roger Gosselin.

The vessel *Pogo* as operated by the Gatineau Sea Cadet Corps.

The tender to HMCS *Chippawa* in Winnipeg originally was built in Riverton, Manitoba, as a cabin cruiser with the name *Latinozza* and was designed to operate on the choppy waters of Lake Winnipeg. Acquired by the Canadian Navy in 1976 to replace the division's previous tender (*Cree*, see below), it was renamed *Service*, after the division's motto, and designated *PB-198*. During its naval service, it participated in the unit's exercises on Lake Winnipeg and the Red and Assiniboine Rivers, and supported both the Summer Youth Employment Program (SYEP) and the Sea Cadet summer camps in Hnausa and Gimli, Manitoba. One of its last excursions occurred during the 1990 Western Canada Summer Games, where it led the sail past in the opening ceremonies with His Royal Highness Prince Edward taking the salute. It remained HMCS *Chippawa's* tender from 1976 until officially deactivated on 27 September 1995; it was then turned over to the Crown Assets Distribution Centre for sale, and was eventually purchased for commercial use on the Newfoundland shores.

As discussed above, many of the small wartime construction Ville-class tugs served as tenders to NRDs. One of these, *Burrard* (582), bore the names *Adamsville* and *Lawrenceville* during its naval auxiliary career. It was a tender to HMCS *Discovery* until May of 1977, when transferred to HMCS *Nonsuch* in Edmonton, Alberta. For that role, it was moved by rail to Lake Wabamun, around 65 kilometres west of Edmonton (the lake is about 24 kilometres long and 8 kilometres at it widest, and is about 10.5 metres deep). Launched there on 20 May 1977, it was docked at the Calgary Power pier during the summers and at that of the provincial Department of Environment in the winters. Locally given the unofficial name *Norcott*, it was used in local exercises and as a training platform for the SYEP from the late-1970s through the 1980s, although it could not operate in 1988 because of the drought suffered by the prairies that lowered the water level in the lake. It was broken into and vandalized twice in 1989 and once in 1990. It last appeared in *Nonsuch's* records in 1990.

Most of the other wartime Ville-class tugs were assigned as tenders to divisions located more typically on large bodies of water such as the coasts or the Great Lakes. Although commissioned during the war, the Ville-class harbour tugs were paid off after the conflict and employed as auxiliaries or tenders. Soon after the war, *Listerville* (578) was allocated to HMCS *Donnacona* before being transferred to HMCS *Cataraqui* in 1979 with its name changed to *Cavalier* (578); it remained there, except for a brief period in 1982 when it served at Hamilton, until disposed of circa 1991. *Plainsville* (587) provided the same services more regularly with HMCS *Star* in Hamilton as early as 1962, and was a familiar feature for years at Canada Cup events until disposed of in the early 1990s. *Marysville* (585) was transferred to HMCS *Chatham* in Prince Rupert, British Columbia, in May 1947. HMCS *Griffon* also had one, *Queensville* (586), from early after the war until disposed of in the mid-1990s. *Scotian* operated *Parksville* (591) from 1948 for only a short while until withdrawn from service in 1949. *Otterville* (580) served HMCS *Brunswicker* after the war until moved elsewhere, leaving the division with only harbour craft as a large tender until the arrival of HMCS *Llewellyn*. *Loganville* (589) was with HMCS *Cataraqui* from the early 1950s until disposed of in the early-1990s. *Youville* (588) is recorded as being with *York* only from the early sixties; after unification of the forces in 1968, *York's* chief petty officers and petty officers used it for a "burial service" of their former service badges. It remained with *York* until transferred to HMCS *Champlain* in 1988, with which she remained until disposed of in 1997 and sold to a commercial party. The ex-*Lawrenceville*, *Cree* (584), served *Chippawa* in Winnipeg from 1972 for a few years before being paid off. Many of these small tugs were involved in the Canadian Olympic Regatta at Kingston (CORK) in 1976. *Lawrenceville* (*Cree*) and *Listerville* (*Cavalier*) were renamed in 1977 to avoid confusion with tugs of the new Ville class bearing the same names. As proof of their endurance and credit to their builder, evidence could be found as late as 2007 that many still sail as pleasure or commercial vessels.

Class: Ville (Old)	**Type:** Harbour Tug	**LOA:** 12.2 m
Beam: 3.2 m	**Draft:** 1.4 m	**Crew:** 4
Displacement: 16.3 tonnes	**Maximal Speed:** 8 kt	**Armament:** None

Back on the West Coast, HMCS *Malahat* has enjoyed a variety of small vessels as tenders over the years besides those already mentioned. In August 1953, the division received the 8.5-metre motor launch *E-427*, quickly christened *Lady Malahat*. Another was the

Department of National Defence, IE80-210.

A Huey Helicopter from 408 Squadron lifts a pair of SAR technicians off the deck of CFAV *Burrard* while working jointly with the Naval Reserves from HMCS *Nonsuch*, September 1980.

wartime-built Yard Tug Light (YTL) *Wildwood* (553), 19 metres long and displacing 62 tonnes, and on loan to *Malahat* from Queen's Harbour Master (QHM) Esquimalt for approximately one year before its disposal (1995–96). Built in 1944 by Falcon Marine Industries of Victoria as an ASW (anti-submarine warefare) towing vessel and assigned to HMC Dockyard Esquimalt, it previously spent many years, until 1991, at the Canadian Forces Maritime Experimental and Test Range (CFMETR) Nanoose Bay as a torpedo recovery vessel. *Wildwood* was purchased soon after disposal in 1996, converted to a pleasure vessel, and once again was for sale in 2008.

HMCS *Discovery's* divers were very active in the late 1980s and, to support visiting warships in Vancouver, the division acquired a small 14-metre work boat, *YMU-118*, from QHM Esquimalt. Many of *Discovery's* junior officers, boatswains, and divers were able to develop their shiphandling skills on a single-screw vessel while it was attached to the unit, and it was slightly modified in the second year to ease recovery of the divers. The class designator was later changed to YFU, and subsequent to its disposal through the Crown Assets Distribution Centre in the 1990s, *YFU-118* was purchased by one of *Discovery's* ex-diving officers for personal use as a runabout in the Gambier Island area.

The reserve fleet saw a great improvement in July 1982, when the Department of Transport transferred two vessels to the Reserve Training Unit (Atlantic), RTU(A) — *Rally* (141) and *Rapid* (142) — to join the Portes and *Fort Steele*. They were popular because of their small crew requirement and good speed. Both served in that capacity until their retirement in 1992. Stood up in April 1975, RTU(A) was the keeper of the vessels assigned for reserve training for the East Coast and its counterpart on the West Coast was the Training Group Pacific formed in January 1973.

Class: R-class	**Type:** Patrol	**LOA:** 29.0 m
Beam: 6.1 m	**Draft:** 2.2 m	**Crew:** 18
Displacement: 118.6 tonnes	**Maximal Speed:** 20 kt	**Armament:** None

Another class of training platforms used by the naval reservists was the 22.9-metre wooden Yard Auxiliary General, or YAG, boats. Late in the seventies, the YAGs were designated as training vessels and regrouped under the control and operation of the Small Boats Unit (SBU) in HMC Dockyard Esquimalt. Like many naval vessels, their designation was changed in the 1990s, and as such "YFP" was also used; they did not have official names but some unofficially adopted those of wartime armed yachts (for example, *Beaver*, *Raccoon*, *Otter*, and *Wolf*). Like the gate vessels during winter and fall, they could be signed out by NRDs for weekends or a longer period, and the admittedly incomplete records indicate that

Department of National Defence, HS82-4443.

HMC Ships *Rapid* and *Rally*.

some were assigned to certain NRDs as follows: *YFP-309* to *Queen Charlotte* in 1964, *YFP-319* to *Discovery* in 1967, and *YFP-306* to *Discovery* in 1976. They required a much smaller crew to operate than the Portes but had the advantages of carrying a substantial number of extra bunks, as well as being fitted with two propellers (allowing for more complicated shiphandling exercises), and being available as a group provided opportunities for one NRD to sign out more than one at a time so as to practice officer-of-the-watch manoeuvres and other multi-vessel evolutions. They were disposed of as their Orca-class replacements came into service (see below). The coastal diving tenders, such as *YTD-8* or *YTD-10*, were also used in this capacity when available.

Class: YAG	**Type:** Training	**LOA:** 22.9 m
Beam: 5.5 m	**Draft:** 1.1 m	**Crew:** 16
Displacement: 73.6 tonnes	**Maximal Speed:** 10 kt	**Armament:** None

All these vessels served these units well, but with age maintenance became problematic, and they were all disposed of in the second half of 1990s without being replaced at the unit level and with a gap of over a decade before the new Orca class would be acquired. Ironically, this occurred just after the Naval Reserve underwent a reorganization in the late

Department of National Defence, ETC97-65-34A.

A YAG.

1980s under which much more time at sea was required. In a sweeping change, each NRD was divided into wartime crews and all personnel were assigned a mobilization billet. Not every NRD had the same establishment and some crews could be operated by more than one NRD, but the main crew components were: Coastal Surveillance Vessel (CSV) of around 30 personnel; Inshore Surveillance Vessel (ISV), and Harbour Surveillance Vessel (HSV) each with some 10 persons; Maritime Coastal Defence Office (MCDO) with some 25–30 people; Naval Liaison Office (NLO) with three persons; Convoy Commodore Unit (CCU) with six persons; Diving Unit with 10 persons; Naval Control of Shipping Office (NCSO) with 20 persons; Naval Reporting Office (NRO) with 12 persons; and finally a training cadre of some 10–12 persons that would stay at the NRD and train the next wave. The demand for more sea time arose from the coincident introduction of the regular force concept of "Combat Readiness Requirements" (CRR), many of which required teams to be embarked in a platform to be credited. In consequence, with the retirement of the aged unit tenders, inland personnel had to travel more frequently to the coasts to use vessels in Esquimalt or Halifax.

The eight vessels of the Orca class began entering service in late 2006. They are built of steel and, although only slightly longer overall than the YAGs, are a much more imposing and capable vessel. They are fulfilling many of the same functions and can be used by Naval Reserve units on request, but the arrival of the Orcas also freed the Kingston class from serving as initial training platforms for junior officers; the Orcas eventually may also provide a secondary inshore patrol capability on the West Coast where they all are stationed. They were given official names but are not commissioned: *Orca* (55), *Raven* (56), *Caribou* (57), *Renard* (58), *Wolf* (59), *Grizzly* (60), *Cougar* (61), and *Moose* (62); they are designated PCT (patrol craft training) to indicate their potential secondary role.

Department of National Defence, ISX2009-0034.

The Orca *Renard.*

Class: Orca
LOA: 33.0 m
Draft: 2.0 m
Displacement: 190.9 tonnes

Type: Training/Patrol
Beam: 8.3 m
Crew: 24
Maximal Speed: 18 kt

Possible Armament: one 12.7mm machine gun

For the last several decades of the twentieth century, the regular navy kept four of the six remaining Bay-class patrol vessels in operation for year-round officer training out of Esquimalt, the two remaining vessels being in refit or out of routine in rotation. In anticipation of acquiring the Kingston class, a fifth Bay vessel was operated by a Naval Reserve crew during the summer to support the training of reservists, with the ship working in conjunction with its sister ships during that period. This practice began with HMC Ships *Cowichan* (162) in 1988 and *Chaleur* (164) in 1989, and continued during the first half of the 1990s. All Bay-class vessels were paid off in the late 1990s and disposed of through the Crown Assets Distribution Centre.

Class: Bay	Type: Patrol/Training	LOA: 46.3 m
Beam: 8.5 m	Draft: 2.4 m	Crew: 38
Displacement: 354.5 tonnes	Maximal Speed: 16 kt	Armament: None

In passing, it has been noted elsewhere in this volume that one aspect in which the Naval Reserve was many years ahead of its permanent counterpart has been in the embarkation of women, who have been a fixture at sea in reserve vessels since the early 1970s, generally without any problem, even if it took some time for the vessels to be modified to accommodate both genders. And the appointment of the first female commanding officer of a Canadian warship, HMCS *Kingston*, occurred on a reserve ship almost five years before a regular force ship.

With the White Paper of 1987, the Naval Reserve was assigned the new tasking of mine countermeasures, and with that came a change in the definition of what was meant by a "reserve vessel." The first sign was the change in RTU(A)'s mission from pure training to operations in preparation for the forthcoming mine countermeasures vessels and, with that, its eventual dissolution in 1994 to become part of the present Fifth Maritime Operations Group (MAROPSGRU 5 or more simply MOG 5). This all placed enormous demands on the abilities of part-time personnel to develop the skills required for the new task, and the effort to ease the transition included, on the West Coast the activation discussed above of the fifth Bay-class vessel, and on the East Coast the acquisition in the late 1980s of two civilian ocean-going offshore supply vessels that were quickly modified to provide basic training in the discipline of warfare; designated minesweeper auxiliary (MSA), they were HMCS *Anticosti* (110) and HMCS *Moresby* (112). These vessels were a significant increase in capability over any previous vessels operated by the Naval Reserve in time of peace: whereas the diminutive Portes displaced about 360 tonnes, the Anticostis were much larger vessels with twice the displacement and an enormous range. Crewed on a full-time basis by reservists until a proper class (the Kingstons) could be built to fulfill the role, as these came on line, the *Anticosti* and *Moresby* team was broken up and *Moresby* was transferred to the Pacific coast in company with HMCS *Edmonton* in 1997. Shortly afterward, however, both ships had to be paid off as personnel could not be found to man them, nor could a proper role be secured for them, and both were sold for civilian uses. The Anticostis, like so many vessels before them, had also served as training platforms for part-time reservists while not engaged in minesweeping training or exercises. They visited, as a pair or individually, many NRDs in the Maritimes, along the St. Lawrence River, and on the Great Lakes, to fulfill their training role. Many personnel from the MSAs became the initial crews of the maritime coastal defence vessels (MCDVs) when those ships joined the order of battle.

Class: Anticosti	Type: Auxiliary Minesweeper	Armament: two 12.7-mm
LOA: 58.2 m	Beam: 12.5 m	(2 x I) machine guns
Draft: 5.2 m	Crew: 23	
Displacement: 976.1 tonnes	Maximal Speed: 13.5 kt	

Department of National Defence, SWC93-436-14.

In May 1992, a contract was let to Halifax Shipyards Ltd. to build the 12 MCDVs of the Kingston class. They were designed to commercial standards and intended to conduct a wide variety of what have come to called "sovereignty" or "homeland defence" tasks, including: coastal patrols, minesweeping, route survey, fisheries patrols, law enforcement, pollution surveillance, and general response such as search and rescue duties. The ships are fitted with easily exchanged modular payloads to carry out the assigned duties. They also support training at sea for both reserve and permanent force officers, but their propulsion system (unique in the Canadian Navy) did not make them popular with the permanent force officers, and the class was relieved of this role when the Orcas entered service in the early years of the 21st century. With the Anticostis and then the Kingstons, the Naval Reserve extended its reach, with these vessels operating as far and wide as the Baltic Sea, both coasts of Mexico, Hawaii, and the Arctic region.

The MCDVs are evenly distributed with six vessels on each coast, of which normally five are active at one time, the sixth being in a routine maintenance period until returning to service and replacing the next one scheduled to go into maintenance. The MCDVs on the Atlantic coast are: HMC Ships *Glace Bay* (701), *Goose Bay* (707), *Kingston* (700), *Moncton* (708), *Shawinigan* (704), and *Summerside* (711). On the Pacific they are: HMC Ships *Brandon* (710), *Edmonton* (703), *Nanaimo* (702), *Saskatoon* (709), *Yellowknife* (706), and *Whitehorse* (705). It is unclear, at the moment, what might be the future of the Kingston-class vessels as they quickly approach their planned mid-life anniversaries, whether to refit or retire them.

Department of National Defence, SW2007-0288-58.

HMCS *Summerside* demonstrates the great manoeuvrability of an MCDV in a high speed turn while going astern.

Class: Kingston
LOA: 55.3 m
Draft: 3.4 m
Displacement: 881.8 tonnes

Type: Minesweeper
Beam: 11.3 m
Crew: 37
Maximal Speed: 15 kt

Armament: one 40 mm gun and two 12.7 mm machine guns (2 x l)

Indeed, the fate of the Kingston class portends a weightier rephrasing of the question that opened this appendix — what will be the future for Naval Reserve vessels? Many options exist, including the possibility of reservists manning the Arctic offshore patrol ships (AOPS) that should enter service in the middle of the coming decade. These vessels, with their estimated displacement of around 7,000 tonnes, length of 110 metres, maximum speed of 20 knots, and capacity to operate a helicopter, would be the most massive and combat-capable ships the Naval Reserve will have operated in time of peace.

Class:
LOA: 109.6 m
Draft: 7.0 m
Displacement: 6,940.0 tonnes

Type: Arctic Patrol
Beam: 18.2 m
Crew: 45
Maximal Speed: 20 kt

Armament: one 35 mm gun and two 12.7 mm machine guns (2 x l)

Truly, if there is one notion to be gained from this brief survey, it is that the definition of what is a Naval Reserve vessel has evolved along with the definition of a reservist. Both may be different in the future.

International Radio Call Sign (IRCS)
Vessels of the Canadian Naval Reserve

(In alphabetic order)

VESSEL'S NAME	HULL NUMBER	IRCS	CLASS
Acadian	194	CGNH	65-ft Detachment
Adversus	191	CGJG	65-ft Detachment
HMCS *Anticosti*	110	CGAA	Anticosti
HMCS *Beaver* (II)	706	CZGS	Fairmile-B
HMCS *Blue Heron*	782	CGZH	Bird
HMCS *Brandon* (II)	710	CGJI	Kingston
HMCS *Brockville*	178	CYQP	Bangor (diesel)
Burrard	582	CGEC	Ville (old)
Captor	193	CGLN	65-ft Detachment
Caribou	57	CGAA	Orca
Cavalier	578	CGCA	Ville (old)
HMCS *Chaleur* (II)	164	CZDS	Bay
HMCS *Chignecto* (III)	160	CGTX	Bay
HMCS *Cordova*	158	CYWV	YMS-400
HMCS *Cormorant* (I)	781	CGTN	Bird
HMCS *Cougar* (II)	704	CYXC	Fairmile-B
Cougar	61	CGCY	Orca
HMCS *Cowichan* (III)	162	CGZR	Bay
Cree	584		Ville (old)
Crossbow (ex *FMU-116*)	197	CGJD	
Detector	192	CGKE	65-ft Detachment
HMCS *Edmonton*	703	CGAW	Kingston
Egret	925	CFL5358	
HMCS *Elk* (II)	724	CZDL	Fairmile-B
HMCS *Forte Steele*	140	CGMQ	
HMCS *Fundy* (III)	159	CYWE	Bay
HMCS *Glace Bay* (II)	701	CGAU	Kingston
HMCS *Goose Bay*	707	CGBV	Kingston
HMCS *Granby*	180	CYQX	Bangor (Diesel)
Grizzly	60	CGCA	Orca

HMCS *Kingston*	700	CGJX	Kingston
Lawrenceville	584	CGJM	Ville (old)
Listerville	578	CGKD	Ville (old)
HMCS *Llewellyn*	141	CYZB	Llewellyn
Loganville	589	CGDB	Ville (old)
HMCS *Loon*	780	CGLO	Bird
HMCS *Mallard*	783	CZCU	Bird
Marysville	585	CGNC	Ville (old)
HMCS *Miramichi* (III)	163	CGWY	Bay
HMCS *Moncton* (II)	708	CGJC	Kingston
HMCS *Moose* (II)	711	CYQF	Fairmile-B
Moose	62	CGCZ	Orca
HMCS *Moresby*	112	CGAB	Anticosti
HMCS *Nanaimo* (II)	702	CGAV	Kingston
Nicholson	196	CGRA	75-ft Detachment
Orca	55	CGAB	Orca
Otterville	580		Ville (old)
Parksville	591	CGKC	Ville (old)
Plainsville	587	CGDK	Ville (old)
Pogo	104	CGFP	
HMCS *Porte Dauphine*	186	CZGL	Porte
HMCS *Porte de la Reine*	184	CYVB	Porte
HMCS *Porte Quebec*	185	CYVO	Porte
HMCS *Porte Saint Jean*	180	CYWJ	Porte
HMCS *Porte Saint-Louis*	183	CYWS	Porte
Queensville	586	CGQB	Ville (old)
HMCS *Raccoon* (II)	779	CYQT	Fairmile-B
Rally	141	CYQF	R
Rapid	142	CYQG	R
Raven	56	CGAM	Orca
HMCS *Reindeer* (II)	716	CYQY	Fairmile-B
Renard	58	CGAS	Orca
HMCS *Revelstoke*	140	CZCM	Llewellyn
HMCS *Saskatoon* (II)	709	CGJG	Kingston
HMCS *Sault Ste. Marie*	176	CYVS	Algerine
HMCS *Scatari*	514	CZFZ	
Service	198	CGKY	
HMCS *Shawinigan* (II)	704	CGAX	Kingston
Sidney	195	CGQT	55-ft Detachment
Standoff	199	CGMU	75-ft Detachment
HMCS *Summerside* (II)	711	CGJJ	Kingston
HMCS *Thunder* (III)	161	CZCY	Bay
HMCS *Whitehorse*	705	CGAZ	Kingston

Wildwood	553	CGQQ	
HMCS *Wolf* (II)	762	CGWR	Fairmile-B
Wolf	59	CGBP	Orca
YAG-306	306	CFH8051	75-ft YAG
YAG-312	312	CFH8054	75-ft YAG
YAG-314	314	CFH8055	75-ft YAG
YAG-319	319	CFH8056	75-ft YAG
YAG-320	320	CFH8057	75-ft YAG
YFU-118	118		
YMT-177	177		
HMCS *Yellowknife*	706	CGAY	Kingston
Youville	588	CGDI	Ville (old)

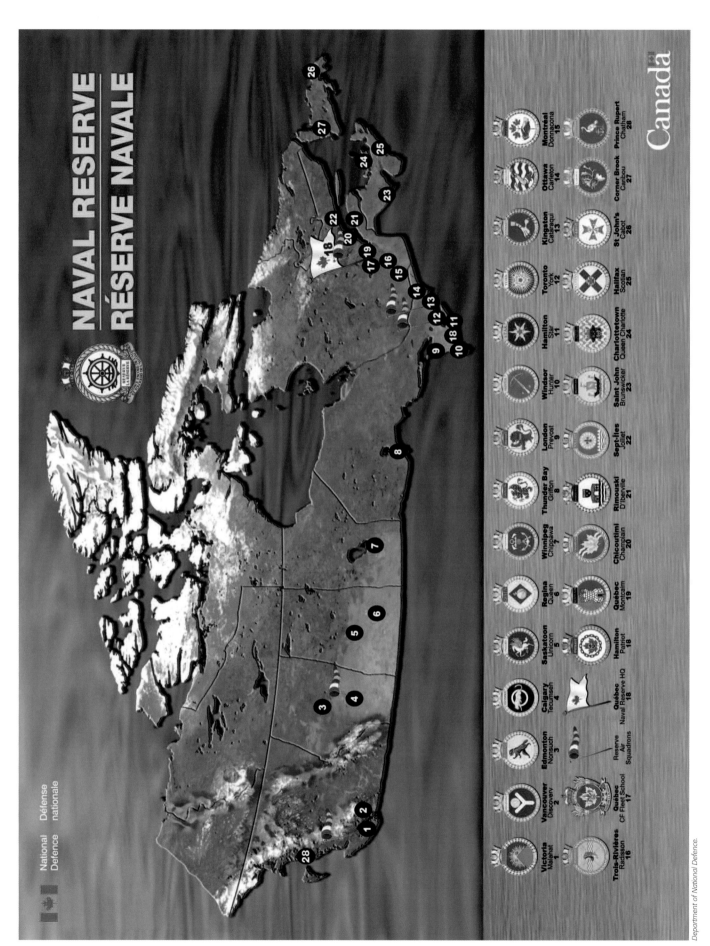

Naval Reserve Divisions across Canada.

Department of National Defence.

Naval Reserve Divisions

Richard Gimblett and Colin Stewart

Department of National Defence

The Naval Reserve badge.

1. HMCS *Malahat* (Established 1914–20; 1944–46; 1947–)

Motto: *Navis exercitatione parata* ("A ship prepared by training")

The Victoria naval enthusiasts who began drilling in 1913 formed the "No. 1 Company Royal Naval Canadian Volunteer Reserve" in May 1914. Disbanded in June 1920, it was reopened in January 1944 as the Naval Reserve Divisional Headquarters for Vancouver Island and commissioned HMCS *Malahat*. It served principally as a recruiting centre for the West Coast during the Second World War. Closed again in 1946, *Malahat* was recommissioned as a Naval Reserve division in April 1947. It was soon joined by Naval Air Squadron VC 922, which provided air crew training from 1953 to 1964. Its seagoing expertise supported reserve training from other divisions, as well as the training squadron of the permanent force. Its members have served abroad in peacekeeping operations.

First housed in the historic Customs House on the Victoria waterfront, the division was subsequently relocated in a variety of temporary facilities in Esquimalt. With the opening of its new building in 1992 at the entrance to Victoria's inner harbour, *Malahat* is a frequent host to port security exercises and diving operations.

COMMANDING OFFICERS

Lieutenant-Commander D.S. Scott	1944–46
Lieutenant-Commander G.A. Powell	1946
Lieutenant-Commander W.M. Gage	1946
(The division was paid off between 1946 and 1947)	
Captain R. Jackson	1947–52
Captain G.A.V. Thomson	1952–58
Captain J.D. Garrard	1958–63
Captain P. Thomas	1963–65
Commander W.F. Walker	1965–69
Captain E.K. Lee	1969–74
Captain M.L. Hadley	1974–78
Commander M.B. Ellis	1978–81
Commander A.R. Horner	1981–85
Commander S.J. Churlish	1985–89
Captain D.R. Macrae	1989–92
Commander D.W. Craig	1992–95
Commander J.J. Bennett	1995–98
Commander M.B.C. Carter	1998–2000
Commander D.P. Gagliardi	2000–04
Lieutenant Commander L.J. Zezza	2004–07
Commander P.D. MacNeill	2007–09
Commander S.V. Pokotylo	2009–

Department of National Defence, COND-7426-40.

HMCS *Malahat*, in the former Customs House on Wharf Street, August 1961.

2. HMCS *Discovery* (Established 1914–18; 1923–)

Motto: "Steadfast and Vigilant"

HMCS *Discovery*'s beautiful buildings are situated on the picturesque and historic military reserve of Deadman Island. Originally constituted as the "No. 2 Company Royal Naval Canadian Volunteer Reserve" in 1914, it was disbanded after the First World War. Brought back to life with the creation of the modern naval reserve in 1923, the Vancouver Half-Company was commissioned as HMCS *Discovery* in 1941, named after the vessel commanded by Captain George Vancouver, RN, while surveying the northwest coast of North America. Although a major recruiting centre, *Discovery* was busiest at war's end as a demobilization centre for the entire West Coast.

Deadman Island's location is of growing importance to maritime security operations for the Port of Vancouver. With its own helipad and sea access, it offers a secure command and control capability and an ideal location to coordinate efforts between the Department of National Defence, the port, and other federal departments. For example, in 2010, HMCS *Discovery* provided maritime security for the 2010 Winter Olympics and Paralympics, Canada's largest peacetime domestic operation to date.

COMMANDING OFFICERS

Commander J.W. Hobbs	1924–29
Lieutenant H.R. Wade (transitional as senior lieutenant)	1929–30
Lieutenant H.R. Wade	1930–36
Lieutenant-Commander C.E. Donaldson	1936–39
Lieutenant J.V. Brock	1939
Lieutenant-Commander H.R. Wade	1939–41
Lieutenant-Commander N.C.S. Gooch	1941
Lieutenant W.H. Richardson	1941–42
Lieutenant C.S. Glassco	1942–43
Commander K.C. McRae	1943–47
Commander W.R. Stacey	1947–50
Commander G. McDonald	1950–53
Commander J.H. Stevenson	1953–58
Captain A.W. Ross	1958–64
Commander A. Holland	1964–68
Captain D.R. Learoyd	1968–71
Captain J.M. Thornton	1971–75
Commander D.M. Johnston	1975–78
Captain S.B. Alsgard	1978–81
Captain J.E. Newbery	1981–84
Commander R.H. McIlwaine	1985–88
Commander B.A. Cook	1988–91

Commander A.W.F. Hastings 1991–93

Captain C.V. Newburn 1993–96

Commander D. Eakins 1996–98

Lieutenant-Commander M. Locke 1998–01

Lieutenant-Commander K. Wan 2001–05

Lieutenant-Commander M. Fletcher 2005–08

Lieutenant-Commander E. Fisher 2008–

Department of National Defence, E-67263.

Aerial view of HMCS *Discovery*, June 1962.

3. HMCS *Nonsuch* (Established 1923–64; 1975–)

Motto: *A Campis ad Maria* ("From the Prairies to the Sea")

The Edmonton Half-Company was stood up on 27 March 1923, with its first home in the local armoury. The move in 1939 to what had been the stables for the Hudson's Bay Company led to the ship's being formally commissioned in 1941 as HMCS *Nonsuch* in recognition of the company ketch of the same name that had opened up the Canadian interior to trade.

During the fall of 1946, the delivery of a Swordfish aircraft to the air reserve squadron attached to *Nonsuch* caused much discussion when the pilot chose to set the aircraft down only two blocks away, in the Ross Flats area, instead of the local airport. The division was a temporary casualty of the drive to reduce defence expenditures, lowering its ensign in 1964, but was recommissioned in 1975 at its present location.

Among community activities over the years, *Nonsuch* contributed the crew of a fur trader–style York boat to Expo 86 in Vancouver. It continues to live up to its motto.

COMMANDING OFFICERS

Commander A.B. McLeod	1923–38
Lieutenant-Commander E.P. Shaver	1939–41
Lieutenant C.S. Glassco	1941–42
Lieutenant G.L. Crawford	1942–43
Commander J.A. Dawson	1943–45
Lieutenant W.C.C. Webster	1945–46
Lieutenant-Commander R. Steward	1946
Commander F.R. Pike	1946–48
Commander L.R. Hoar	1948–51
Captain G.P. Manning	1951–55
Commander N.S. Cameron	1955–58
Commander L.J.D. Garrett	1958–60
Commander C.H. Rolf	1960–64
(The division was paid off 1964–75)	
Commander H.F. Wallace	1975–78
Commander J.M. Hinz	1978–81
Commander D.B. Logan	1981–85
Commander G.E. Power	1985–88
Captain E.E. Brownfield	1988–91
Commander A.S. Gent	1991–93
Commander R.R. Blakely	1993–97
Commander C.R. McNary	1997–2000
Lieutenant-Commander J.A. Bennett	2000–01
Lieutenant-Commander J.P. Smith	2004–07

Commander C.T. Persson 2007–10
Lieutenant-Commander F.A. van Staalduinen 2010–

HMCS *Nonsuch* is still located in the same building seen in this image from November 1961.

Department of National Defence, COND-7426-58.

4. HMCS *Tecumseh* (Established 1923–)

Motto: *In pace bellum para* ("In peace, prepare for war")

Established in March 1923, Calgary's Naval Reserve division was christened HMCS *Tecumseh* in 1941, after the Shawnee chief who served with the British and Canadian military forces in the War of 1812. The division has moved only once, and has been at its present location since 1943.

As with other reserve divisions, *Tecumseh* was a major source of recruits during the Second World War, including naval pilot Robert Hampton Gray, the only member of the Canadian Navy to be awarded the Victoria Cross. Air squadron VC 924 was attached to the division from 1955 through 1959. *Tecumseh* also lays claim to fostering the first female flag officer in the Canadian Forces, when Commodore Laraine Orthlieb was appointed senior naval reserve adviser in 1989.

Tecumseh survived various postwar challenges, including defence cuts, armed forces unification, and a major fire in 1981. Rebuilt since the fire, *Tecumseh* is a fully modern training facility. In recent years, personnel from *Tecumseh* have participated in both domestic and international operations such as Operation Assistance in 1997 and Operation Apollo in 2003.

COMMANDING OFFICERS

Lieutenant R. Hinton	1923–34
Lieutenant R. Jackson	1934–40
Lieutenant-Commander R. de Winton	1940–41
Lieutenant H.D. Bulmer	1942–43
Lieutenant-Commander D. Dattels	1943–45
Lieutenant D. Elliott	1945–46
Lieutenant-Commander W. Spicer	1946
Captain R. Jackson	1946–52
Acting Commander W.F. Moreland	1952–55
Commander K. Wynot	1955–58
Commander J.F. McKenzie	1958–61
Captain A.R. Smith	1961–67
Commander R.A.F. Montgomery	1967–70
Captain J. Newberry	1970–72
Acting Commander B. Harasymiv	1972–75
Commander A.W.G. Hale	1975–78
Commander M.P. Hayes	1978–80
Commander W. Evelyn	1980–83
Captain L.F. Orthlieb	1983–87
Commander G.G. McKenzie	1987–90
Captain C.D. Waddell	1990–93

Commander G.K. Wong 1993–96
Commander G.A. Whitehead 1996–2000
Lieutenant-Commander M.J. Ervin 2000–03
Lieutenant-Commander D.L. Carroll 2003–06
Lieutenant-Commander E.A. Shirley 2006–09
Lieutenant-Commander R.K. MacLeod 2009–

HMCS *Tecumseh* in the "prefire" building, November 1961.

Department of National Defence, COND-7426-61.

5. HMCS *Unicorn* (Established 1923–)

Motto: *Unicus est* ("One of a Kind; Unequalled")

The Saskatoon Half-Company was established in April 1923 as one of the original RCNVR divisions, under the command of a First World War veteran. The division initially shared space with the militia in the local armoury and moved twice before arriving at its present home in 1943. Commissioned as HMCS *Unicorn* on 1 November 1941, over 3,000 "prairie sailors" joined the RCNVR here, serving in the Battle of the Atlantic, on the Murmansk Run, in the Caribbean, in the Mediterranean, and on D-Day.

The division is named after one of the first vessels to enter Hudson Bay in search of the Northwest Passage, and perpetuates the battle honours of all its namesake Royal Navy vessels, including engagements of the Spanish Armada, the Napoleonic Wars, and the Second World War.

Following the Second World War, HMCS *Unicorn* continued to play a prominent role in Saskatoon and in operations at home and abroad. *Unicorn* sailors served during the Korean Conflict and the Cold War, and in peacekeeping missions around the world and disaster relief efforts in Canada.

COMMANDING OFFICERS

Acting Lieutenant J.W. McEown	1923–24
Sub-Lieutenant L.P. Danis	1924–28
Lieutenant J.W. McEown	1928–33
Lieutenant W.F. Campbell	1933–34
Lieutenant-Commander H.W. Balfour	1934–40
Lieutenant C.F.R. Wentz	1940–41
Lieutenant R.M. Wallace	1942
Lieutenant-Commander C.A.E. White	1942–45
Captain O.K. McClocklin	1945–56
Commander C. McLeod	1957–60
Commander D.M. Keith	1960–63
Commander E.C. Boychuk	1963–67
Captain W.J. McCorkell	1968–71
Commander R.L. Cheesman	1971–74
Commander W. Borycki	1974–77
Captain D.P. Ravis	1977–83
Captain J.M. Dalzell	1983–88
Commander T.C.D. Gordon	1988–92
Commander R.L. Hanson	1992–94
Commander L.A. Christ	1994–98
Lieutenant-Commander M.E.Z. Cebryk	1998–2001
Lieutenant-Commander R.F. Chow	2001–04

Commander L.A. Christ 2004–07
Commander R.L. Hanson 2007–

HMCS *Unicorn*, spring 2010.

Courtesy Louis Christ.

6. HMCS *Queen* (Established 1923–64; 1975–)

Motto: *Augusta Invictaque* ("Majestic and Invincible")

Originally established in 1923 with a complement of three officers and 45 men, the Regina Half-Company trained in a series of rented or borrowed facilities until eventually moving to the Regina Armoury in the 1930s. Having rapidly expanded during the war years, *Queen* finally found a proper home on 4 June 1955, in the Queen Building in Wascana Park.

A victim of mid-1960s budget constraints, on 30 November 1964 the White Ensign was hauled down from the Queen Building and the keys were turned over to Air Command. A relentless lobbying effort to have the division reopened bore fruit when HMCS *Queen* was recommissioned on 1 July 1975.

Although one of the smaller divisions in the Naval Reserve, *Queen* habitually has "punched above her weight," from providing boats and personnel during the 1926 Wascana Creek floods through to the 1997 "Flood of the Century" in Manitoba. In recognition of the important contribution to the community, the street where *Queen* is located was renamed by the City of Regina. The new address is 100 Navy Way.

COMMANDING OFFICERS

Lieutenant A.L. Geddes	1923–27
Lieutenant-Commander A.C. Ellison	1927–36
Commander A.T. Hall	1936–38
Lieutenant-Commander D.A. Grant	1938–40
Lieutenant-Commander A.C. Ellison	1940–43
Lieutenant-Commander N.L. Pickersgill	1943–44
Lieutenant-Commander F.C. Aggett	1944–45
Commander N.E. Whitmore	1945–47
Commander W.W. Spicer	1947–51
Commander D. Clarke	1951–53
Commander W. Haggett	1953–57
Commander T.L. Clark	1958–61
Commander W.M. Stan	1961–64
(The division was paid off 1964 to 75)	
Commander R.L. Cheesman	1975–76
Commander J.O. Burgess	1976–81
Commander K.W. McCaw	1981–86
Acting Commander R.B. Routley	1986–90
Commander P.B. Weber	1990–94
Lieutenant-Commander W.T. Bowes	1994–97
Lieutenant-Commander T.K. Daniel	1997–2001
Lieutenant-Commander L.M. Mushanski	2001–04

Lieutenant-Commander J.A. Bell 2004–07
Lieutenant-Commander C.J. Thiemann 2007–

HMCS *Queen* is still located in the same building seen in this image from November 1961.

Department of National Defence, COND-7426-15.

7. HMCS *Chippawa* (Established 1923–)

Motto: "Service"

Formed in March of 1923 as one of the "Original Six" Naval Reserve divisions, HMCS *Chippawa* has, throughout its history, lived up to its motto. During the Second World War, despite being the furthest inland of all naval establishments, *Chippawa* became the third largest source for naval recruits in Canada, and the second largest contingent of volunteers for the Women's Royal Canadian Naval Service.

Chippawa was ready when in 1997 the "Flood of the Century" covered much of Southern Manitoba. The unit became the main staging area for all small boat operations, and was awarded the Deputy Chief of the Defence Staff Unit Commendation — the first reserve division to receive this honour. As home to one of the Naval Reserve's five bands, HMCS *Chippawa* acted as the "home unit" for the 2007 National Band of the Naval Reserve summer tour. In recent years, *Chippawa* has been at the forefront of the Total Force concept, such that, as of the winter of 2010, *Chippawa* had deployed more than a dozen sailors to Task Force Afghanistan since 2005.

COMMANDING OFFICERS

Captain E.A. Brock	1923–30
Commander H.G. Nares	1931–33
Lieutenant-Commander F.J. Kelly	1933–36
Captain C.R. Frayer	1936–40
Commander H.G. Nares	1940–41
Captain E.T.C. Orde	1941–42
Commander R.F. McRimmon	1943–44
Commander G.E. Kernohan	1944–45
Commodore J.V. Brock	1945–46
Captain C.R. Frayer	1946
Acting Captain H.J. Craig	1946–48
Lieutenant-Commander J. Boyd	1948
Commander L.D.G. Main	1949–52
Commander F.H. Pinfold	1952–53
Captain L.B. McIlhagga	1953–60
Captain J.W. Dangerfield	1960–66
Captain C.R. Godbehere	1966–69
Commander T.S. Durham	1969–73
Captain W.N. Fox-Decent	1973–78
Commander C.E. Thain	1978–81
Commander B.P. Duggan	1981–85
Commander R.W Siemens	1985–90
Lieutenant-Commander E.F. Smith	1990–93

Commander D.R.A. Schultz   1993–96

Lieutenant-Commander, J.O. Dawson   1996–2000

Lieutenant-Commander C. Michon   2000–04

Lieutenant-Commander H.P. Collins (Heuthorst)   2004–09

Lieutenant-Commander M.R. Morlock   2009–

Front angle view of HMCS *Chippawa*, November 1961.

Department of National Defence, COND-7426-21.

8. HMCS *Griffon* (Established 1937–)

Motto: *Prima in lacubus* ("First on the Lakes")

Founded in 1937 as the Port Arthur Division of the RCNVR, HMCS *Griffon*, as it became, was established through a combination of local factors: the influence of the shipping industry on the Great Lakes, especially the Port Arthur Shipbuilding Company, and the association with the sea cadet program. Such was the level of local enthusiasm that the division had to draw up a waiting list for recruits.

With no home of its own, the division originally shared space with the militia at the Port Arthur Armoury, and then another interim location before moving to its current quarters in 1944. During the war, sailors recruited from the prairies were often routed through *Griffon* on their way east for training.

Located at the western end of the Great Lakes, *Griffon* provides an important connection to the navy far inland, frequently hosting Kingston-class vessels and other units of the Atlantic fleet when they deploy to the Lakehead. In addition, the shipping activity in the area provides its sailors ready access to practical training for operations in a busy maritime environment.

COMMANDING OFFICERS

Acting Lieutenant D. Black	1937–38
Lieutenant J.M. Hughes	1938–41
Lieutenant F.A. Bryan	1941–43
Acting Lieutenant-Commander H.S.C. Wilson	1943–44
Acting Lieutenant-Commander W.A Johnson	1944–45
Acting Lieutenant-Commander R.E. Eakins	1945
Lieutenant-Commander D.W. Gardiner	1945–46
Lieutenant-Commander C.W. King	1946–49
Captain E.O. Ormsby	1949–56
Commander T.C. Luck	1956–60
Commander D.H. Botley	1960–63
Commander D.A. Binmore	1963–66
Commander E.A. Fallen	1966–72
Commander A. Tooms	1972–76
Commander J.L. Bryant	1976–80
Commander E.V. Dalton	1980–83
Captain D.B. Coulson	1983–87
Commander R.A. Zuliani	1987–91
Lieutenant-Commander S.L Newman	1991–94
Lieutenant-Commander J.S. Mill	1994–97
Lieutenant-Commander K.R. Dawe	1997–2000
Commander E.P.A. Zuliani	2000–04

Lieutenant-Commander C.J. Marrack 2004–07

Lieutenant-Commander J.A Bell 2007–

HMCS *Griffon* is still located in the same building seen in this image from November 1961.

Department of National Defence, COND-7426-26.

9. HMCS *Prevost* (Established 1938–64; 1990–)

Motto: *"By Valour, Not Deception"*

On 8 August 1938, a half division of the Royal Canadian Navy Volunteer Reserve was established in London, Ontario, and with the declaration of war in 1939 it mobilized a full division. Officially commissioned HMCS *Prevost* on 1 November 1941, it was named after the schooner HMS *Lady Prevost* in the Lake Erie Squadron during the War of 1812. In 1941, 1942, and 1943, *Prevost* won the Commodore Walter Hose Efficiency Trophy, which became the permanent property of the division. During the war, *Prevost* served also as an English-language training centre for francophone sailors.

Converted to a permanent Naval Division at the close of hostilities in 1945, *Prevost* conducted seamanship training on vessels based at Port Stanley, Lake Erie, 45 minutes south of London. In 1964, *Prevost* was paid off in response to budget cuts. Reactivated as a detachment of HMCS *Star* in 1978, *Prevost* was recommissioned on 29 September 1990, and in the years since has established itself as an integral member of the Naval Reserve and local communities of London and Port Stanley.

COMMANDING OFFICERS

Lieutenant E.E. Hart	1938–40
Lieutenant-Commander J.R. Hunter	1940–43
Lieutenant-Commander R.N.D. Carmichael	1944–46
Lieutenant D.A. Jackson	1946–46
Commander W.A. Childs	1946–49
Lieutenant-Commander T. F. Owen	1949–50
Commander F.R.K. Naftel	1950–52
Commander E.G. Gilbride	1952–57
Captain G.A. MacLachlan	1957–63
Commander H.W. Littleford	1963–64
(The division was paid off 1964–90)	
Commander B.E. Lodge	1990–93
Commander B.R. Struthers	1993–95
Commander P.F. Earnshaw	1995–96
Lieutenant-Commander W.R. Glover	1996–97
Lieutenant-Commander M.J. Hoare	1997–2000
Lieutenant-Commander M.J. Van Den Bossche	2000–03
Lieutenant-Commander J.A. Offer	2003–06
Commander T.P. Gijzen	2006–08
Lieutenant-Commander J.S. White	2008–

Department of National Defence, COND-7426-19.

HMCS *Prevost* was re-established in the same building seen in this image from November 1961.

10. HMCS *Hunter* (Established 1940–)

Motto: *"Ready When Required"*

With the expansion of the Naval Reserve upon the outbreak of the Second World War, a Windsor division was established in March 1940 and formally commissioned on 1 November 1941 as HMCS *Hunter*, named after a British vessel that served on the Great Lakes in the War of 1812.

During the Second World War, the local training expanded so much that a second facility known as *Hunter II* was opened. In 1944, *Hunter* consolidated and moved to the division's current location. In addition to recruits for Canada's war effort, *Hunter* trained a large contingent of Polish-American volunteers (because of its proximity to the United States), who eventually transferred to the Polish Navy.

In 1965, *Hunter* acted as host for the naval funeral of Rear-Admiral Walter Hose, the "father of the Naval Reserve;" the funeral procession included seven admirals and commodores. *Hunter* has seen a number of firsts for the Naval Reserve, including the appointment in 1981 of Lieutenant-Commander Marilyn O'Hearn as the first female commanding officer of a Naval Reserve division and in 1996 the first formation chaplain.

COMMANDING OFFICERS

Lieutenant J. Marshall	1939–40
Lieutenant-Commander N. Bruce	1940–42
Lieutenant R.K. Baker	1942–43
Commander A.R. Webster	1943–45
Lieutenant-Commander A. Kirkpatrick	1945–46
Lieutenant-Commander J. Loaring	1946–47
Commander B. Wilkinson	1947–52
Captain W.G. Curry	1952–61
Commander D. Charters	1961–65
Commander A. Harris	1965–68
Commander T. Smith	1968–71
Commander F. Knight	1971–74
Commander R. Del Col	1974–77
Commander K. Towers	1977–81
Commander M. O'Hearn	1981–85
Commander W. Pastorius	1985–88
Captain M. Pandzich	1988–91
Commander R. Del Col	1991–94
Commander B. Lodge	1994–98
Lieutenant-Commander D. Kazmirchuk	1998–2000
Commander B. Lodge	2000–02

Lieutenant-Commander P. Kelly 2002–05

Lieutenant-Commander D. Baars 2005–08

Lieutenant-Commander N. Bell 2008–09

Commander P.J. Fleming 2009–

HMCS *Hunter* is still located in the same building seen in this image from November 1961.

Department of National Defence, COND-7426-39.

11. HMCS *Star* (Established 1923–)

Motto: *Diligentia* ("Diligence")

The Hamilton Half-Company of the RCNVR was established on 31 January 1923, although the expanding ship's company required a number of moves before a permanent home was found on the harbour waterfront. The commissioning of the unit as HMCS *Star* on 1 November 1941 honoured a Lake Ontario naval presence dating to the War of 1812, when HMS *Star* had defended Canada against American invasion.

From 1943 until unification in 1968, *Star* shared its premises with HMCS *Patriot*, the headquarters of the Commanding Officer Naval Divisions (COND), the forerunner to the present-day Naval Reserve Headquarters, as well as the Great Lakes Training Centre, or what would now be called Fleet School (Hamilton). For the period 1954–64 a sub-unit tender to *Star* was established in Kitchener.

Star's unique ability to accommodate large vessels at its adjacent berth has resulted in many opportunities to host important events and visits, including the Royal Yacht HMY *Britannia* in 1959. In 2003, *Star* made room for HMCS *Haida*, now a National Historic site and constant tribute to our naval heritage.

COMMANDING OFFICERS

Lieutenant-Commander R.H. Yeates	1923–29
Lieutenant W.G. Beaver	1929–34
Lieutenant-Commander H.L.G. Westland	1934–37
Lieutenant J.C. Hart	1937–40
Lieutenant W.R. Morrison	1940
Lieutenant F.E. Waterman	1940–41
Lieutenant W.H.B. Thomson	1941
Commander J. McFetrick	1941–44
Commander R. Jackson	1944–45
Commander C.S. Glassco	1945–46
Lieutenant R.G. Baker	1946
Lieutenant W.H. Adamson	1946
Commander S.F. Ross	1946–50
Commander G.H. Parke	1950–53
Commander J.H. Curtis	1953–58
Captain W.T. Houghton	1958–63
Commander R.G. Wilson	1963–64
Commander H.C. Tilbury	1964–66
Commander R.T. Bennett	1966–69
Commander C.D. DiCenzo	1969–71
Commander F.J. Lee	1971–75
Commander M.J. Pandzich	1975–79

Commander R.H. Bowman   1979–82
Commander D. Woodliffe   1982–85
Commander R.J. Williamson   1985–88
Commander D.Y.S. Mark   1988–91
Commander A.J.M. Woodrow   1991–95
Lieutenant-Commander P.W. Duynstee   1995–98
Lieutenant-Commander D.J. Martin   1998–2002
Lieutenant-Commander N.S. Bell   2002–05
Lieutenant-Commander G.E. Swing   2005–08
Lieutenant-Commander D. Baars   2008–10
Lieutenant-Commander S.P. Gothi   2010–

HMCS *Star*, November 1961. An aerial view of the new building, also on the Hamilton harbour waterfront, is pictured in chapter 4.

Department of National Defence, COND-7426-41.

12. HMCS *York* (Established 1923–)

Motto: *Bon espoir* ("Good Hope")

Established as the Toronto Half-Company in April 1923, HMCS *York* was formally commissioned in 1942. As with most reserve divisions, *York* moved many times in its early years, finally shifting to its current location in 1947. Throughout the Second World War, the division distinguished itself as one of the premier naval recruiting depots in the British Commonwealth, with almost 17,000 men and women joining the navy through its doors.

York was home to the first Naval Reserve air squadron, VC 920, from its establishment in 1953 until it was disbanded in 1963. Equipped with Avengers, it was the only reserve air squadron to be carrier-qualified.

Based in Canada's largest city, HMCS *York* forms an important part of the Naval Reserve's mission of bringing the navy to Canadians, aided by its being home to one of the five bands in the Naval Reserve. Its location on Lake Ontario means that it has been host to a number of exercises and it frequently acts as the local host for port visits by units of the fleet.

COMMANDING OFFICERS

Lieutenant-Commander G.B. Jackson	1923–27
Commander A.D. MacLean	1927–31
Captain W.G. Sheddon	1931–40
Commander A.C. Turner	1940–42
Commander G.C. Bernard	1942–43
Captain E.T.C. Orde	1943
Captain J.J. Connolly	1943–45
Commander G.F. McCrimmon	1945–47
Captain F.R. Base	1947–51
Captain R.I. Hendy	1951–55
Captain L.D. Stupart	1955–58
Captain J.W.F. Goodchild	1958–63
Commander P.J. Wilch	1963–66
Commodore J.W.F. Goodchild	1966
Captain T.C. Turner	1966–71
Commander F.R. Berchem	1971–73
Commander W.H. Wilson	1973–76
Commander D.S. Asley	1976–78
Commander E.E. Sparling	1978–81
Captain R.N. Baugniet	1981–85
Captain G.J. Oman	1985–88
Commander A.E. Pitts	1988–91

Commander R.K. Bonnell 1991–95

Lieutenant-Commander L.L. Barwick 1995–98

Lieutenant-Commander P.N. Duynstee 1998–99

Commander H.W. McEwen 1999–2002

Commander K. Kubeck 2002–04

Commander R.L. Perks 2004

Commander C.J. Ross 2004–07

Commander M.P. Davies 2007–

Department of National Defence, COND-7426-14.

The rear (harbour) view of HMCS *York*, still located in the same building seen in this image from November 1961.

14. HMCS *Carleton* (Established 1923–)

Motto: *Vincemus armis* ("With these arms we shall conquer")

The Ottawa Half-Company was established in 1923, and was formally commissioned on 1 November 1941, taking its name after the two-masted schooner HMS *Carleton*, a vessel that had distinguished itself at the Battle of Valcour Island in 1776. HMCS *Carleton* moved into its present home on Dow's Lake in December 1943, and during the course of the war saw to the training of some 4,620 officers and men.

After hostilities ended, *Carleton* continued to serve as a training facility for sailors, cadets, and a branch of the Woman's Royal Canadian Naval Service. For a short period, 1955–58, a sub-unit tender to *Carleton* was established in North Bay.

As with other Naval Reserve divisions, Carleton is actively involved in the community, lending support to many festivals, ceremonies and charitable causes within the National Capital Region. Continuing the role it fulfilled so well during the Second World War, Carleton continues to provide trained sailors and officers to both domestic and international operations.

COMMANDING OFFICERS

Lieutenant R. Shippley	1923–25
Lieutenant H.B Burney	1925–26
Commander E.C. Sherwood	1926–39
Lieutenant F.H. Sherwood	1939–40
Lieutenant T.D. McGee	1940
Lieutenant-Commander W.J.F. Hose	1940–41
Lieutenant C.A.E. White	1941–42
Commander W.G. Shedden	1942
Lieutenant D.C. MacKintosh	1942
Lieutenant J.G. Fraser	1942–43
Lieutenant H.C. McGowan	1943
Lieutenant W.C.L. Barker	1943
Lieutenant S.P.A. Redgrave	1943
Lieutenant-Commander A.A. Hargraft	1943–44
Lieutenant-Commander G.L. Bott	1944–46
Commander L. Audette	1946–48
Commander T.G. Fuller	1948–51
Captain R.P. White	1951–1956
Captain W.R. Inman	1956–1962
Captain J.M. Robertson	1962–68
Commander E.J. Cooper	1968–69
Commander P.B. Curzon	1969–70
Commander R.B. Duncombe	1970–74

Commander R.J. Wilson	1974–76
Commander P.J. Godbout	1976–77
Lieutenant-Commander R.N. Baugniet	1977–78
Commander P.J. Godbout	1978–79
Lieutenant-Commander R.N. Baugniet	1979–80
Commander J.G. Daniels	1980–84
Commander G.H. Weston	1984–87
Captain H.F. Wallace	1987–90
Commander D.G. Arnaud	1990–91
Commander J.M. Levesque	1991–92
Commander D.G. Arnaud	1992–94
Commander J.M. Levesque	1994–95
Commander R.J. Thibault	1995–98
Commander E.F. Boettger	1998–2001
Commander K.I. Sanford	2001–04
Lieutenant-Commander, R.J. Roberts	2004–07
Commander D. Bancroft	2007–09
Commander M.A. Hopper	2009–

Department of National Defence, COND-7426-42.

The view of HMCS *Carleton* as seen from Dow's Lake is little changed from this image taken in November 1961.

15. HMCS *Donnacona* (Established 1923–)

Motto: "Hand on"

The Montreal unit of the RCNVR was established in 1923 as separate anglophone and francophone half-companies, designated "Montreal E" and "F," respectively. These were merged into one full company in 1933, only to be split again in 1939 to accommodate the high recruiting intake on the outbreak of war. These were commissioned in 1941 as HMCS *Montreal* and NCSM *Cartier* and merged in 1944. Meanwhile, *Montreal* had been recommissioned in 1943 as HMCS *Donnacona* to free the name for a frigate, and that became the combined division name. Also in 1943, both moved to 2055 Drummond Street where the division became a downtown fixture for more than 60 years. In 1944, HMCS *Donnacona*'s football team won the Grey Cup for Montreal, defeating the Hamilton Wildcats 7–6.

Since then, the division has remained in service without interruption. As with most divisions, *Donnacona* has a portion of its ship's company on full-time service, both in the fleet and at shore establishments. HMCS *Donnacona* was moved to a new purpose-built facility at 3525 St. Jacques Street in the summer of 2007.

COMMANDING OFFICERS

Lieutenant F.C.C. Mead	1923
Lieutenant D.J. Desbarats	1923–28
Lieutenant H.G. Gonthier	1928–29
Lieutenant J.C.K. McNaught	1929–30
Lieutenant T.H. Beament	1930–34
Commander E.R. Brock	1934–39
Lieutenant J.F. Stairs	1939

HMCS *Montreal*

Commander E.R. Brock	1939–40
Commander P.W. Earl	1940–41

HMCS *Cartier*

Lieutenant P.S. Major	1939–41
Commander M.R. Campbell	1942–44

HMCS *Donnacona*

Commander P.W. Earl	1941–42
Commander M.R. Campbell	1942–44
Commander J. McFetrick	1944–45
Captain M.R. Campbell	1945–46
Lieutenant-Commander E.P. Earnshaw	1946
Captain R.B. Warwick	1946–47
Captain O.G.L. Holmes	1947–51

Commander P.A.F. Langlois 1951–52
Commander G.St.A. Mongenais 1952–56
Captain A.R. Webster 1956–58
Commander R.G. Bell 1958–62
Captain R.G. Stapley 1962–68
Commander M.S. Bistrisky 1968–71
Commander W.J. Law 1971–72
Commander G.R. Telfer 1972–75
Commander A. Comeau 1975–77
Commander R. Langlais 1977–78
Captain P. Langlais 1978–85
Commander L. Flavelle 1985–88
Commander P. Charland 1988–92
Commander H. Létourneau 1992–95
Lieutenant-Commander P. Parker 1995–97
Commander R. Dominique 1997–2001
Lieutenant-Commander A.C. Grant 2001–04
Lieutenant-Commander S.M.D.R. Dethier 2004–08
Commander K. Kubeck 2008–

Department of National Defence, COND-7426-20.

Front view of
HMCS *Donnacona*,
November 1961, in
the old Drummond
Street location.

16. HMCS *Radisson* (Established 1986–)

Motto: *Fortitudo in perseverantia* ("Preserve with courage")

HMCS *Radisson* was named after the famous explorer Pierre Esprit Radisson (1636–1710). The unit was established at Trois-Rivières during the second phase of the Naval Presence in Quebec project. The division was stood up in August 1986 in the premises of the Canadian Forces Recruiting Centre, which, at the time, occupied the floors above the historic Trois-Rivières post office. In June 1987, the unit moved to the former d'Youville School at 175 Saint-Alphonse Street, Cap-de-la-Madeleine. Two days later, the first 74 recruits were sworn in. The commissioning ceremony for HMCS *Radisson* took place on 3 October 1987.

On 14 December 1990, National Defence Headquarters in Ottawa granted the heraldic crest of HMCS *Radisson*. In the centre of the crest is the bust of Pierre Radisson. Behind him, two oars cross over a gold background; through the middle of the crest are three wavy blue lines symbolizing the three rivers. A few months later, the unit was granted its motto.

In 1992, the minister of national defence inaugurated the unit's permanent building on Saint-Christophe Island. Constantly progressing, the *Radisson* has quickly made a name for itself within the great Naval Reserve family.

COMMANDING OFFICERS

Lieutenant-Commander D. Prévost	1986–88
Lieutenant-Commander B. Allard	1988–93
Lieutenant-Commander M. Charron	1993–95
Lieutenant-Commander R. Tremblay	1995–98
Lieutenant-Commander R. DeNobile	1998–2004
Lieutenant-Commander M. Brisson	2004–07
Lieutenant-Commander B. Beaulieu	2007–10
Lieutenant-Commander J.P.A Gervais	2010–

Department of National Defence.

HMCS *Radisson*.

17. Canadian Forces Fleet School Quebec (Established 1995–)

Motto: *Servir la marine* ("To serve the fleet")

The Canadian Forces Fleet School Quebec (CFFSQ) opened in May 1995 in response to the Canadian government's 1980s project to increase the naval presence in Quebec. Initially mandated to instruct the Initial Cadre Training (ICT) for crews of the Kingston-class vessels, it has expanded to provide specialized instruction to both the Naval Reserve and the Canadian Forces in areas ranging from logistics to military intelligence and basic leadership. Apart from the main facility in Quebec, the Fleet School operates a Training Detachment at CFB Borden to conduct basic recruit training.

As part of the Pointe à Carcy Naval Complex where it shares space with HMCS *Montcalm*, Fleet School's location on the waterfront at the base of the Old City of Quebec makes it a part of the fabric of the daily life of its host city. In addition, it has been the home for the Compagnies Franches de la Marine, a historical drill unit providing a direct link to the French naval infantry units that provided part of the defence of New France.

CFFS QUEBEC COMMANDANTS

Lieutenant-Commander P.W. Stiff	1995
Commander A. Nadeau	1995–2000
Commander J.P.R. Drolet	2000–01
Commander J.A.C. Gauthier	2001–03
Commander C.J. Deere	2003–07
Commander R. Brisson	2007–09
Commander D. Trudeau	2009–10
Commander A. Fry	2010–

Department of National Defence, VLC99-109-15A.

Canadian Forces Fleet School
Québec amidst the Point-à-Carcy
Naval Complex.

18. Reserve Formations and Commanders

After the establishment of the reserve forces in 1923, the senior reserve authority rested in the hands of the director of reserve divisions. This was a staff position at Naval Service Headquarters under the aegis of what became the naval personnel branch. The expanding war effort led to the creation of two formal reserve officer appointments: first, in December 1942, the commanding officer reserve divisions (CORD) at HMCS *York* in Toronto; and then on 15 January 1944, a new seat on the Naval Board for the chief staff officer reserves (CSOR). They were responsible for all reserve promotions, appointments, honours, and awards, as well as the maintenance of morale. Both positions ended 1 December 1945.

Although the reserves were reorganized in 1947, a commanding officer naval divisions (COND) was not reinstituted until April 1953, held by a regular force officer. Initially co-located within HMCS *Star*, the separate facility HMCS *Patriot* (both in Hamilton) opened on 1 February 1956.

Armed Forces unification initiated the first proper position of senior naval reserve adviser in 1967. The appointment was held by a reservist who reported to the commander maritime command. The initiative to make the Naval Reserve more operationally focused argued for the shift of this advisory function into one of actual command. This was formalized with the relocation of Naval Reserve Headquarters to Quebec City and the onset of the Total Force concept. Two incidents of special note in this period were the appointment in 1989 of Commodore Laraine Orthlieb as senior naval reserve adviser, thus making her the first female flag officer in the Canadian Forces, and the creation in 1993 of the position of commander naval reserve.

Commanding Officer Reserve/Naval Divisions (CORD/COND)

Commodore (2nd class) E.R. Brock	1942–45

Chief Staff Officer Reserves (CSOR)

Captain P.B. Cross	1944–45
Captain P.W. Earl	1945

Commanding Officer Naval Divisions (COND / Regular Force officers)

Commodore K.F. Adams	1953–55
Rear-Admiral K.F. Adams	1955–58
Commodore E.W. Finch-Noyes	1958–60
Commodore P.D. Taylor	1960–65
Commodore G.C. Edwards	1965–66

Senior Naval Reserve Adviser (SNRA)

Commodore B.S.C. Oland	1967–71
Commodore D.R. Learoyd	1971–74
Commodore R.T. Bennett	1974–77
Commodore T.A.M. Smith	1977–83
Commodore W.N. Fox-Decent	1983–86

Commodore G.L. Peer	1986–89
Commodore L.F. Orthlieb	1989–92
Commodore J.-C. Michaud	1992–93

Commander Naval Reserves (COMDNAVRES)

Commodore J.-C. Michaud	1993–95
Commodore R.N. Baugniet	1995–97
Commodore R.A. Zuliani	1997–2000
Commodore W.F. O'Connell	2000–04
Commodore R.R. Blakely	2004–07
Commodore J.J. Bennett	2007–

Courtesy Kévin Jutras.

Naval Reserve Headquarters in Quebec City.

Top: The badge of the Commanding Officer Naval Divisions, 1956–66.

19. HMCS *Montcalm* (Established 1923–)

Motto: *Disponible pour server* ("Ready to serve")

One of the first French-speaking units of the Canadian Navy was founded on 21 April 1923. Named Québec Half-Company, the unit's first mission was to recruit volunteers and provide them with training in seamanship. The unit grew with time and became the Québec Division in 1935. The unit was commissioned on 23 November 1941 and was named HMCS *Montcalm*. The VC 923 Naval Air Squardron provided training from 1954 to 1959.

The unit played a major role as the main channel through which French-speaking Canadians could join the Canadian Navy and do their part during Second World War. The end of the fighting brought with it a transformation of the unit, but by no means the end of its activities.

After many years near the Quebec Citadelle, HMCS *Montcalm* moved into its current location in the Pointe-à-Carcy Naval Complex in May 1995, where it continues to play a major role within the Naval Reserve of the Canadian Forces. The unit distinguishes itself by outreach to and ongoing involvement with the community, notably with the Compagnies Franches de la Marine.

COMMANDING OFFICERS

Sub-Lieutenant C.L. Gauvreau	1923–25
Lieutenant L.J.M. Gauvreau	1925
Sub-Lieutenant J.C.A. Pettigrew	1925–35
Lieutenant-Commander J.M.E. Beaudoin-Lemieux	1935–37
Sub-Lieutenant J.C.A. Pettigrew	1937–38
Lieutenant-Commander F.A. Price	1938–40
Lieutenant K.L. Johnson	1940–42
Lieutenant R.M.S. St-Laurent	1942–43
Lieutenant E.F. Noël	1943–1946
Lieutenant T.S.R. Peacock	1946
Lieutenant M.J.A.T. Jetté	1946–47
Lieutenant J.B.A. Bérubé	1947–49
Lieutenant E.F. Noël	1949–51
Lieutenant M.J.A.T. Jetté	1951–52
Lieutenant-Commander W.G. Mylett	1952–56
Commander P. Langlais	1956–62
Lieutenant-Commander W.G. Mylett	1962–63
Commander J.-P. Jobin	1963–68
Commander P.J. Gwyn	1968–71
Commander R. Langlois	1971–74
Commander J. Dallaire	1974–77

Commander P. Houle 1977–81
Commander J.-C. Michaud 1981–86
Commander P. Houle 1986–89
Commander J. Léveillé 1989–93
Lieutenant-Commander C.R. LeClerc 1993–94
Lieutenant-Commander P. Tessier 1994–96
Lieutenant-Commander G. Ross 1996–98
Commander A. Dubuc 1998–2003
Lieutenant-Commander M. Audy 2003–06
Commander L. Morin 2006–09
Lieutenant-Commander É. Landry 2009–

Department of National Defence, COND-7426-23.

Front view of the old premises of HMCS *Montcalm* on the Plains of Abraham, November 1961.

20. HMCS *Champlain* (Second of name) (Established 1985–)

Motto: *Se préparer à se défendre* ("Preparing to defend")

The opening of a Naval Reserve unit at Chicoutimi, now Ville de Saguenay, marked the beginning not only of the second phase of the Naval Presence in Quebec project, but also contributed to the revitalization of the Naval Reserve as a whole. Activated in 1985 and commissioned on 15 August 1986, *Champlain* was the first of a series of new divisions; it had been decades since new divisions had been established. Named in honour of the famous French mariner and explorer Samuel de Champlain (c.1570–1635), it also revived the name of one of the earliest destroyers commissioned in the RCN in the interwar years.

Originally, the division was located in an old shopping centre, at 141 Racine Street East, but the move to its present permanent location in the Vieux Port de Chicoutimi in 1993 provides it with docking facilities capable of berthing ships of the Canadian Navy. In addition to training men and women to meet the various needs of the Naval Reserve and the Navy, *Champlain* has been involved closely in social, cultural, and charitable activities in the region.

COMMANDING OFFICERS

Lieutenant-Commander P.N. McKoegh	1985–89
Lieutenant-Commander P.A. Guindon	1989–91
Lieutenant-Commander D.W. Shubaly	1991–93
Commander J.A.C. Gauthier	1993–94
Lieutenant-Commander M. Otis	1994–96
Lieutenant-Commander J.A. Auclair	1996–98
Lieutenant-Commander B. Girard	1998–2002
Lieutenant-Commander R. Gauthier	2002–06
Lieutenant-Commander J.L.A. Thibeault	2006–10
Commander J.A.C. Gauthier	2010–

Department of National Defence, BNC95-2937.

HMCS *Champlain* on the
Chicoutimi waterfront.

21. HMCS *d'Iberville* (Second of Name) (Established 1986–)

Motto: *Ensemble* ("Together")

The historical name *d'Iberville* commemorates Pierre LeMoyne, Sieur d'Iberville, a Canadian sailor and explorer who was born in Ville-Marie (present-day Montreal) in 1661 and died in 1706. He fought the English in Hudson Bay and around Newfoundland (1686–97), then established Louisiana, becoming the territory's first governor.

On a heritage note, the first HMCS *d'Iberville* was a naval school commissioned in October 1952 in the city of Quebec for the purpose of increasing the presence of francophones in the Royal Canadian Navy. The school was paid off in 1961.

The second HMCS *d'Iberville*, the current Rimouski Naval Reserve division, was authorized in July 1986 and formed in August. It was formally commissioned on 14 November 1987 in temporary facilities. HMCS *d'Iberville* was established as part of Phase II of the Naval Presence in Quebec, spearheaded by the Department of National Defence to recruit more francophones into the Canadian Navy and encourage them to stay and build their careers.

In May 1994, the unit's permanent facilities were inaugurated. Co-located with port facilities in Rimouski East, HMCS *d'Iberville* has a crew of approximately 100 people from Greater Rimouski.

COMMANDING OFFICERS

Lieutenant-Commander G. Lafontaine	1986–89
Lieutenant-Commander J.B.M.S. Allard	1989–92
Lieutenant-Commander D.J. Forestell	1992–96
Lieutenant-Commander P.E. Elistive	1996–99
Lieutenant-Commander A.S. Quenneville	1999–2002
Lieutenant-Commander J.A.G. Mercier	2002–04
Lieutenant-Commander M.C.D. Moutillet	2004–07
Commander J.A.C. Gauthier	2007–10
Lieutenant-Commander J.-F. LeBlanc	2010–

Department of National Defence.

HMCS *d'Iberville.*

22. HMCS *Jolliet* (Established 1989–)

Motto: *Omnia perrumpimus* ("Nothing can stop us")

HMCS *Jolliet* is the 22nd Naval Reserve division of Canada, the last one to be established in the Province of Quebec. The commissioning ceremony took place on 7 October 1989, presided over by the Honourable Mary Collins, Associate Minister of National Defence. A number of other dignitaries were in attendance as well, including Vice-Admiral R.E.D. George, Commander Maritime Command.

HMCS *Jolliet* was named after the great explorer and cartographer Louis Jolliet, who lived from 1645 to 1700. He sailed in the Canadian midwest and discovered the Mississippi River. He is even believed to have owned a few acres of land in Moisie, near Sept-Îles; Louis Jolliet died a poor man on one of the Mingan Islands, and it is believed that his remains are still there. Jolliet was the kind of person who let nothing deter them, hence the motto of the HMCS *Jolliet*.

The first building to house HMCS *Jolliet* was a former elementary school, École Saint-Paul, located at 652 Dequen, that had been leased from the school board. In November 1993, construction was completed, and HMCS *Jolliet* moved into its own permanent facilities at 366 Arnaud. The complex is comprised of a main drill hall, a boathouse and an indoor firing range.

COMMANDING OFFICERS

Lieutenant-Commander D. Prévost	1988–91
Lieutenant-Commander R. Cardin	1991–93
Lieutenant-Commander J.M. Levesque	1993–94
Lieutenant-Commander J.A. Gagné	1994–97
Lieutenant-Commander P.M. Huppé	1997–98
Commander J.A.C. Gauthier	1998–99
Lieutenant J.M. Cormier	1999–2000
Lieutenant J.A.G. (Gaston) Mercier	2000–02
Lieutenant J.A.G. (Gilles) Mercier	2002–03
Lieutenant-Commander R.J.E.G. Leblanc	2003–06
Commander J.C.G. Goulet	2006–

Courtesy Gilles Goulet.

HMCS *Jolliet.*

23. HMCS *Brunswicker* (Established 1923–)

Motto: *Pacis tuendae causa* ("In the cause of peace")

Saint John was a rarity among the original RCNVR divisions, for it was established in 1923 as a full company of 100 sailors, although it was reduced in 1927 to a half-company of 50. Throughout the interwar period, in addition to basic seamanship skills such as semaphore and rope work, the company personnel trained in the use of the 12-pounder, Lewis gun, rifle, and cutlass. With the onset of the Second World War, the division became the primary recruiting and training establishment of the RCN in the province of New Brunswick. As the war progressed, the division was commissioned in 1941 as HMCS *Brunswicker*, a name long associated with both the city and the province.

HMCS *Brunswicker* was housed "temporarily" for 27 years in an annex of the Barrack Green Armoury in South Saint John. *Brunswicker's* new facilities inaugurated in May 1995 are situated prominently on the city waterfront. Participation in civic events, combined with a demanding training commitment, keeps the ship's company especially active and always prepared to answer the call "In the cause of peace."

COMMANDING OFFICERS

Lieutenant H.A. Morrison	1923–25
Lieutenant P.B. Cross	1925–37
Acting/Lieutenant N.J. Magnusson	1938–39
Acting/Lieutenant F. Brock	1939–40
Commander P.B. Cross	1940–41
Lieutenant-Commander F.B. Cooms	1941–42
Lieutenant G.A.M. Brown	1942–44
Lieutenant-Commander G.M. Butler	1944–45
Commander J. McAvity	1945–45
Lieutenant-Commander G.G.K. Holder	1945–46
Captain C.H. Bonnycastle	1946–51
Captain J.A. Mackinnon	1951–58
Commander R.M. Black	1958–62
Commander W. Mellalieu	1962–66
Commander R.B. Macauley	1966–69
Captain T.L. McGloan	1969–72
Captain G.L Peer	1972–79
Commander D.W.S Hamilton	1979–82
Commander L.M. LaFontaine	1982
Commander J.F. Montague	1982–87
Commander W.F. O'Connell	1987–91
Lieutenant-Commander J.A. McCrae	1991–95

Lieutenant-Commander L.R. Brown 1995–99
Commander J.M. Henderson 1999–2003
Lieutenant-Commander J.P. Seyffarth 2003–06
Lieutenant-Commander S.C. Robinson 2006–10
Commander E.A. Syversten-Bitten 2010–

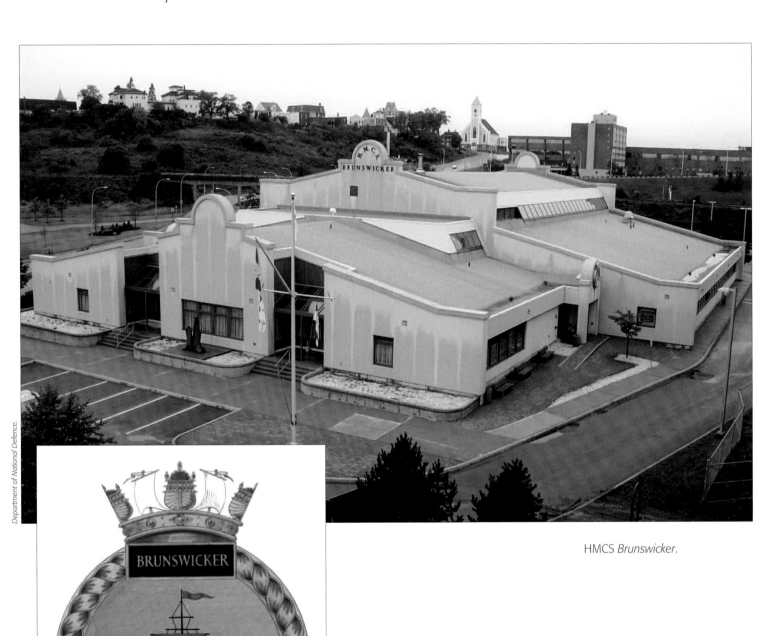

Department of National Defence.

HMCS *Brunswicker*.

24. HMCS *Queen Charlotte* (Established 1923–64; 1994–)

Motto: none

The Charlottetown Half-Company of the RNCVR was established in September of 1923 as the naval presence in Prince Edward Island. As with many of the early Naval Reserve divisions, it shared space with local militia units, moving twice before the outbreak of war in 1939.

The division was commissioned HMCS *Queen Charlotte* in 1941, after a British schooner that fought in the War of 1812. Throughout the Second World War, *Queen Charlotte* acted as a training division, not only for local recruits, but also for the overflow from other naval divisions across the country. After the war, *Queen Charlotte* acted as a demobilization centre.

Even though a new building was constructed for the division in 1959, it fell victim to budget cuts in 1964, and the facilities were turned over to the militia (it remains known as the Queen Charlotte Armoury). As part of the revitalization of the Naval Reserve in the early 1990s, HMCS *Queen Charlotte* was recommissioned in September 1994, and moved into a new permanent home in 1997.

COMMANDING OFFICERS

Lieutenant-Commander G.H. Buntain	1923–35
Lieutenant-Commander J.J. Connolly	1935–40
Lieutenant-Commander K. Birtwistle	1940–41
Acting Lieutenant-Commander E.S. Cope	1942
Acting Lieutenant-Commander M.G. McGarthy	1942–43
Lieutenant-Commander C.P. Mackenzie	1943–46
Acting Lieutenant-Commander D.R. Baker	1946–47
Lieutenant-Commander V.D.H. Saunders	1947–48
Captain J.J. Connolly	1948–51
Lieutenant-Commander J.J. Trainor	1951–52
Acting Lieutenant-Commander K.A. Mackenzie	1952–53
Commander J.N. Kenny	1953–60
Surgeon-Captain L.E. Prowse	1960–64
(The division was paid off 1964–94)	
Commander M.D. Conroy	1994–99
Lieutenant-Commander M.J. McCormick	1999–2002
Lieutenant-Commander A.A. Dale	2002–06
Lieutenant-Commander P.N. Mundy	2006–10
Lieutenant-Commander P.J. Gallant	2010–

Department of National Defence, COND-7426-54.

The old quarters of HMCS *Queen Charlotte* on the Charlottetown waterfront, November 1961.

25. HMCS *Scotian* (Established 1925–39; 1943–46; 1947–)

Motto: *Fèin Earbsa Troimh Sheirbheis* ("Self Reliance Through Service")

The Halifax Half-Company existed from 1925 to 1939 in the dockyard. On the outbreak of the Second World War, the entire company volunteered for active service and was disbanded. Re-established in March 1943 as HMCS *Haligonian*, it served essentially as a recruiting centre until VE day, when it became a final discharge centre for thousands of sailors returning from overseas. HMCS *Haligonian* was paid off in 1946.

Recommissioned on 23 April 1947 as HMCS *Scotian*, it was assigned the role of a seaward defence training division in 1951. Over the years that has evolved along with the reserve itself. Today many Scotians are crewing the Kingston-class vessels, port security units, and Naval Control and Guidance for Shipping (NCAGS) units. The division was intricately involved in the Swissair recovery operation off Peggy's Cove in 1998, and has contributed to deployed operations in Afghanistan and elsewhere.

Scotian was granted the Freedom of the City of Halifax on the occasion of its 50th anniversary, and moved into its present modern building at the south end of the Canadian Forces Base Halifax Dockyard in 1985.

COMMANDING OFFICERS

Halifax Half-Company

Lieutenant J.P. Connolly	1925–31
Lieutenant-Commander J.P. Connolly	1931–37
Commander J.P. Connolly	1937–39

HMCS *Haligonian*

Lieutenant W.E. Flavelle	1943–44
Lieutenant C.S. Boucher	1944
Acting Lieutenant-Commander H.S.C. Wilson	1944–45
Lieutenant-Commander J.C. Mackintosh	1945–46

HMCS *Scotian*

Captain W.E.S. Briggs	1947–51
Commander W.G. Allen	1951–55
Commander D.J. O'Hagen	1955–58
Captain G.A. Brown	1958–63
Captain B.S.C. Oland	1963–67
Captain D. Brownlow	1967–71
Commander L.A. Cormier	1971–74
Commander R.C. Marshall	1974–77
Captain B. Waterfield	1977–81
Captain J.T. Stuart	1981–85

Captain J.G. MacLeod 1985–88
Commander J.M.A. Brownlow 1988–91
Captain H.L. Davies 1991–92
Commander J.D.G. MacMillan 1992–95
Commander M.A. Hickey 1995–98
Captain D.A. Edmonds 1998–2002
Captain C. Walkington 2002–05
Commander M.N. Cameron 2005–07
Commander J. MacInnes 2007–08
Commander R.H. Oland 2008–

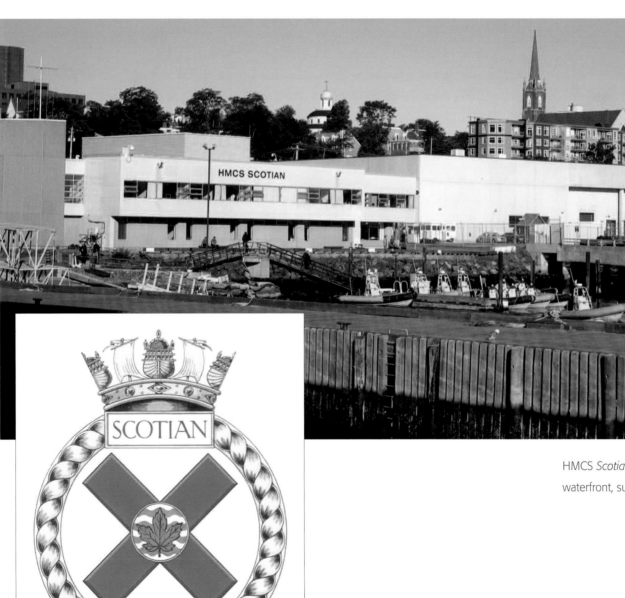

Courtesy Richard Gimblett.

HMCS *Scotian* on the Halifax waterfront, summer 2010.

26. HMCS *Cabot* (Established 1949–)

Motto: none

HMCS *Cabot* was commissioned in 1949 to represent the navy in Canada's new province. Initially housed at Buckmaster's Field as part of a tri-service headquarters, it experienced rapid growth, prompting a move to Pleasantville, and finally to Pier 27 in St. John's harbour. *Cabot* has always been an integral part of the local community, hosting many social functions and participating in many sporting activities, including rowing in the annual Royal St. John's Regatta, a tradition recently re-established. This service to the community has continued, such as when *Cabot* and its sailors provided temporary lodgings to 483 people stranded in St. John's when the terrorist attacks on the World Trade Center towers in New York on 11 September 2001 grounded all commercial flights.

Beginning with the division's first cruise with its tender, the Llewellyn-class minesweeper HMCS *Revelstoke*, to Bermuda in 1951, sailors from *Cabot* have always been "Ready Aye Ready" to serve Canada at sea and ashore. They have done so in both small and large vessels of the fleet and at port security units.

COMMANDING OFFICERS

Commander H. Garrett	1949–53
Commander F. O'Dea	1953–56
Commander H. Garrett	1956–60
Commander G.G.R. Parsons	1960–65
Commander W.J. Gushue	1965–67
Lieutenant-Commander F. Riche	1967–69
Commander M.R. Andrews	1969–76
Commander R. Lucas	1976–80
Commander E. Stack	1980–83
Commander R. Lucas	1983–84
Commander R. Rompkey	1984–88
Captain E.J. Cahill	1988–91
Commander Y. Hepditch	1991–94
Lieutenant-Commander J. Prowse	1994–98
Lieutenant-Commander M. Morris	1998–2003
Lieutenant-Commander M. Harvey	2003–07
Lieutenant-Commander B. Walsh	2007–10
Lieutenant-Commander D.E. Botting	2010–

Department of National Defence, NFD-8141.

HMCS *Cabot* in the old Pleasantville location, January 1964.

27. HMCS *Caribou* (established 1953–1958)

Motto: none

HMCS *Caribou* was commissioned on 23 August 1953, as the second naval division to be located in the then-new province of Newfoundland. The name was chosen in part because that animal is prominent on the provincial emblem, and to perpetuate the name of the Newfoundland Government ferry SS *Caribou*, torpedoed and sunk in Cabot Strait on 14 October 1942. Located in Corner Brook, on the Bay of Islands on the Gulf of St. Lawrence coast, the new division was in a natural setting for afloat training. Although initial support was encouraging, especially the donation of a portion of the Bowater paper mill warehouse (the vice-president of which was a former officer in the RCNVR), it soon proved difficult to sustain sufficient interest to keep the division viable. HMCS *Caribou* was paid off on 31 March 1958.

COMMANDING OFFICERS

Commander F.L. Rowsell	1953–57
Lieutenant-Commander H.W. Strong	1957–58

Directorate of History & Heritage, Caribou PRF file.

The entrance to HMCS *Caribou*.

28. HMCS *Chatham* (established 1924–26; 1929–40; 1946–64)

Motto: none

The RCNVR half-company in Prince Rupert, British Columbia, was established in 1923, but initial recruiting was slow and it was closed down in 1926. Recommissioned in 1928, by 1931 the complement consisted of five officers and 75 ratings. When war was declared, the entire ship's company engaged for active service. The unit was paid off in June 1940, and the quarters turned over to the Fisherman's Reserve.

Shortly afterward, the establishment was recommissioned on 1 April 1942 as HMCS *Chatham*, named after the consort ship of HMS *Discovery* in which Captain George Vancouver, RN, explored the West Coast of North America in the 1790s. However, during the war, *Chatham* was not considered to be a reserve division, and served instead as a routing centre for convoys and patrols along the northern British Columbia coast until paid off in August 1945.

HMCS *Chatham* was recommissioned formally as a peacetime Naval Reserve division on Trafalgar Day, 21 October 1946, in modern and far more spacious accommodation than the pre-war facilities. However, the unit was paid off as a cost-saving measure in 1964.

COMMANDING OFFICERS

Lieutenant R.P. Ponder	1924–26
(The division was paid off 1926–29)	
Lieutenant W. Hume	1929–35
Lieutenant-Commander W. Hume	1935–38
Lieutenant L.H. Haworth	1938–39
Lieutenant O.G. Stuart	1939–40
(The division was paid off 1940–42, and did not serve as an NRD in 1942–45)	
Lieutenant-Commander O.G. Stuart	1946–48
Lieutenant-Commander J.D. McRae	1948–52
Commander T.A. Johnston	1953–54
Lieutenant-Commander J.D. McRae	1957–58
Lieutenant-Commander E.W.K. McLeod	1958–62
Lieutenant-Commander J.O. Pearson	1962–64

Department of National Defence, E-67298.

HMCS *Chatham*, July 1962.

Suggested Readings

Armstrong, John Griffith. *The Halifax Explosion and the Royal Canadian Navy: Inquiry and Intrigue.* Vancouver and Toronto: UBC Press, 2002.

Bernier, Serge, Jacques Castonguay and André Charbonneau et al., *Québec: ville militaire, 1608–2000.* Montreal: Art Global, 2008.

Bernier, Serge, and Jean Pariseau. *Les Canadiens français et le bilinguisme dans les Forces armées canadiennes, Tome II 1969–1987: Langues officielles: la volonté gouvernementale et la réponse de la Défense nationale.* Ottawa: Department of Supply and Services Canada, 1991.

Boutilier, James A. ed. *The RCN in Retrospect.* Vancouver: UBC Press, 1982.

Brodeur, Nigel D. "L.P. Brodeur and the Origins of the Royal Canadian Navy." In Boutilier, James A., ed. *The RCN in Retrospect.* Vancouver, UBC Press, 1982. 13–22.

Canada. *Histoire de la Réserve navale: 1923–1998 — 75e anniversaire de la Réserve navale du Canada.* Ottawa: Department of National Defence, 1998.

DeGagné, Chelsea, Michel S. Beaulieu, and David Ratz. "*Prima in Lacubus:* Over a Century of Naval Activity at the Lakehead." The Thunder Bay Historical Museum Society Papers & Records, 37 (2009), 46–59.

Douglas, W.A.B. ed. *The RCN in Transition 1910–1985.* Vancouver: UBC Press, 1988.

Douglas, W.A.B., Roger Sarty, and Michael Whitby. *No Higher Purpose: The Official Operational History of the Royal Canadian Navy in the Second World War, 1939–1943*, Vol. 2, Part 1. St. Catharine's: Vanwell Publishing Limited, 2002.

Douglas, W.A.B., Roger Sarty, and Michael Whitby. *A Blue Water Navy: The Official Operational History of the Royal Canadian Navy in the Second World War, 1943–1945*, Vol. 2, Part 2. St. Catharine's: Vanwell Publishing Limited, 2007.

Easton, Alan. *50 North: An Atlantic Battleground.* Toronto: Ryerson Press, 1963.

Freeman, David J. *Canadian Warship Names.* St. Catharines: Vanwell Publishing Limited, 2000.

Garner, Hugh. *Storm Below.* Toronto: Ryerson Press [1949], 1968.

Gimblett, Richard. "Re-Assessing the Dreadnought Crisis of 1909 and the Origins of the Royal Canadian Navy." *The Northern Mariner/Le Marin du Nord*, Vol. 4, No. 1 (January 1994), 35–53.

Glover, William. "Commodore Walter Hose: Ordinary Officer, Extraordinary Endeavour." In Whitby, Michael, Richard H. Gimblett, and Peter Haydon, eds. *The Admirals: Canada's Senior Naval Leadership in the Twentieth Century*, Toronto: Dundurn Press, 2006, 56–68.

Glover, William. "Officer Training and the Quest for Operational Efficiency in the Royal Canadian Navy, 1939–1945." Ph.D. diss., King's College, London, 1998.

Gough, Barry Morton. "The End of Pax Britannica and the Origins of the Royal Canadian Navy: Shifting Strategic Demands of an Empire at Sea." In Douglas, W.A.B. ed. *RCN in Transition 1910–1985.* Vancouver: UBC Press, 1988, 90–102.

Hadley, Michael L. *U-Boats against Canada: German Submarines in Canadian Waters.* Kingston and Montreal: McGill-Queen's University Press, 1985. (For the Battle of the St. Lawrence see especially "The First St. Lawrence Sorties: 1942," 82–111; "The Battle of the St. Lawrence," 112–143; and "After Normandy," 224–48).

Hadley, Michael L., and Roger Sarty. *Tin-Pots and Pirate Ships: Canadian Naval Forces and German Sea Raiders 1880–1918*. Montreal and Kingston: McGill-Queen's University Press, 1991.

Hadley, Michael L., Rob Huebert, and Fred Crickard, eds. *A Nation's Navy: In Quest of Canadian Naval Identity*. Kingston: McGill-Queen's University Press, 1996.

Hébert, Christian. *NCSM MONTCALM: Le français dans la Marine canadienne 1923–2008*. Sillery: Les Éditions du Septentrion, 2008.

Hopkins, Anthony, ed. *Songs from the Front and Rear: Canadian Servicemen's Songs of the Second World War*. Edmonton: Hurtig Publishers, 1979.

Hunter, Mark C. *To Employ and Uplift Them: The Newfoundland Naval Reserve 1899–1926*. St. John's: ISER Books, Memorial University of Newfoundland, 2009.

Lamb, James. *The Corvette Navy: True Stories from Canada's Atlantic War*. Toronto: Macmillan, 1977.

Lawrence, Hal. *A Bloody War: One Man's Memories of the Canadian Navy 1939–45*. Toronto: McClelland and Stewart, 1979.

Lawrence, Hal. *Tales of the North Atlantic*. Toronto: McClelland and Stewart, 1985.

Lynch, Thomas G., and James B. Lamb. *Gunshield Graffiti: Unofficial Badges of Canada's Wartime Navy*. Halifax: Nimbus Publishing, 1984.

MacPherson, Ken, and Ron Barrie. *The Ships of Canada's Naval Forces 1910–2002*. St. Catherines: Vanwell Publishing Limited, 2003.

Mayne, Richard. *Betrayed: Scandal, Politics and Canadian Naval Leadership*. Vancouver: UBC Press, 2006.

McKee, Fraser. *Volunteers for Sea Service*. Toronto: Houstons Standard Publications, 1973.

McKee, Fraser. *The Armed Yachts of Canada*. Erin, ON: The Boston Mills Press, 1983.

McKillip, R.W.H. "Staying on the Sleigh: Commodore Walter Hose and a Permanent Naval Policy for Canada." Unpublished Masters Thesis, Royal Military College, Kingston, 1991.

Milner, Marc. *Canada's Navy: The First Century*. Toronto, Buffalo, London: University of Toronto Press, 1999.

Milner, Marc. *North Atlantic Run: The Royal Canadian Navy and the Battle for the Convoys*. Toronto: University of Toronto Press, 1985.

Morgan, Jean-Louis, and Linda Sinclair. *Ne tirez pas!* Montreal: L'Archipel, 2008.

Parsons, W.D., and E.J. Parsons. *The Best Small-Boat Seamen in the Navy*. St. John's: DRC Publishers, 2008.

Stead, Gordon W. *A Leaf Upon the Sea: A Small Ship in the Mediterranean, 1941–1943*. Vancouver: UBC Press, 1988.

Sarty, Roger. "Hard Luck Flotilla: The RCN's Atlantic Coast Patrol 1914–18" In *RCN in Transition 1910–1985*, edited by W.A.B. Douglas. Vancouver: UBC Press, 1988, 103–25.

Schull, Joseph. *The Far Distant Ships: An Official Account of Canadian Naval Operations in the Second World War*. Ottawa: Queen's Printer, 1952.

Tucker, Gilbert Norman. *The Naval Service of Canada: Its Official History*, 2 vols. Ottawa: The King's Printer, 1952.

Whitby, Michael, Richard H.Gimblett, and Peter Haydon, eds. *The Admirals: Canada's Senior Naval Leadership in the Twentieth Century*. Toronto: Dundurn Press, 2006.

Winters, Barbara. "The Wrens of the Second World War: their Place in the History of Canadian Servicewomen." In Hadley, Michael L., Rob Huebert, and Fred Crickard, eds. *A Nation's Navy: In Quest of Canadian Naval Identity*. Montreal and Kingston: McGill-Queen's University Press, 1996, 280–96.

About the Contributors

Bob Blakely (CD, LL.B., LL.D.) was born on the prairies and soon became interested in "things nautical." He claims to have joined the Naval Reserve because girls liked men in naval uniform much more than those in any other suit of clothes. A labour lawyer by profession, plumber and steamfitter by trade, labour leader by inclination, and a naval officer by choice, he rose through the ranks of the Naval Reserve to eventually command the formation from 2004 to 2007 as commander naval reserves in the rank of commodore. "Fortunate enough to become sea-command qualified," as he puts it, he commanded all the various classes of ships that the Naval Reserve operated during his period as a sea-going officer. A claim to fame is the fact that in 1996 he gave the last helm order ever given in a gate vessel. It was HMCS *Porte de la Reine* (also the first ship he had served aboard). He and Geraldine Rajotte have a blended family of three children, two grandchildren, and one spoiled and precocious cat.

Louis Christ (CD, LL.B., M.A.) joined the Naval Reserve as it seemed an interesting summer job. It became a passion. He has served in Esquimalt and Halifax, but for most of the past 16 years was on the staffs for command and staff courses at the Canadian Forces College in Toronto. Currently a naval captain, he is director naval reserve training and education. Louis has twice commanded Saskatoon's Naval Reserve division, HMCS *Unicorn*, and has served as the logistics branch adviser for the Naval Reserve. He studied history and law at the University of Saskatchewan. A noted middle-distance runner, he was inducted into the University of Saskatchewan Athletics Wall of Fame and the Saskatoon Sports Hall of Fame. He was a member of three national track & field teams and a two-time national university champion. For the past 10 years he has worked in marketing, research, and business development — since 2002 with the law firm MacPherson Leslie & Tyerman LLP. Louis is an avid photographer and plays saxophone in a swing-era "big band." Louis and his wife Janet married in 1982 and have been living happily ever after.

François Ferland (CD, B.Mus.), a musician by training and inclination, joined the Régiment du Saguenay in 1986 as director of music, because the summer jobs were better than unemployment during the off season of privately teaching the flute. He moved to the Naval Reserve in 1998, serving full time in Naval Reserve Headquarters, in Quebec City, first as staff officer bands and director of music for the National Band of the Naval Reserve, then, from 2003, after six national band tours and 18 straight summers away from home, as translator and copy editor, a position he still holds. With retirement from the CF looming, he is looking forward to getting back to music full time, both as a performer and a music publisher. Having met in a choir of which they are still members, he and Marie Bouret were married in 1976; they are the very proud parents of two grown children, even though they have not (yet) been gifted with grandchildren.

Carl Gagnon (CD, B.A.) is a native of Chicoutimi, now Ville de Saguenay, Quebec, who joined the Canadian Forces in December 1983 and the Naval Reserve in 1988. He has been a staff officer at the Naval Reserve divisions HMC Ships *Champlain*, *Queen Charlotte*, and *Carleton*; Fifth Maritime Operations Group; Canadian Forces Fleet School (Quebec); and the Canadian Naval Centennial 1910–2010 Project. He holds the rank of lieutenant. He has a Bachelor's degree in history from Université du Québec à Chicoutimi and completed his academic studies for a masters degree. With his interest in Canadian military and naval history, he has hobbies in graphic arts and in heraldry.

Richard Gimblett (CD, Ph.D.) was a career officer in the regular force navy, the highlights of which included serving as training officer in HMCS *Porte de la Reine* for the summer of 1981, and 10 years later as combat officer aboard HMCS *Protecteur* in the Persian Gulf. Before becoming the command historian of the Canadian Navy, he at one point in retirement collected eight months' pay as a reservist. He is the past president of the Canadian Nautical Research Society, is a contributor to volume one of the official history of the RCN (1867–1939), and edited *The Naval Service of Canada 1910–2010: the Centennial Story* (2009). His many published works include studies on Canada's role in the Persian Gulf. He is convinced that his wife Muriel married him in 1979 and has followed him since largely out of curiosity, a pastime in which she is now joined by daughters Meaghan and Beth.

Michael L. Hadley (CD, Ph.D., FRSC) fell under the spell of the sea as a youngster living at Pachena Point Lighthouse (British Columbia), and later while working with Union Steamships. Inspired by the mentoring and seafaring yarns of a Newfoundland uncle, he joined the reserve in 1954 as a member of the University Naval Training Division. He subsequently served in seven classes of vessel from cruiser to submarine, as well as in three different reserve divisions, and the German training vessel *Deutschland*. He commanded Victoria's HMCS *Malahat* (1974–78), and variously skippered HMC Ships *Porte Quebec*, *Porte de la Reine*, and *Porte Dauphine*. He retired in the rank of captain. In civilian life he is Professor Emeritus of German (University of Victoria) with books on naval and maritime history. For years he played trumpet in a concert band, later "big band" and jazz. His swan song was with "old boys" of the Kitsilano Boys Band at Vancouver's "Show Boat" in 2008. He lives in Victoria with his wife Anita and his mistress — his sloop *Peregrine*.

Ian Holloway (CD, Q.C., RANR Retired) has had a maritime career involving five navies. After many years as a sea cadet, he joined the Canadian Naval Reserve as a signalman in 1977. He was promoted to the rank of chief petty officer in 1990 at the age of 29. In 1998 he was commissioned as a lieutenant in the Royal Australian Navy. His service afloat has included frigates, a destroyer, supply ships, an aircraft carrier, and three of the five gate vessels. He holds the distinction — probably unique in the Commonwealth navies — of having served as a yeoman at sea for three different flag officers, and for commanding officers of every rank from lieutenant up to and including vice-admiral. Ashore, he has served in establishments in Canada, Australia, Great Britain, the United States, and Norway. In civilian life, Holloway is the dean of law at the University of Western Ontario. He is a member of the bars of Ontario and Nova Scotia, and an elected member of the American Law Institute.

Hugues Létourneau (CD, M.A.) is a native of Montreal who joined the Canadian Naval Reserve in 1970. He has served in many capacities in the Naval Reserve, including commanding officer of HMCS *Donnacona* (Montreal) from 1992 to 1995. He holds the rank of naval captain. His positions in civilian life include director of information services at the Board of Trade of Metropolitan Montreal and senior marketing writer for the Montreal high-tech firm Memotec. He holds a Master's degree in public policy and public administration from Concordia University, a Bachelor's degree in political science from Saint Mary's University, and a certificate in immigration and inter-ethnic relations from the Université du Québec à Montréal. He is currently a consultant living in Quebec City.

Fraser Murray McKee (CD) was born in Toronto and joined the RCNVR as an ordinary seaman in March 1943. Commissioned a year later, he served in an armed yacht, two ocean escorts, and shore bases. He returned to Toronto in 1946 and took a degree in forestry, later working in the communications and advertising industries until retirement in 1984. He remained in the Naval Reserve until 1975, having specialized in anti-submarine warfare, and served in vessels ranging from an RN submarine to aircraft carriers. He once commanded HMCS *Porte Saint Jean*. He retired as a commander. For 16 years he edited two successive naval newsletters for the Naval Officers Association of Canada, and has written seven books on the Canadian Navy and its Merchant Navy. A past president of the Navy League of Canada, he was also president of the Grey County Historical Society, and contributes maritime book reviews to various journals. He lives in Toronto and has four children, one a retired lieutenant-colonel in the Canadian militia.

Richard Oliver Mayne (CD, Ph.D.) received his M.A. from Wilfrid Laurier University, and his Ph.D. from Queen's University. He now works for the Department of National Defence as a military analyst, and is an author for the study on Future Shocks being prepared in the Directorate of Future Security and Analysis. While employed for eight years as a historian at the Directorate of History and Heritage he was assigned to the teams responsible for volumes two and three of the Official History of the Canadian Navy. He is the author of two books, *Betrayed: Scandal, Politics and Canadian Naval Leadership* (2006) and an edited volume with Dr. Richard Gimblett entitled *People, Policy and Programmes* (2008); he has also published many articles on Canadian naval history. A serving officer in the Naval Reserve for over 17 years, Dr. Mayne has had the privilege of serving on a wide variety of ships, units, and shore appointments.

W. David Parsons (M.D.) was born in St. John's, Newfoundland, and graduated in Medicine from McGill University in 1951. He practised in Twillingate, Fogo, and St. John's before training in internal medicine. From 1970–71 he served as president of the Newfoundland Medical Association, and later as senior district medical officer for the Department of Veteran's Affairs in St. John's. As consultant to the Veterans Pavilion, he maintained contact with many veterans of both world wars. He served in the COTC (Canadian Officers Training Corps), RAFTC (Royal Air Force Transport Command), and RCAMC(M) (Royal Canadian Army Medical Corps), retiring in the rank of major. He is a member of the Advisory Council of the Royal Newfoundland Regiment. His publications include *Pilgrimage: a Guide to the Royal Newfoundland Regiment in World War One* (1994, Second Edition 2009) and, with Dr. Ean Parsons, *The Best Small Boat Seamen in the Navy* (2008). He has written articles on military and medical history as well. He has conducted tours of the Western Front, is a member of the Western Front Association, and is founding member of the St. John's Medical History Association.

Colin Stewart (CD, LL.B., M.B.A.) is the Logistics Officer at HMCS *Chippawa* in Winnipeg. Having enrolled as a medical assistant in 1987, on receiving his call to the Bar in 1998 he technically became a "lower deck lawyer." He was commissioned from the ranks in 2001, and has instructed at the CF Medical Services School, Fleet School Quebec, and the recruit schools at both St. Jean and Borden. Highlights of his career include service with the United Nations on the Golan Heights in 1990, the CF response to the 1997 Manitoba flood, and most recently as adjutant for the Theatre Support Element of Task Force Afghanistan at Camp Mirage from June to December 2006. Along the way he somehow convinced his wife Tamara that marrying him was a good idea, and so far his children Titus and Siobhan seem to think he is pretty cool.

Barbara Winters (CD, M.A., LL.B.) was a member of the Naval Reserve from 1980 until 1997, serving as a medic, ship's diver, and later MARS officer, based in the reserve divisions HMC Ships *Carleton*, *Cataraqui*, *Discovery*, and *Malahat*. She trained and served aboard various gate vessels and minesweepers. She trained briefly aboard the destroyer HMCS *Saskatchewan* and was not unhappy when that ship was scuttled. Of all her many fond experiences in the Naval Reserve, Barbara remembers best the florescence that sparkled during a night dive and the solitude of a stormy, black sea. Sadly, Barbara chose law over history and a part-time life at sea. Sometimes, in the quiet stillness of some tedious file review, a sigh and lament can be heard from her office " … I miss the condensed milk and the crappy coffee."

List of Acronyms and Abbreviations

AMC	Armed Merchant Cruiser
AOPV	Arctic Offshore Patrol Vessel
BWK	Bridge Watchkeeping Certificate (also WK)
CGS	Canadian Government Ship
CND	Continuous Naval Duty
COND	Commanding Officer Naval Divisions
CPF	Canadian Patrol Frigate
CPO	Chief Petty Officer
DAMS	Defensively Armed Merchant Ship (First World War)
DEMS	Defensively Equipped Merchant Ship (Second World War)
DND	Department of National Defence
HMCS	His/Her Majesty's Canadian Ship (see NCSM)
HMS	His/Her Majesty's Ship (British)
JLC	Junior Leadership Course
MarS	Maritime Surface/Sub-surface (officer classification; also MARS)
MCDO	Maritime Coastal Defence Organization
MCDV	Maritime Coastal Defence Vessel
MCM	Mine Countermeasures
MPA	Maritime Patrol Aircraft
MSA	Minesweeping Auxiliary (Vessel)
MTR	Military Technical Revolution
NATO	North Atlantic Treaty Organization
NCM	Non-commissioned Member (see NCO)
NCO	Non-commissioned Officer
NCS	Naval Control of Shipping
NCSM	Navire canadien de Sa Majesté
NCSO	Naval Control of Shipping Officer
NCSORG	Naval Control of Shipping Organization
NOIC	Naval Officer-in-Charge (Organization)
NPQ	Naval Presence in Quebec
NR	(see RCNR)
NRD	Naval Reserve Division
NROC	Naval Reserve Officer Cadet (Program)
NSA	New Ship-borne Aircraft
OBE	Order of the British Empire

OJT	On-the-Job Training
PSU	Port Security Unit
Q-ship	Anti-submarine decoy ship
RCAF	Royal Canadian Air Force
RCMP	Royal Canadian Mounted Police
RCNR	Royal Canadian Naval Reserve
RCNVR	Royal Canadian Naval Volunteer Reserve
RMA	Revolution in Military Affairs
RN	Royal Navy (British)
RNCVR	Royal Naval Canadian Volunteer Reserve
RNR	Royal Naval Reserve (British)
RNVR	Royal Naval Volunteer Reserve (British)
RNWMP	Royal Northwest Mounted Police
ROE	Rules of Engagement
ROUTP	Reserve Officer University Training Plan
SNRA	Senior Naval Reserve Adviser
SSEP	Summer Student Employment Program
UNTD	University Naval Training Division
VR	Volunteer Reserve, or Volunteer Reservist (see RCNVR)
WK	Watchkeeping Certificate
WRCNS	Women's Royal Canadian Naval Service (known as "Wrens")
Wrens	(see WRCNS)

Index